OXFORD CLASSICAL MONOGRAPHS

Published under the supervision of a Committee of the Faculty of Literae Humaniores in the University of Oxford

OXFORD CLASSICAL MONOGRAPHS

The aim of the Oxford Classical Monographs series (which replaces the Oxford Classical and Philosophical Monographs) is to publish outstanding theses on Greek and Latin literature, ancient history, and ancient philosophy examined by the faculty board of Literae Humaniores.

Ovid and the *Fasti*

AN HISTORICAL STUDY

Geraldine Herbert-Brown

CLARENDON PRESS · OXFORD

1994

Oxford University Press, Walton Street, Oxford OX2 6DP

Oxford New York Toronto
Delhi Bombay Calcutta Madras Karachi
Kuala Lumpur Singapore Hong Kong Tokyo
Nairobi Dar es Salaam Cape Town
Melbourne Auckland Madrid
and associated companies in
Berlin Ibadan

Oxford is a trade mark of Oxford University Press

Published in the United States
by Oxford University Press Inc., New York

British Library Cataloguing in Publication Data
Data available

Library of Congress Cataloging in Publication Data
Ovid and the Fasti: an historical study
Geraldine Herbert-Brown.
Includes bibliographical references and indexes.
1. Ovid, 43 B.C.–17 or 18 A.D. Fasti.
2. Rome—History—Augustus, 30 B.C.–14 A.D. —Historiography.
3. Elegiac poetry, Latin—History and criticism.
4. Rites and ceremonies in literature.
5. Rome—Religious life and customs.
6. Rites and ceremonies—Rome.
7. Festivals in literature. 8. Calendar in literature.
9. Rome in literature. 10. Festivals—Rome. 11. Calendar—Rome.
11. Calendar—Rome. I. Title. II. Series.
PA6519.F9H47 1994   871'.01—dc20   93–14179
ISBN 0–19–814935–2

1 3 5 7 9 10 8 6 4 2

Set by Hope Services (Abingdon) Ltd.
Printed in Great Britain
on acid-free paper by
Bookcraft (Bath) Ltd., Midsomer Norton

FOR MICHAEL

PREFACE

OVID'S *Fasti* is, after the *Aeneid*, the longest extant poem to reflect a contemporary's view of the ideology of the Augustan regime. It is the only work to reveal a living witness's interpretation of the mature Augustus' own view of his place in Roman history, and of the mythology created in the late Augustan Principate. It is the only political poem in the period to bridge two regimes, and to disclose its author's understanding of events when Tiberius succeeded Augustus. It is the only poem to mirror the attitudes to the Principate of two personae in the one author: on the one hand Ovid is an interested witness of his times, a financially independent, socially confident, popular Roman poet outside the political mainstream; on the other, a plaintive victim of political vagaries, stripped of *dignitas*, banished to the far-flung reaches of the empire, forced to plead with friends and questionable friends alike, in order to secure his recall.

It is remarkable, therefore, that Ovid's versification of the Roman calendar has not attracted greater attention and more substantial study from historians of the Augustan Age. The attention it has attracted has done little to expose the wealth of historical insights the work has to offer. Literary critics have been content to use it as a source for parallel passages of elegiac motifs, or to distil every possible word of the text into just another 'stilkritische' allusion to Callimachean literary criticism. Barsby (1978, 25) confidently asserted that it was 'on the literary side of the *Fasti* that the most interesting work is to be done'. Others, such as Warde Fowler (1899), Wissowa (1912), Frazer (1929), and Latte (1960), exploited it solely as an antiquarian curiosity. They saw it as a repository of facts for Roman religion isolated from contemporary politics and dissociated from the author, who, as a product of a specific cultural environment, was writing the poem for a particular reason and from a particular standpoint. The same approach was essentially adopted by Bömer (1957–8), even though he concentrated on language as well as on content. Others such as Allen (1922) and Scott (1930) saw in the work merely exaggerated flattery of the ruler, without taking into account the genre of the poem or its political milieu. Others again, such as Phillips (1983) Wallace-Hadrill (1987), and Hinds (1992), have deemed it 'subversive', or found it to be out of step with establishment culture. Such judgement has often been formed by critics who are unwise enough to compare the ideology of Ovid's 'epic' with Virgil's, a work by a poet of very different temperament, writing in a different age under a ruler of a very different stamp. Syme (1978) concentrated on the anniversaries which Ovid left out, thus directing his great scholarship to an essentially negative treatment of the *Fasti*.[1]

The purpose of the present study is to show that the *Fasti* is an important contemporary witness to late Augustan ideology and dynastic politics. My hope is that the poem will at last receive the attention it deserves from historians. The text I have followed throughout is that of Alton, Wormell, and Courtney (Leipzig, 1988). I explain my reasons for doing so where alternate readings exist which affect the sense of the text. Translations of passages cited are my own.

The poem as we have it is only half complete, yet it still comprises some 5,000 lines. A rigorous selection of passages has therefore had to be made. In making that selection I have concentrated on the entries incorporating members of the contemporary ruling family, for the following reason. The *Fasti*, containing numerous categories of unconnected information such as Greek and Roman ritual, old and new festivals, etymology, mythology, astronomy, and legend, provides no narrative history. However, in the 'Julian anniversaries', the more overtly 'political' entries which punctuate the poem as the calendar dictates, it depicts portraits of individual members of the ruling family in a particular guise, according to the anniversary of the day in question. These are the sections in which Augustus, as a ruler concerned about the way in which he was presented in literature, and as dedicatee of the work, would be most interested. These Julian anniversaries are the focus of the *Fasti* in its capacity as Ovid's poetic 'militia' or service to the state, as his 'munera' to Caesar Augustus (*F* 2. 9, 17). For this reason the present study concentrates on those sections of the poem which incorporate into the Roman calendar

[1] I have not seen J. F. Miller's *Ovid's Elegiac Festivals* (1992) which appeared after this manuscript was completed.

cameos of Augustus, Julius Caesar, Livia, Tiberius, and Germanicus over a range of politico-religious roles, with constant reference being made to the cultural, religious, and political environment which produced the poem. Chapters 2–5 are devoted to those entries.

An historical study of the *Fasti* cannot ignore the artistic temperament, personality, and circumstances of its author. It is this which is crucial to an understanding of Ovid's style and presentation of Augustus and the ruling family, both before and after exile. A biographical scheme has therefore been adopted and is evident throughout, most particularly in Chapters 1 and 5.

The *Fasti* is the amatory elegist's first departure from the popular *recusatio* tradition, his first attempt to hazard his reputation in a new, and dangerous, field. It is his first 'political' poem. Yet Ovid's decision to versify the calendar has been criticized by modern scholars without regard for the political pressures and cultural influences of the late Augustan Principate. The background to that choice of subject matter, and the options available to a poet, require investigation. While there is no doubt that Greek literary models heavily influenced the metre and form of the *Fasti*, it is not practicable to review the enormous literature on the subject in this short monograph. In the present enquiry I have deliberately chosen to put the emphasis on Ovid's personal choice in an Augustan context. This is carried out in Chapter 1.

Although this study of the *Fasti* is not a literary analysis, a vigilant eye is kept on the nature of the evidence, on the fact that it is a literary work in metrical form employing a great variety of techniques: formal modes, stock phrases, situations, sound effects, echoes of other literary texts, irony, and humour. The atmosphere is dictated by the genres he has selected, as are words and epithets by metrical requirements. Ovid delivers his 'historical' information in an elegiac package.

The dating of the *Fasti* is not, to my mind, in dispute. Ovid himself says that his banishment in AD 8 interrupted its composition (*T* 2. 549–50) and I have found no reason to disbelieve him. Syme (1978) argued that the poet ceased writing the work by mid-AD 4, specifically at the adoption of Tiberius in June of that year. In the Appendix I hope to demonstrate that the omissions in the *Fasti* to which Syme has drawn attention serve to indicate that the poet was witnessing the politically turbulent years AD 5–8.

Where the question of Ovid's sources is raised in the course of this book, equal consideration is given to the Augustan building programme, to the Roman calendar, and to literary texts. The *Fasti* reveals that Ovid was acutely aware of the policies and ideals of the Princeps. For such information he did not, as a man living in Rome, always have to look in books to get a general feel for the current of the times. Ovidian 'Quellenforschung' has not, I believe, given enough recognition to the fact that all the poet had to do to gain much information was personally to examine the topographical lay-out of the Palatine, or to take a stroll around the Roman and Augustan *fora*.

Finally, the poet's own plea from exile could not provide a better guide for an historical study of the *Fasti* (*T* 3. 14. 27–30):

> quod quicumque leget—si quis leget—aestimet ante,
> compositum quo sit tempore quoque loco.

Whoever shall read this—if anyone reads it—let him first take stock of when and in what place it was composed.

ACKNOWLEDGEMENTS

SIMON PRICE first drew my attention to the *Fasti* as an unmined source for the late Augustan regime. During the years that followed he patiently supervised my excavations, cast a critical eye over my findings, and often rescued me from bottomless pits and quicksands which threatened to engulf me. To him go my heartfelt thanks. I am also deeply indebted to Barbara Levick, who has been unfailingly generous with putting her great scholarship at my disposal, and who, in the midst of her own work, has found time to read and comment on every page of the draft. Sincere thanks go to Fergus Millar, Robin Nisbet, Peter Parsons, and Nicholas Purcell, who have been most generous in giving me the benefit of their comments and constructive criticism. The late Elizabeth Rawson's encouragement and helpful insights in the initial stages have not been forgotten. She has been, and still is, sorely missed. Very special thanks go also to the Commonwealth Scholarship Commission, without which I would not have been able to study at Oxford.

It is impossible to enumerate all those scholars whom I encountered and who offered insight and challenge during the years of my research. However, mention must be made of Alessandro Barchiesi, Mary Beard, Ian Du Quesnay, Janet Fairweather, Elaine Fantham, Stephen Harrison, Carole Newlands, John North, C. Robert Phillips, Michael Reeve, John Scheid, the late Sir Ronald Syme, Andrew Wallace-Hadrill, and Peter Wiseman, all of whom gave me, in varying degree, the benefit of their views and great learning.

In the course of writing my thesis at Oxford I also received constant stimulus from discussions with some of my postgraduate colleagues, and as a token of my appreciation I would like to name them here: Tim Bateson, Eugenia Bolognesi, Richard Burgess, Margaretha Debrunner-Hall, Marie Diaz, Hugh Elton, Susan Fischler, Nicholas Hardwick, Margaret O'Hea, Tim Parkin, and Louise Stephens. The staff of the Ashmolean reading room, notably Jane Jakeman and Danny Darwish, have my deepest gratitude for calmly locating any journal and book required for the final stage when, as the submission deadline approached, panic threatened to overcome me.

Finally, I wish to pay tribute to two outstanding teachers, Brian Brennan and Edwin Judge, who first introduced me to Augustan Rome: their inspiration and influence pervade this work.

CONTENTS

I

WHY *FASTI*?

'To versify and adorn an almanac was not a sound proposal.'[1]
Many critics have concurred with this verdict on Ovid's decision
to compose the *Fasti*. Yet it is a judgement based on criticism of
the artistic results of the half-finished work without reference to
the environment which produced it. It is time the verdict was
reconsidered in the light of the options available to a Roman poet
trying to adapt his talents to the service of the ruler in the highly
politicized climate of the years immediately prior to AD 8.

In those years Ovid was at the height of artistic maturity, at the
peak of a successful career, keenly desirous of maintaining his
claim to immortal fame through his art (*Met.* 15. 875–9). It is difficult to believe that he would choose something as problematic
and unwieldy as the Roman calendar to set to verse unless extra-
neous pressure were being applied. For this reason it is more feasible that Ovid's decision to produce a major work as a tribute to
Caesar Augustus came first; his decision to versify the calendar
was the result.

This chapter will be concerned with a consideration of the cultural influences working on Ovid which prompted him to create
the *Fasti* as a tribute to the ruler, and gave him reason to believe
in its potential success, both artistic and practical.

Technical Difficulties of the Enterprise

The technical difficulties confronting a poet in versifying the
Roman calendar were not inconsiderable.[2] The scope of the subject would mean a major work: twelve months to be separated

---

[1] Fränkel (1945) 148. Also Syme (1978) 105: 'Not a good idea.'
[2] Fränkel (1945) 148 believes Ovid was well aware of the difficulties involved in
versifying an almanac, but displays no curiosity as to why the poet still went ahead
with it.

into twelve books, a number which Virgil had already proved
appropriate to frame his great national epic. Yet each book representing a month would need to be further divided into days, each
of which was marked in the official calendar as having its own
particular character.[3] The calendar also marked some days as celebrating major religious festivals, others minor ones; some days
were left blank, while yet others were marked as celebrating
major and minor festivals simultaneously. Sometimes several
days were bracketed where games were extended over that
period.[4] The subject matter of the festivals themselves comprised
heterogeneous and discordant themes for an author looking for
material for a structured work.

Moreover, the poet would have seen that the rigid and relentless divisions and subdivisions in the calendar would impose a
framework allowing no natural climatic structure, nor scope for a
continuous, symmetrical, full-length narrative. It could provide
only a superficially unifying frame for a series of unrelated
episodes and categories of information, the selection of which
would be primarily dictated, not by the poet, but by the day of
the year. (An example of a story beginning abruptly for no good
reason other than the fact that the day demands it (4. 417): 'exigit
ipse locus raptus ut virginis edam'). That selection, furthermore,
would have to be treated in the order in which the episodes
occurred. The poem would have to progress painstakingly, day
by day through the year, just as the calendar ordained. Such a
plan was hardly one to inspire spontaneity or versatility; hardly a
framework to inspire poets to compete for the privilege of being
the first to try it as an innovation in poetry. At this point we
might concur with Fränkel's verdict on Ovid's decision to compose the *Fasti*.

As if these inherent obstacles were not problem enough, Ovid
elected to compose this extensive work, designed to comprise
approximately 10,000 lines (the magnitude of the *Aeneid*), in elegiac couplets.[5] Virgil had appropriately chosen hexameters for his
epic; Ovid himself had chosen the more freely flowing hexameter

---

[3] By the letters C, N, NP, F, to be discussed below.

[4] Degrassi (1963) reproduces the inscriptions of the calendars.

[5] The over-running of couplets in the narrative proper of the *Fasti*, i.e. not in
speech, simile, or catalogue, is extremely rare, almost non-existent. See Otis (1970)
42.

verse for his great fifteen-book *Metamorphoses*, which provided
technical scope for the ingenious transitions in the huge medley
of discontinuous narratives to give an impression of constant, forward, narrative movement,[6] of *perpetuum carmen*. The choice of
elegiac metre for the *Fasti* checks such a possibility, even without
the fetters of the calendrical framework. The closed couplet succeeds in dragging the progression of a story even more:[7] the
metre is more suited to the rapid fire of direct speech, commands,
apostrophes, questions, interjections, parentheses, and short dialogue.[8] In short, elegy was more suited to poetry on a small scale;
thus Ovid had not only decided upon a very difficult subject and
framework for his poem, but had added to his problems by
selecting a very unlikely and inappropriate metre as its medium.
The concern here now is not with the artistic results of the half-
finished product but with the question of why a mature poet
made such apparently unlikely choices. We shall first see how he
turned his choice of metre to advantage.

Why elegy for a work of epic proportions? Horace assists a little
with part of this question. In the *Ars Poetica* he obligingly sets
out the rules for the writing of poetry, states that the subject to be
written about must be equal to the talents of the writer (38–41),
and that the metre chosen must accord with the weight and content of the prospective poem and its poetical purpose (73–98).[9]
Propertius, who confined all his poetry to the elegiac metre, certainly concurred with the idea in his practice. He insists, more
than once in his poems, that his medium is simply not appropriate to celebrating events such as wars between gods and giants, or
the genealogy of Caesar. His poetic field is the lightweight theme
of love, that is the area in which his skill is greatest (2. 1. 39–46,
34. 45; 3. 1. 14–18, 3. 13–26).

Ovid picks up Propertius' theme of elegy being suitable to love
and infuses into it a spirit of burlesque. The opening lines of the
first of his *Amores* read thus:

> Arma gravi numero violentaque bella parabam
> edere, materia conveniente modis.

[6] Wilkinson (1955) 280.   [7] Otis (1970) 333.   [8] Wilkinson (1955) 280.
[9] The sharp difference between hexameter and elegiac narratives, and the dis-
crimination of poetry by metre is a characteristic of Augustan poetry. It did not
exist in the earlier Roman poets, nor in the poetry of Callimachus. See Otis (1970)
24–5.

> par erat inferior versus; risisse Cupido
> dicitur atque unum surripuisse pedem.

I was preparing to tell of arms and war and violence in heroic metre, with the topic in harmony with the rhythm. The second line was the same length as the first; Cupid laughed, they say, and snatched away one foot.

Cupid's snatching a foot from the second hexameter line of his poem and so making it a pentameter line of an elegiac couplet, Ovid jokes, has forced him to alter the subject of his poem from war to love.[10] With mock regret he bids farewell to the hexameter epic he had intended to write[11] and settles for the subject of love which the elegiac couplet determines as a theme. He ends the poem with the same conceit (*Am.* 1. 1. 27–30; cf. 2. 1. 29–38):

> sex mihi surgat opus numeris, in quinque residat;
> ferrea cum vestris bella valete modis.
> cingere litorea flaventia tempora myrto,
> Musa per undenos emodulanda pedes.

Let my poem rise with six feet and fall back to five. Goodbye, iron warfare, and the metre that goes with you. Bind your golden temples with the myrtle of the shore, Muse, whose verses must be completed in eleven feet.

By the time that Ovid was writing, elegiacs had become associated primarily with the theme of love. The genre of amatory elegy is said to have begun with Gallus (69–26 BC), who derived and combined aspects of style and content from the Alexandrian poets and earlier Roman poets. Tibullus and Propertius refined it and turned it into elegiac convention, a self-conscious literary exercise.[12] Both poets confined their compositions to the elegiac metre. Tibullus is not known to have ventured away from the sphere of amatory elegy (see Ovid's tribute to Tibullus in *Am.* 3. 9), and Propertius did so only briefly in his final book (see below). The genre was already created for Ovid and he absorbed the stock-in-trade of his predecessors. He in fact associated himself specifically with the love elegists even when in exile, even after he had created other works outside that genre *T* 4. 10. 53–4). That he

[10] See Newman (1967) 182.

[11] Compare the first line with 'arma virumque cano', the first line of the *Aeneid*. His audience must have recognized an echo—Otis (1970) 14.

[12] Otis (1970) 8 f.

should concern himself mainly with amatory elegy, infusing it with his own individual stamp of wit and burlesque which his predecessors never arrived at, should come as no surprise. Epic was dead. Who would rival Virgil on his own ground? Any would-be imitator of Virgil's style of themes could succeed only in steering himself on to a direct course to oblivion.

It is important to realize that the audience of the poets would also be conditioned to expect the lighter themes that the genre of amatory elegy had come to represent. By the time Ovid began the *Fasti*, he had already composed the three books of his *Amores*, and the mock-didactic *Ars Amatoria* and *Remedia Amoris*.[13] Ovid had worked long in the elegiac tradition himself and his renown was primarily based on amatory elegies. He even sends up his reputation as a love elegist in *Amores*, 3. 1. 15–20.

But the *Fasti*, while composed in elegiac couplets and even comprising many traces of the love elegist's amatory interests,[14] is not a love elegy. Ovid reminds his audience of this, thus signalling the fact that he is making an advance into new territory. In the earliest extant proem of the work he distinguishes between the type of poetry he had hitherto written, and the work he is now composing (*F* 2. 3–8):

> nunc primum velis, elegi, maioribus itis:
>   exiguum, memini, nuper eratis opus.
> ipse ego vos habui faciles in amore ministros,
>   cum lusit numeris prima iuventa suis.
> idem sacra cano signataque tempora fastis:
>   ecquis ad haec illinc crederet esse viam?

Now for the first time, elegiacs, are you sailing with a wider canvas. Recently you were, I remember, an insignificant art-form. I myself treated you as obliging servants of love when my early youth played with its own measures. The same poet is now celebrating the sacred rituals and seasons marked in the calendar. Who would believe that there was a way from that to this?

---

[13] On the chronology of Ovid's love poetry see Syme (1978) ch. 1. Not all Ovid's poetry permits dating, but the *Amores* and the *Ars* are indisputably earlier than the *Fasti*. The first edition of the *Amores* was written in his youth (*T* 4. 10. 57), and the *Ars* (1. 182) refers to Gaius' departure against the Parthians in 2 BC (see Ch. 2, 'Avenger of Caesar and Crassus').

[14] See e.g. the section on Priapus and Lotis, beginning at 1. 415; Ariadne at 3. 460; Faunus at 2. 303.

Ovid has stepped into the shoes of a new persona. Before he had
played the role of love elegist; now he was at the service of a wor-
thier cause of singing about sacred rites and seasons marked in
the calendar. To contemporaries familiar with his love poetry,
this new role would contrast markedly with his former role as
'vates' forced into service of love by Cupid in the first poem of
the *Amores* (1. 1. 6 and 24), and in whose service he had spent a
long career.

The theme of the self-consciousness of the poet in his new
identity recurs and is lengthily treated at the beginning of book 4
(1–18). Venus teasingly reminds him of his former role of love
elegist, and wonders what he could want from her now that he
was engaged in loftier themes ('maiora'). Ovid reassures her that
she is no less important to him now in his new role than formerly
in his old; it's just that now he has graduated from the juvenile
themes that were appropriate to his youth to those of an 'area
maior'. Venus too was capable of adopting a new persona: she
smoothly makes the transition from goddess of love to patroness
of the month of April and ancestral deity of the city of Rome to
adapt to the poet's new role (*F* 4. 1–18).

The new identity of the poet is further reiterated in his claim to
be a 'vates' now writing about 'tempora' and 'sacra' at the beginning of books 1, 2, 4, and 6. His audience is not bombarded with
reassertions of his new role, yet his reminders of the fact come at
regular and strategic points. The new Ovid also receives acknowledgement from deities within the work itself, thus adding an
unobtrusive emphasis on the contrast between the former and the
present persona: Janus addresses him as 'vates operose dierum'
(1, 101), and Mars as 'Latinorum vates operose dierum' (3. 177). It
is Juno, though, who says it all (6. 21–4):

> 'o vates, Romani conditor anni,
> ause per exiguos magna referre modos,
> ius tibi fecisti numen caeleste videndi,
> cum placuit numeris condere festa tuis.'

'Oh poet, compiler of the Roman year who have dared to register great
things in a humble mode, you have earned yourself the right to lay eyes
on a heavenly divinity since you chose to compile the festivals in your
own metre.'

It is Juno's address to the poet which perhaps most succinctly
reflects Ovid's intentions regarding his choice of metre for the

Fasti. By daring to record the great things that are the religious festivals of the Roman year in elegiacs, Ovid is staking a claim to be creating a new genre. 'Magna' are no longer the preserve of the heroic hexameter, or of wars and conquest. Convention is broken. Great things are now being treated in a lighter vein without degrading or undermining them. His new persona is that of a more serious and dignified elegist than his audience had hitherto known, but nevertheless still an elegist and so still very distinct from the impersonal grandiose poets of epic verse.

The reason for Ovid's choosing elegiacs over hexameters for his new large work is clear. For a poem that was to celebrate 'Magna' in approximately the same number of books and lines as the *Aeneid*, an overt distinction had to be made. He was not trying to write another *Aeneid*. Yet he was not cleaving to elegiacs here simply because it was the medium in which he was most skilled (like Propertius for example). His brilliant handling of the hexametric *Metamorphoses* demonstrates that the choice was his. He could have been tempted, with good reason, to compose the *Fasti* in hexameters, particularly in view of the technical difficulties confronting him which have been outlined above. But Ovid, a generation younger than Virgil, was catering to an audience a generation removed from Virgil's. Elegiacs, the ideal metre for light witticisms, pointed epigrams, clever conceits, familiar asides to his protagonists or his audience, for a more personal touch, might well meet a demand from a post-war generation. And the manifold aspects of the calendrical subject matter, the disconnected categories of information, could sit well within the elegiac domain.[15]

Ovid's chosen metre is as good as a statement: no grand historical narrative is to be expected here, despite the size of this poem. Great things are to be celebrated, but from a different perspective now, and they are to be handled in a lighter vein than hitherto. Nothing too tragic, and doses of Ovidian humour and cheek may be anticipated. This is a new genre, a middle road between the opposite extremes of frivolous amatory elegy, and the sublime grandeur of the epic.[16]

How valid is Ovid's claim to have created a new genre?

[15] Otis (1970) 43.

[16] Santini (1973–4) 45. See Otis (1970) 23–4 for the differences between epic and elegy.

'Tempora . . . Latium digesta per annum': is this a new genre simply for Ovid, or for Roman poetry in general? Who, or what, could have influenced his selection of a chronologically precise, diurnal calendar as both subject and framework for his verse? No attempt will be made here to identify his sources of information,[17] but merely to review that calendar in his poetic heritage and environment.

The Calendar in the Poetic Tradition

The theme of days, months, and seasons marked by the rising and setting of constellations had attracted the attention of poets since the time of Hesiod. But whether a poet before Ovid actually constructed a poem around the framework of a calendar is, in view of paucity of evidence, difficult to say. In the Greek world it is rather improbable that any did so, given the absence of a fixed calendar. Time-reckoning varied so greatly from city to city, each *polis* had its own month-names, and uncertainty long prevailed concerning the actual duration of the solar year.[18] Simias of Rhodes (*c*.300 BC) wrote an elegiac poem on the months and origins of their names,[19] but it is unlikely that it was structured on a day-to-day framework. The work is lost.[20]

Callimachus of Cyrene (*c*.305–*c*.240 BC), court poet to the Ptolemies in Alexandria, is said by Suidas to have written a prose work called Μηνῶν προσηγορίαι κατ᾽ ἔθνος καὶ πόλεις.[21] The names of what months, exactly, that he was discussing are unknown as this work too is lost. A work in prose, however, would not in any case have the same difficulties to overcome. But Callimachus also wrote an elegiac poem in four books called *Aitia*, which treated in a series of episodes all sorts of aetiological legends connected with Greek history, customs, and rites. This work had a very great influence on Roman poets,[22] especially Propertius (as he often

---

[17] Already attempted by Merkel (1841) in the prolegomena to his edition of the *Fasti*. See also Frazer (1929), p. xii in the preface to his edition of same, and Peeters (1939) 49–63.

[18] Bickerman (1980) 30ff.

[19] Fränkel (1945) 240 n. 9; Wilkinson (1955) 242.

[20] Powell, *Collectanea Alexandrina*, p. 112 fr. 8. The fragments of Simias are discussed by Fränkel (1915).

[21] Herter, 'Kallimachos (6)', *PW* Suppl. v (1931) 403. Pfeiffer (1949–53) i. 339.

[22] See Wimmel (1960). Miller (1982) 372 n. 2 cites notable examples from the

himself acknowledges: 2. 1. 40, 34. 32; 3. 1. 1, 9. 43; 4. 1. 64.) and Ovid.[23] The *Fasti* itself is riddled with Callimachean features such as frequent dialogues between poet and deities, the personal approach of the poet, his pose as an inquirer after antiquarian information, sacred rites, etc.[24] Indeed, its very first line pays it tribute 'tempora cum causis . . .' (repeated *F* 4. 11), and so establishes the fact that aetiology itself is to be a fundamental concept of the poem.

It is tempting to ask whether *tempora*, the calendar, provided the overall scheme of Callimachus' poem as it did of Ovid's; the four books could have corresponded conveniently to the four seasons. All statements about the *Aitia* rest on partial evidence, since the work survives only in fragments. But so far as that evidence goes we find no hint of either of the calendars (Macedonian or Egyptian) which would have been in use in contemporary Alexandria. Certain poems centre on the Thesmophoria,[25] or mention the Pithoigia and Choes,[26] festivals from the Athenian year, others deal with religious observances from other parts of the Greek world; but these represent only one element in a mixed bag of aetiological topics.[27] This miscellany was indeed carefully organized: an internal structure may have been provided by groupings, or recurrences, of thematically related material.[28] As to external structure, it seems that books 1–2 had a narrative framework, the dialogue between the poet and the Muses; books 3–4 were framed by the two long court poems, *Victory of Berenice* and *Lock of Berenice*, which begin and end them.[29] But in this organization temporal sequence apparently has no importance.

In the case of the Roman poets, it is no difficult task to track

vast literature on the subject. The older fragments of the *Aitia* are collected by Pfeiffer; additional texts in Lloyd-Jones and Parsons, *Supplementum Hellenisticum* (1983), frr. 238–77.

[23] Heinze (1919) examines the elegiac narrative in the *Fasti* against the backdrop of Propertius' narratives in bk. 4 and fragments of the *Aitia*.

[24] See also Wilkinson (1955) 248; Fränkel (1945) 145–6.

[25] Thesmophoria, fr. 63.

[26] Pithoigia and Choes, part of the setting for Pollis' feast, fr. 178.

[27] For a convenient summary of contents as then known, see P. M. Fraser, *Ptolemaic Alexandria* (1972) i. 721–32.

[28] Some possible examples are discussed by A. S. Hollis, *CQ* 32 (1982), 118–19, *ZPE* 93 (1992) 6–8.

[29] See most recently A. Kerkhecker, *ZPE* 71 (1988), 16–24.

down those who touched on themes or topics such as *aetia, orig-ines*, festivals, legends, myths, and constellations (the second line of the *Fasti* ('signa') is a tribute to Aratus) which proliferate both in the *Aitia* and the *Fasti*.[30] It is not so easy to trace one who ver-sified a calendar, even though the idea of celebrating holidays had been floated by Horace before 16 BC (*Od.* 4. 2. 41–4):

> concines laetosque dies et urbis
> publicum ludum super impetrato
> fortis Augusti reditu Forumque
> litibus orbum.

You shall hymn the holidays and the public games of the city in honour of the granted return of the brave Augustus, and the forum devoid of law suits.

If Iullus Antonius, addressee of the ode, did take up Horace's suggestion, there remains no trace. There was, however, a certain Sabinus who is mentioned by Ovid as having been at work on an 'opus dierum' at the time of his death (*Ex P.* 4. 16. 15–16). The sound of this 'opus' certainly smacks of a calendrical poem, although Ovid does not draw an analogy between the work of Sabinus and his own. Propertius, Ovid's older contemporary, is the only poet whose extant work shows us how 'dies' was employed as a theme before the creation of the *Fasti*. It is one of the three topics announced for his projected aetiological elegies in book 4 (1. 69):

> sacra diesque canam et cognomina prisca locorum

I shall celebrate rites and days and ancient names of places

The echo in Ovid's assertions in the two proems of the *Fasti* is unmistakable (1. 1; 2. 7). But unlike Ovid, Propertius does not live up to his claim. Not one of his subsequent elegies really concerns 'dies'. Only one deals primarily with an aspect of a sacred rite (*Bona Dea*, 4. 9. 25), and one with an ancient Roman place name (*Mons Tarpeius*, 4. 4). And intriguing is the fact that Propertius intended to avoid fulfilling his stated aims. No sooner does he say he will sing about sacred rites, days, and ancient place names than he has Horos, the Egyptian astrologer, immediately interrupt him to warn him not to neglect his allotted task of writing love elegy,

---

[30] Wilkinson (1955) 242.

his 'fallax opus' wherein lay his 'castra' (4. 1. 135). Apollo had for-
bidden the poet to partake in public life, and now Horos' intervention is designed to warn him to avoid matters of public
interest in his poetry as well (4. 1. 133 ff.). This intervention
appears to be nothing short of a 'whimsical apology' for
Propertius' not having persevered with his stated intention.[31]
With regard to 'dies', in fact, he never really began. The implication is that such topics as he announced were not in the domain of
love elegists. (Tibullus promised to celebrate the triumph of
Messalinus, but never did (2. 5. 113 ff.).[32] But why did the self-
styled 'Callimachus Romanus' (4. 1. 64) not carry out his
promise?

It must be remembered that, following the Callimachean
precedent, Roman poets had made it a conventional motif to
reject the epic genre in favour of the elegiac. The prologue to the
Aitia, in which Apollo demands, not grand epic, but a slender
song from the poet,[33] is, of all passages in Greek poetry, the one
most quoted by the Romans.[34] To embark upon an epic theme
only to be interrupted by an admonition of Apollo to stick to
slender ones, is a recurring conceit that appears for example in
Virgil (*Ecl.* 6. 3–5), Horace (*Od.* 4. 15. 1–4), and Propertius (3. 3.
13–24, 39–46). Ovid stamps his own personality on it by replacing
Apollo with his mistress as the admonisher (*Am.* 2. 18. 13–19).

Propertius also punctuates his elegies with variations on this
conceit. For example, he often betrays a reluctance to treat
themes that strayed very far from the personal, or more specifically here, to treat themes with an Augustan orientation.
Augustus' patron of letters, Maecenas, was evidently trying to
induce him to write such poems, as his other celebrated clients,
Virgil and Horace, had done. The poet protests to Maecenas
quite openly. If he had the power, he says, he would sing of the
wars and the deeds of Caesar (2. 1. 17–26), but his Callimachean
elegy is not up to dealing with heroic topics such as Caesar's
Phrygian ancestry (2. 1. 40–2). He repeats his protest thus (3. 9.
3–4):

> quid me scribendi tam vastum mittis in aequor?
> non sunt apta meae grandia vela rati.

---

[31] Ibid. 243.   [32] Newman (1967) 115.   [33] See Pfeiffer fr. 1. 21–8.
[34] Wilkinson (1955) 48.

Why are you pushing me out upon so vast an ocean of writing? Huge
canvasses are not suitable for my craft.

and adds that, if Maecenas changes his way of life and enters
public office, then, and only then will he accept his commands
('iussa') and celebrate in poetry the themes he demands (3. 9.
21 ff.).[35] Even Augustus himself does not escape the poet's direct
refusal. In the future, Propertius tells him, when he is in his
prime, he will celebrate his wars; in the meantime he is still too
weak for the mighty task and can only offer him 'vilia tura' (2. 10).

Although Callimachus and his *Aitia* are said to have inspired
the Roman poets' refusal to write epics, and so to have created a
conventional motif in Augustan literature, it must also be
assumed that the Romans would adopt such a motif only if it
were congenial to their own environment and appropriate to the
message they had to convey. Propertius seems to have added
extra emphasis to his *recusatio*, possibly because elegy, the
medium in which he specialized, was not regarded as suitable for
epic themes. Pressure for heroic poetry, then, was still floating in
the literary atmosphere.[36] His address to Maecenas and Augustus
leaves no doubt as to where that pressure was coming from, or as
to the type of (Augustan) themes required. The *recusatio* of
Propertius in particular provides insight into what it was in
poetry that could be of service to the state, or 'militia' in poetic
terms, as Ovid puts it (*F* 2. 9). It is evident also that there were
plenty of poets around who were endeavouring, even after Virgil,
to write epic. Ovid rescues some of their names from obscurity:
Ponticus (*T* 4. 47), Macer (*Am.* 2. 18. 1–2; *Ex P.* 2. 10. 10 ff.; 4. 16.
6), Rabirius (*Ex P.* 4. 16. 5), Severus (*Ex P.* 4. 16. 9; 4. 2. 2),
Montanus (*Ex P.* 4. 16. 11), and others.

Propertius' refusal to write on national and Augustan themes is
not, in the context of the Callimachean/Roman *recusatio*, so
remarkable. The frankness with which he names and addresses
those who were applying the pressure belies any notion that that
pressure was menacing or sinister, or that he lived in fear of censure or rebuke for non-compliance. Yet in his fourth book, which
contains five aetiological elegies, despite Horos' warning he does
succeed in breaking out of the love elegy mould by treating what

---

[35] Griffin (1984) 195.   [36] Newman (1967) 184.

may be termed Roman, if not national and Augustan themes, with the topography of contemporary Rome as a scheme.[37]

It has been suggested that Propertius finally decided upon composing the Callimachean *aition* with a Roman setting as an effort to comply with Maecenas' request.[38] Another suggestion is that, after 18 BC and the passing of Augustus' moral legislation, Augustus wished to take over more direct control of literature to encourage support for his moral programme and so applied heavier pressure on writers.[39] The latter suggestion would be more convincing if Propertius' final poem (4. 11), a funeral elegy eulogizing Cornelia, daughter of Scribonia, and her status of *univira*, had not reflected something of a defiance of that very legislation, which decreed that all widows of child-bearing age had to marry again. It also implicitly holds up to unfavourable comparison Cornelia's half-sister Julia, forced by her father into a number of marriages for dynastic purposes. Perhaps it was the fall of Maecenas from favour which caused 'encouragement' for Augustan themes to come more directly from the Princeps himself. Yet if Propertius bowed to that pressure, he nevertheless still felt free enough to express such themes as he wished. And Propertius, as the first to apply the Callimachean model to a poetic description of Roman themes, was an undoubted influence on Ovid.

Nevertheless, there is no indication in his fourth book that Propertius had planned a scheme of a poetical calendar, as has been suggested by some critics.[40] And it is most unlikely that the Roman Callimachus saw any calendrical system in the Alexandrian *aitia* either. As noted before, Propertius does not use 'dies' as a theme at all. His book is rather a collection of elegies with a separate elegy on each topic.[41] The poet gives no indication that his elegies were meant to be read as one poem. As is appropriate to his elegiac medium, he has kept his work on a small scale. If there is any unifying focus at all, it is a topographical, not a calendrical scheme.[42]

One can only speculate why Propertius chose not to write

---

[37] Miller (1982) 381.   [38] Ibid.   [39] Williams (1978) 59.

[40] Otis (1970) 22 and 29 claims that Ovid completed the Propertian scheme of a poetical calendar intended as a conversion of the analogously structured *Aitia* of Callimachus.

[41] Wilkinson (1955) 242–3.   [42] Miller (1982) 381.

about 'dies' after all. Horace had already floated the idea, as we have seen, but perhaps the names of ancient places were of more topical interest at the time he wrote book 4.[43] More likely, he was only too aware of the pitfalls awaiting him. At any rate, while Propertius indubitably showed Ovid the way towards Callimachean treatment of Roman themes, there is no evidence that he might have influenced Ovid's decision to write elegy on an epic scale, or to versify the entire Roman calendar. Thus we have reached a dead end. While Ovid's literary heritage and environment certainly influenced his choice of genre and the idea of setting Roman themes to an Alexandrian tone, no extant literary predecessor really explains why an elegist should decide to structure a poem on something as large and divisive as a twelve-month calendar. No elegist had attempted such a mammoth task before. Ovid was indeed breaking new ground in poetry.

We must turn now to non-poetical influences to proceed with the enquiry. Ovid provides clues in the *Fasti* itself which suggest the importance which he thought Augustus attached to the calendar. First, apart from mention of a rather vague 'annales prisci' (1. 7; 4. 2), calendars are his only acknowledged source of information for the sacred rites and seasons (3. 87–96). (And rightly so, in tune with the calendar theme and his pose as a peripatetic enquirer after information.) Second, he says that the *Fasti* is his 'militia' or service to the state and compensation for not bearing arms (2. 9). This is a neat reversal of Propertius' 'castra' and his dedication to 'militiam Veneris' (4. 1. 135 ff.). Perhaps also a dig at his older contemporary's *recusatio* for not fulfilling his aim to sing of 'sacra diesque'. At any rate 'militia' now leads us to expect a work with national, Augustan topics. That expectation is fulfilled in the portraits of Augustus and members of the ruling family which punctuate the poem. Third, he dedicates the *Fasti*, his proposed 'epic with a difference', to Caesar Augustus (*F* 2. 17–18; *T* 2. 551).

These clues prompt an enquiry into the contemporary significance of the Roman calendar in the late Augustan principate, its connection with Caesar Augustus, and what might have prompted a poet into thinking it would serve as an appropriate vehicle for performing a service to the state.

---

[43] No poem of Propertius can be put later than 16 BC. See Syme (1978) 4.

History and Contemporary Significance of the Calendar

The Roman calendar had had a somewhat chequered history, both in its function as a device for measuring time, and as a guide to the religious, political, legal, and business activities for Roman citizens, by the time Ovid decided to set it to verse. The problematic nature of the Republican calendar as a time chart is well documented by the *Fasti Antiates Maiores* (*Ant. Mai.*), the only extant Republican calendar.[44] It is fortunate that we have this evidence, as it allows for assessing the extent of the political and religious changes that took place in Rome by comparing it with fragments of over forty extant calendars that have survived after the Julian reform, which chart the evolution.

A summary of the method of time-reckoning in the Republican period is necessary in order to appreciate fully the impact of the Julian reform of the Roman calendar in the mid-first century BC. The *Fasti Antiates Maiores* comprises twelve months, four of 31 days, seven of 29 days and one of 28, totalling 355 days a year. A thirteenth column shows an intercalary month, inserted every other year, at which time February was reduced to 23 days. Twenty-two or 23 days were added after the Terminalia (23 Feb.). The five remaining days of February were added at the end of the intercalary month, so that the 'intercalaris' or Mercedonius, consisted of 27 or 28 days.[45]

The peculiar features of the pre-Julian calendar, the length of the months and the intercalation system, were seen by Censorinus (AD 238) as an effort to synchronize the civil and solar years (*De die natali*, 20. 6). If this is so, it was not successful. The Roman quadrennial system comprised 355 + 378 + 355 + 377 days, a cycle which added up to 1,465 days, four days longer than the 1,461 days of the solar year. Thus the calendar crept forward four days every quadrennium in relation to the solar year and the four seasons.[46]

Difficulties in coping with the charting of time in the Republican period are evinced by a long history of attempts by the Romans to align the civil and solar year. Livy records that Numa inserted intercalary months (1. 19); Macrobius (*Sat.* 1. 13)

---

[44] Degrassi (1963) 1 ff.   [45] Bickerman (1980) 43; Michels (1967) 16 and 145.
[46] Bickerman (1980) 44; Michels (1967) 17.

shows how intercalation produced more problems than it solved; he does not mention that any other solution was considered. Quoting Tuditanus, an earlier source, he says that the Decemviri, in preparing a code of Laws (*Lex XII Tabularum*) brought before the people (*c*.450 BC) a bill concerning intercalation into the calendar (1. 13. 21).[47] The *Lex Acilia de calandando*, belonging to the consulship of Manius Acilius Glabrio (191 BC), was another attempt to deal with the problems of reckoning time. It was clearly unsuccessful, as in this period (after the Hannibalic War), the practice of intercalation became neglected, so that in 190 BC the calendar was ahead by 117 days. This discrepancy was reduced to 72 days in 168 BC, indicating that intercalation must have been reintroduced during the intervening 22 years.[48]

With the trial and error methods of attempting to align the civil with the solar year, it comes as no surprise to find that Cato, writing about farming in the second century BC, reckons time mainly by the stars. He uses the civil calendar only for business contracts, and the formula of the contracts is telling: it contains the clause 'si intercalatum erit' (*De Agr.* 150. 2). Polybios (9. 14–15), discussing at length the methods by which a general should calculate time for military manœuvres, does not mention the calendar, for in his day it had no regular relation to the seasons.[49]

At some unknown time schematic intercalation was abandoned and power for making intercalations for correcting inexactitudes was vested in the pontiffs, so Censorinus informs us (20. 6). The standard was to be that the same sacrifices should be performed at the same seasons—'Quod ad tempus ut sacrificiorum libamenta serventur fetusque pecorum . . . diligenter habenda ratio intercalandi est . . .' (Cic. *Leg.* 2. 12. 29). But intercalation became a tool for less than worthy motives, and the pontiffs became responsible for placing in disorder the very thing which was entrusted to them to regulate (Censor. 20. 6). Before surveying the problems that the pontiffs added to the already unreliable calendar, it is necessary at this point to emphasize its manifold functions, and the manner in which it was interwoven into the fabric of Roman religious, political, and social life.

The Roman calendar was a festival calendar and *fasti*, thought

[47] See the *Lex XII Tabularum* in *Remains of Old Latin*, Loeb edn., iii (1951) 504.

[48] Bickerman (1980) 46.   [49] Michels (1967) 16 n. 19.

now to have been so called from the days on which there were no
religious impediments to public business,[50] were divided primarily to ensure proper observance of the state religious festivals.
Each day, in fact, had a mark of religious significance attached to
it, which regulated activities in the law courts and the assemblies.
The character of the days were marked in large letters thus: F
(*fastus*) = day on which citizens might initiate suits in civil law in
the court of the urban praetor when business could be transacted
in court; C (*comitialis*) = when the *comitia* might be summoned to
vote on proposed legislation, in elections, or on the verdict for
criminal offences; N (*nefastus*) = days not available for *legis
actiones* or *comitia*; EN (*endotercisus*) = days split between the
evening and the morning which were N, and the afternoon,
which was F; NP = uncertain (curiously neither Varro, Ovid, nor
Macrobius mention its meaning), but probably means *nefastus
publicus*, as all 49 NP days are named days (the kalends of March,
all the ides, and 36 of the 45 individual name days), displayed in
large lettering on all calendars across the vertical monthly
columns in abbreviated form: TERMI(nalia), AGON(alia),
LUPER(calia), etc.[51] The all-important visual impact of the large
lettering of the Feriae Stativae in both Republican and Julian calendars is identical,[52] so demonstrating the continuity in form and
emphasis, at least in the written documents.

What *feriae* are, exactly, is not an easy question to answer,[53]
but the ancient writers provide hints as to what people actually
did on such days. Varro (*LL* 6. 12) claims that they were days
instituted for the sake of the gods ('dies deorum causa instituti'),
and Macrobius affirms this: 'Festi dis dicati sunt' (*Sat.* 1. 16. 2).
He goes on to distinguish between the festival days on which sacrifices and banquets in honour of the gods and public games are
held, so-called *feriae*, and working days which include court days,
assembly days, adjournment days, appointed days, and battle
days (1. 16. 3). Cicero confirms the notion of festival days as holidays or *feriae* where he states that, on holidays, free men should
rest from lawsuits and controversies, and slaves from labour and

[50] Wiseman (1979) 13.

[51] Livy, 1. 20. 5; Ovid, *F* 1. 45 ff.; Macr. *Sat.* 1. 16. 3; Michels (1967) 173 ff. for
discussion of the character of the days. Also 26–7; 45; 66.

[52] Degrassi (1963) 1 ff.

[53] Michels (1967) 69 ff. discusses all the characteristics pertaining to them.

toil (*Leg. 2. 12. 29*). He further implies that *feriae* were normally days of leisure for all when he complains to Cassius that he has had to spend such days occupied with the composition of speeches, and so absolute leisure was a thing he never knew (*Planc.* 27. 66. 13).

Even those employed on farms, who would least of all be expected to afford time off for *feriae*, were advised what might or might not be done on the land. Among the duties of a bailiff (*vilicus*), Cato decrees, is the observance of the festival days ('feriae serventur') (*Agr.* 5. 1) even though he must perform no religious rites himself ('rem divinam'), except on the occasion of the Compitalia at the crossroads or before the hearth (*Agr.* 5. 4). The housekeeper (*vilica*) was not to engage in religious worship either, as she had to remember that it was the master who did so for the whole household. On the kalends, nones, and ides, or any other 'festus dies', however, she must hang a garland over the hearth and on those days pray to the household gods ('Lares familiares') (*Agr.* 143. 1–2). Columella (2. 21), quoting the practices of Roman ancestors (including Cato) as a guide, instructs the farmer on numerous tasks which might or might not be performed on *feriae* (See also Virg. *Georg.* 1. 268–75; Macr. *Sat.* 1. 16. 10, 11, 24, 25, 28). Religious festivals were celebrated, according to Macrobius, by offering sacrifices to the gods or by a ritual banquet, or by the observance of *feriae*. The chief examples of the *feriae*, he says, were the Agonalia, the Carmentalia, and the Lupercalia. Fines were exacted if *feriae* were desecrated by work being performed, and the pontifex maximus and flamens, not permitted to see work in progress on such a day, gave public warning that nothing of the sort should be done (*Sat.* 1. 16. 4, 6, 9).

Even with the information imparted by the writers, however, it is far from clear how many Romans attended or took part in religious rites performed on the great festival days, even if they had to abstain from certain labours and activities of the normal work day. All that can be surmised is that the public *feriae* were in general terms holidays on which religious rites were performed, civil lawsuits were avoided, and all men, slaves included, were entitled to a period of rest.[54] Furthermore, not all the state *feriae* were

---

[54] Scullard (1981) 39. Michels (1967) 78 shows that, while *feriae* demanded certain observances, some festival days were far more popular than others, and many aspects of the working life of the city were not unduly interfered with.

marked in the calendar. *Feriae conceptivae* were understandably absent from the documents, as the dates, set and announced annually by the pontiffs, varied from year to year (Macr. *Sat.* 1. 16. 6; Varro, *LL* 6. 25–6). Ovid never fails to celebrate every one of the large-lettered major festivals, the *feriae stativae* marked both in the Republican and Julian calendars (they did not vary), but he does omit *feriae conceptivae*. In looking to the calendar as his source material he would not find them there (*F* 1. 657–60):

> Ter quater evolvi signantes tempora fastos,
> nec Sementiva est ulla reperta dies;
> cum mihi (sensit enim) 'lux haec indicitur' inquit
> Musa, 'quid a fastis non stata sacra petis?'

Three or four times I unrolled the calendar marking the seasons, and yet no day of sowing was to be found. The Muse (for she had noticed), says: 'that day is publicly proclaimed: why seek movable festivals in the calendar?'

The Roman state *feriae*, both *stativae* and *conceptivae*, affected the character of a day officially. An example of how this happened is provided by Cicero. The kalends of January was ordinarily marked F, but in the year 58 BC the Compitalia, *feriae conceptivae* fell on this day (Cicero, *Pis.* 8) and so changed it to NP. The 29 December was normally marked C, but in the year 67 BC the Compitalia fell on that day and made it NP so that no *comitia* could be held (most unfortunately for the tribune Manilius, who tried to carry a law on that day).[55]

Religion and the calendar, then, were inextricably intertwined in Roman public life. This fact explains why the power to make intercalations for correcting inexactitudes had been vested in the pontiffs, who also happened to be magistrates. This latter fact unfortunately motivated the priests to manipulate the calendar for partisan political purposes, for by announcing *feriae*, public thanksgivings for victories, or intercalary months, they could provide more or less time for legislation, extend or reduce the tenure of a particular office holder, or the length of a particular public contract.[56] Cases of manipulation of the calendar by the use of festivals to postpone *comitia* for example, are cited by

---

[55] Dio, 36. 42 and Michels (1967) 46.

[56] Liebeschuetz (1979) 2. Censor. *De d. n.* 20. 6; Macr. *Sat.* 1. 13. 2; Michels (1967) 45–6.

Cicero (*Q. Fr.* 2. 4. 4; *Fam.* 8. 11. 1), Caesar (*BG* 2. 35), Plutarch (*Sull.* 8. 3), and Appian (*BC* 1. 56. 5; 59. 6). Dio (49. 62. 1) cites a case where a pontifex attempted to intercalate an extra month for the enactment of the senate's measures. Abuse of the system of intercalation for negligence is cited by Cicero (*Leg.* 2. 12. 29), for impropriety by Suetonius (*Div. Iul.* 40), for corruption by Solinus (1. 43), for political gain by Censorinus (20. 7).

Paradoxically, both despite and because of the Republican cal-endar's inefficiency in time-reckoning, its importance in the political–religious life of the city was paramount. But arbitrary intercalation following no predictable pattern rendered the civil calendar useless to the farmer, the sailor, and the general, who were better off making their calculations by the stars. In 50 BC Cicero still did not know, on 13 February, whether or not there would be an intercalation on the 23rd (*Att.* 5. 21. 14). During the civil wars intercalation was abandoned completely so that, at the beginning of 46 BC, the civil year lagged behind the solar by 90 days.[57] The day celebrated as New Year's day should have been 14 October of the old year,[58] and the Roman harvest thanksgiving was being celebrated long before the harvest had even begun (Suet. *Div. Iul.* 40). Cicero (*Ad Att.* 6. 1. 1), Ovid (*F* 3. 155–165), Suetonius (*Div. Iul.* 40), Plutarch (*Caes.* 59), Dio (43. 26. 1), and Censorinus (20. 6), all testify to the chaos generated by the old calendar which was so often divergent from the course of the sun. Macrobius (*Sat.* 1. 16. 3) describes the year 46 BC, the last of the Republican calendar, as 'annus confusionis ultimus'.

Set against a background of such chaos, the impact of the Dictator's reform of the Roman calendar on religious, political, and civil life can hardly be overestimated. He completely aban-doned the old calendar of 355 days, replacing it with one of 365 days with a single day intercalated every fourth year on 24 February to achieve the total of 365¼. He inserted 90 days in 46 BC, so that from 1 January 45 BC the months were correctly aligned to the seasons and the solar year.[59] In the process of reform, how-ever, he was careful not to alter the religious calendar. This was achieved by placing the ten extra days over the former 355-day year at the end of various months, so that the kalends, nones, ides, and dates of the state festivals remained undisturbed. No

[57] Bickerman (1980) 46.   [58] Balsdon (1969) 58.
[59] Samuel (1972) 155; Bickerman (1980) 47.

addition was made to February lest changes in connection with
the worship of the gods result (Macr. *Sat.* 1. 16. 7), and in each
month *feriae* were kept to their appointed places (Macr. *Sat.* 1.
16. 11). The Divalia, for example, celebrated on 21 December, was
not moved, although the notation of its day changed from X Kal.
Jan. to XII Kal. Jan., as December now had 31 instead of 29
days.[60]

Caesar's reason for not interfering with the state religious festivals of the calendar is not difficult to determine. Many of the
feriae were not only agricultural festivals but also reminders of
Rome's past, celebrations of events in Roman legend or history.
The Parilia, for example, although recognized as a shepherds'
festival, was celebrated as the birthday of Rome. The Regifugium
celebrated the expulsion of the Tarquins (Ovid, *F* 2. 685–8), the
Poplifugia recalled the sack of Rome by the Gauls, the Consualia
the rape of the Sabine women, and the Larentalia recalled Acca
Larentia, who nursed Romulus and Remus (Varro, *LL* 6. 18, 20,
23). The ritual performed at each festival offered to participants a
series of tableaux, evoking various elements of the past, distant or
recent, linking it with the present and evoking on particular *feriae*
diverse aspects of the religious and cultural tradition. This has
been aptly called 'a picture of Romanness', or a conceptual
pageant of Rome and what it was to be Roman.[61]

And just before Caesar's reform, Varro had published his
Antiquitatum rerum humanarum et divinarum libri XLI, the first
twenty-five books dealing with 'res humanae', the remaining six-
teen with 'res divinae' (Aug. *Civ. Dei* 6. 3). The eighth book contained information on festivals, perhaps a kind of commentary on
the calendar, encouraging connections between the religious festivals and the city's ancient beginnings.[62] For the Dictator to
move the festivals about in the process of his reform would have
risked creating confusion in collective Roman identity, and

---

[60] Bickerman (1980) 47. For the date of Caesar's reform cf. Censor. *De d. n.* 20.
8: 'G. Caesar pontifex maximus suo III et M. Aemilii Lepidi consulatu.' Other
sources are Macr. *Sat.* 1. 14. 6 ff.; Plut. *Caes.* 59; App. *BC* 2. 154; Dio, 43. 26; Suet.
Div. Iul. 40; Pliny, *NH* 18. 211; Solin. 1. 45.   [61] Beard (1987) 11.

[62] There were also many antiquarians other than Varro writing on religious
topics in the late Republic. For details on these see Rawson (1985) 233, 298–316.
For how this kind of scholarly antiquarianism institutionalized unintelligibility as
a social control, see Gordon (1990) 189. See Cardauns (1976) 53–6 for Varro's
eighth book on festivals.

affronting both patriotic sentiment and *ius divinum*. He understood that the practical use of the calendar as a device for measuring time was but a single one of the multiple cultural–political–
religious–historical facets that made up the institution of the
calendar.

The days added to the calendar by Caesar were all marked F in
order to make more time for legal business, but not more for
comitia to meet and so increase the number of days a magistrate's
power could exercise undue influence.[63] But the Senate, too, had
a part in shaping the new pattern of the Roman year, and of the
state religion, which was taking place. In 45 BC it honoured
Caesar (in his absence) by establishing *feriae* on the anniversaries
of his victories (Dio, 43. 44. 6; App. *BC* 2. 106. 442;), on his birthday (Dio, 44. 4. 4; 47. 18. 5), and by naming a month Iulius in his
honour (Dio, 44. 5. 2; App. *BC* 2. 106. 443; Macr. *Sat.* 1. 12. 34.[64]
The new Julian *feriae*, although receiving no names, and anno-
tated only in small letters (e.g. 'Feriae, quod eo die C. Caesar est
natus', or 'divi Iulii natalis'),[65] were marked NP, the usual desig-
nation for the great public festivals in the calendar.

If we use the generalizations discussed previously for the character of *feriae* and NP days, we may assume that, on the new
Julian anniversaries, sacrifices were offered at public expense by
the pontiffs (to what god(s) is not known), *legis actiones* were not
permitted, *comitia* were not held, and people were able to take
time off their normal labours if they so chose. As his birthday
took the form of a *supplicatio*, we may assume that everybody had
to take part and wear a laurel wreath (Dio, 47. 18. 5).[66]

The marking of Julius Caesar's anniversaries alongside those of
the state cult initiated the process of the incorporation of the personal cult of that individual into the state religion, the history of
the city, and the Roman collective consciousness. What seems to
have facilitated this process was the merger of private with state
anniversaries. To explain: *feriae* fell into two main categories,
publicae and *privatae*, the latter being special religious observances traditional in a family, such as the celebration of a birthday or the mourning of a death. On these occasions the family or

[63] Macr. *Sat.* 1. 14. 12. The extant Julian calendars show the days added by
Caesar (listed by Macr. 1. 14. 7) as marked F.

[64] Weinstock (1971) 197, 155 ff.   [65] Degrassi (1963) 481–2.

[66] Liebeschuetz (1979) 207; 80.

individual is *feriatus*, but no one else is concerned.[67] Macrobius refers to *feriae* which belonged exclusively to certain families, and mentions not only the Julian but also the Claudian, Aemilian, and Cornelian families (*Sat.* 1. 16. 7), who had been prominent in the Republican era. Livy (5. 52. 2) makes reference to the Roman hero Fabius, who, amidst fierce battle, still braved his way to the Quirinal to celebrate the annual sacrifice to the tutelary deity of his clan, and so won a eulogy from Camillus for allowing no interruption of family rites, even in war. In Livy's message, the observance of family rites on the *feriae privatae* was evidently as important as observance of the state festivals on the *feriae publicae* specified in the official calendar. After the calendrical honours bestowed on Caesar by the Senate, it could only be a matter of time before the Julian household anniversaries and family worship, their *feriae privatae*, also became *feriae publicae* and incorporated in the state worship.

The untimely death of Caesar did not halt the process of change in the calendar. It is probable that, had Antony been the victor at Actium, it would have been his birthday and victories that would have been incorporated in the calendar, as he would have been recognized, *de facto*, as Caesar's political heir. As it happened it was Octavian, Caesar's posthumously adopted son, who was the victor. The result of his hard-won supremacy was that the national calendar became flooded with *feriae* on the Julian (now also Augustus') anniversaries, first of the individual, then of his family. Between the years 45 BC and AD 10, the number of NP days celebrating Roman *feriae* increased by twenty, bringing the number of 49 in the pre-Julian calendar to a total of 69 before the death of Augustus. They replaced twelve days marked C, five marked F, and three marked N.[68] Thus the new calendar was having a gradual yet considerable impact on Roman life, religious, political, and civil.

Just as importantly, the calendrical inscriptions which had been proliferating in the city and outside it since 45 BC were creating a new 'genre'.[69] They represented short-hand epitomes of the

---

[67] Macr. *Sat.* 1. 16. 4–8; Festus, *Gloss. Lat.* 4. 348–9; Cato, *Agr.* 140; Michels (1967) 73.

[68] I have made this calculation from the chart in Degrassi (1963) 346 ff.

[69] How these calendars are also evidence of the degree to which the complexity of Roman religion was linked to the institution of literacy, see Gordon (1990) 184 ff.

Roman religious, cultural, and historical tradition. And the new *feriae* marking the birthday, career, and titles of the ruler, not to mention the new month called 'Augustus', were a constant visible reminder of him and his place at the heart of that tradition. No one who needed to consult a calendar for the next market day, or the next court day, could avoid it. This new 'genre' would thus have reached a far wider audience than that educated and leisured enough to read the literature of the poets which celebrated the ruler.

The history of the calendar even after *annus Iulianus* had not been uneventful, however.[70] Had Caesar not had first a colleague desirous of using the Dictator's name for his own advancement, then a family heir with political ambitions equal to his own, it is most probable that the new Julian festival days would have been very short-lived. The change of the name of the month of Quintilis to Iulius, for example, was ignored after the Ides of March until Antony, as consul, announced that the Ludi Apollinares were to be held 'Nonis Iuliis'. Cicero and the conspirators were shocked, for they wished to retain Quintilis (Cic. *Att.* 16. 1. 1. (8 July 44); 4. 1 (10 July 44), but the new name became legal after the appearance of the comet in July 44 (Dio, 45. 7. 2).[71] And although it had been decreed in 45 that a public sacrifice be performed on Caesar's birthday,[72] it was not, as far as is known, performed in 44 and 43. In 42 it was made obligatory by the triumvirs with threats of severe penalties, religious and secular, for defaulters (Dio, 47. 18. 5). Octavian's subsequent and remarkably enduring political success ensured that the festival was thereafter always observed, for Horace mentions it *c.*20 BC,[73] the *Fasti Amiternini* in *c.* AD 20, the *Fasti Antiates Ministrorum* in *c.*AD 23–37,[74] the *Feriale Duranum* in the third century,[75] and Polemius Silvius in the fifth.[76]

It is also therefore most unlikely that Julian *feriae* would have

[70] 46 BC, the year the calendar was created, is cited by Censorinus as 'annus Iulianus' 20. 11; 21. 7; 23. 16.   [71] Weinstock (1971) 157.

[72] Dio, 40. 4. 4. says in 44, but Weinstock (1971) 200, 270 argues for 45.

[73] *Epist.* 1. 5. 9: 'cras nato Caesare festus / . . . dies.' This must refer to Julius' birthday in July, not Augustus' in late September as l. 11 refers to it as 'aestivam . . . noctem'. See Weinstock (1971) 207 n. 4.

[74] See Degrassi (1963) for the dates of the respective calendars.

[75] Fink *et al.* (1940) 146.

[76] But oddly enough not by the Arvals, as noted by Weinstock (1971) 207.

continued to be commemorated in the calendar had Octavian not won the struggle for the position of Caesar's political heir. Being Caesar's son and Julian family heir, and even having the unique advantage of being 'filius divi' since 42 BC, was not enough. For example, his birthday, 23 September, was not made a public festival until 30 BC, after he had won at Actium and for which it was a reward (Dio, 51. 19. 2). And it was only in 27 BC that the Senate decided to name a month after him and renamed Sextilis 'Augustus'. The right of calendrical honours was thus hard-won for Caesar's heir, which only served to make the calendar of greater significance as an advertisement for his pre-eminence.

An important detail amplifies the significance Augustus placed on the calendar in relation to himself. Both Suetonius (*Aug.* 31. 2) and Dio (55. 6. 6) assert that it was not until 8 BC that Augustus officially accepted the honour of having Sextilis named after him. This fact indeed strains credulity, as the biographer and historian do not stipulate the reason for the delay. One will be postulated here: Augustus decided to recognize the honorific month only after he felt he could be seen to have made a significant contribution to the institution of the calendar itself. That contribution is as follows: after Caesar's assassination in 44 BC the pontiffs misunderstood his directions for intercalation and made the error of inserting a leap day every three instead of every four years. Thirty-six years later (9 BC) the calendar was ahead by three whole days. Augustus, by now Pontifex Maximus and so officially in charge of the calendar, corrected the error by omitting intercalation for the next 16 years (Macr. *Sat.* 1. 14. 13–15), that is, in 5 BC and AD 4.[77] At the conclusion of 16 years, one intercalary day was to be inserted at the beginning of every fourth year, and he had the whole of this arrangement engraved on a bronze tablet to ensure that it should always be observed (Macr. *Sat.* 1. 14–15).

It is possible that Augustus chose the year following his orders for emendation of the calendar, that is, 8 BC, as the appropriate time to accept at last the honorific month voted him by the Senate in 27 BC. Be that as it may, what is certain is that at the end of the period of rectification ordered by Augustus, the Roman calendar began to function normally, for the first time in its history without error. The first year of normal function was AD 8.[78]

---

[77] Samuel (1972) 156. [78] Ibid., and Bickerman (1980) 47.

Two individuals were busy composing calendars in that momentous year: Ovid, and Verrius Flaccus. Verrius was the scholarly freedman of Augustus and former handsomely paid live-in tutor to the Princeps' late grandsons (Suet. *Gram.* 17). He was also the creator of the spectacular *Fasti Praenestini*, an inscription in marble of majestic proportions (nearly 2 metres high and 5.5 broad) containing more detailed annotations than any other extant calendrical fragments. The giant calendar, set up in the forum at Praeneste and so a lavish gift to the town, was very probably dedicated to Augustus (although the opening lines are missing), just as Ovid's *Fasti* was. It is reported that Augustus himself often passed through Praeneste (Suet. *Aug.* 72. 2; 82. 1), so he could not have failed to notice and appreciate it. The scholar who had lived so long under the same roof as his master would have known better than any other what most would have pleased him.

The *Fasti Praenestini* has been dated by Degrassi between AD 6 and 9.[79] Ovid says he was engaged in the composition of his *Fasti* when the fate of his exile interrupted it (*T* 2. 551–2), that is, in AD 8.[80] The connection can never be proved, but the coincidences certainly imply that Ovid and Verrius had the same thing in mind: to pay homage to Augustus at this appropriate time by magnifying in marble and celebrating in verse the new genre that was the Roman calendar, thereby celebrating in an unprecedented way the most prolific record and proof of his preeminence. There can be little doubt that the history and contemporary significance of the Roman calendar in relation to Augustus exerted considerable influence on Ovid as he cast about for a subject for his poem.

Influence of the Contemporary Arts

The calendar recommended itself as appropriate for Ovid's poetic 'militia' on technical grounds as well. A major factor commonly selected by Ovid's critics as the very one which made his choice 'an unsound proposal', that is, that the Roman calendar allowed

[79] Degrassi (1963) 141. For the setting, see Coarelli (1982) 133.
[80] The date of Ovid's exile is to my knowledge no longer in dispute, but for literature on the subject see Levick (1976*a*) 60 and 243 n. 49. Also the views of Syme (1986) 121.

for no continuous narrative, is that which the poet must have recognized as being a great advantage. In wanting to praise
Augustus, he would have had to consider the problems involved
in writing about the achievements of the Princeps in a poem on a
large scale, be it in elegiacs or hexameters. How tricky, and how
dangerous, it would have been, for example, to celebrate in narrative form a career saturated with the blood of civil war, and without being able to refer to the fallen, Roman enemy. Moreover, the
arch villain, Antony, had children who were nephews of the ruler
and had been brought up in his house. Germanicus, grandson of
Antony, had been adopted into the Julian house in AD 4, and was
clearly intended to play a major part in Augustus' dynastic plans.
When Ovid came to rededicate the *Fasti* to Germanicus years
later, it was no doubt with relief that he was able to incorporate
without discomfort the words (i. 13) 'Caesaris arma canant alii',
because he had chosen to reject such an unwise option for his
tribute to Caesar Augustus from the outset.

Ovid's older contemporary, Virgil, had written a narrative epic,
but had got around the problem brilliantly by setting his epic in
the past, with occasional, select, prophetic glimpses to the
Augustan Golden Age.[81] But Virgil was fortunate enough to have
produced his epic relatively early in the regime, before the official
inauguration of the Golden Age at the Secular Games in 17 BC.
Ovid was not so lucky. He had to write his tribute to Augustus at
a time when the Golden Age was over twenty years old and more
than a little tarnished. A scheme on the lines of Virgil's would by
now, even for Virgil, never work. A plan had to be sought that
could both avoid extensive narrative, and accommodate and celebrate Augustus in a manner appropriate to his great achievement
of unprecedented, enduring supremacy in a context of Roman
peace. The Roman calendar, celebrating the ruler not only in
warlike but also in non-combative roles such as Pater Patriae and
Pontifex Maximus, certainly offered potential in that respect.
And its non-narrative character, earlier listed as a technical difficulty for a poet, could now be deemed an advantage.

But in versifying the calendar to honour the contemporary
ruler, how could he best present the vastly greater amount of
information concerning the Roman past registered there, such as

[81] Griffin (1984) 213.

in the large-lettered Republican *feriae*, *aetia* of games and festivals, foundation dates of temples and their gods, astronomical phases, and many other categories which had coherent connection neither with each other nor with the present ruler? One answer to the question would have been found in the medium of contemporary architecture. In 2 BC, six or seven years before he began his poem, the temple of Mars Ultor in the Forum of Augustus had been dedicated. This monument was built 'in privato solo' and so most fully expressed Augustus' own ideas and own statement of how he wanted himself to be seen in relation to Roman history. P. Zanker makes the point that myth and history, borrowed from Virgil's imagery, are woven together in this monument into a vision of salvation; but instead of looking toward the future, as in the epic, the observer is directed from the present back into the past.[82] And it is the past, epitomized in the portrait gallery of the *duces* 'qui imperium populi Romani ex minimo maximum reddidissent' (Suet. *Aug*. 31) which suffers in the comparison with the vision of salvation in the present. Augustus himself invited such a comparison in an edict, lest there be any mistake in interpretation: 'commentum id se, ut ad illorum vitam velut ad exemplar et ipse, dum viveret, et insequentium aetatium principes exigerentur a civibus' (Suet. *Aug*. 31. 5). In response to the challenge the Senate and people conferred on him the title Pater Patriae, and had erected a triumphal quadriga with an inscription proclaiming the new honorific title. In his *Res Gestae*, 35, Augustus makes clear that he considered this achievement the apogee of his long career.

Ovid is the only one of the great Augustan poets to live to see the completion of this monument. He is the only one of the extant poets to have been implicitly invited to compare the achievement of the present ruler with the more modest heroes of the Roman past. Augustus was no longer simply the worthy heir to the heroes of old; now he had superseded them, and was the greatest of them all. The ideology of how to present Augustus in relation to the past was virtually handed to him on a platter.[83]

Further inspiration made itself available to Ovid in the form of contemporary architectural sculpture, which provided guidelines as to what techniques to employ in presenting both 'Julian' and

[82] Zanker (1987) 198.
[83] This theme receives in-depth treatment in Ch. 2, 'Pater Patriae'.

'non-Julian' material in an artistic structure. In observing the
details of the temple dedicated in 2 BC, and that of the temples of
Castor and Concord in the Roman Forum, both currently in the
process of being restored, he must have noticed that the artists
were having to work within a very limited scope to evoke new
imagery. There were no battle scenes or any animated, heavily
populated narrative scenes. This absence was in contrast, for
example, with the vividly narrated stories of early Rome depicted
on the frieze of the late Republican Basilica Aemilia.[84] Instead
there were only carefully chosen symbols of groups of divinities
and mythological figures which fitted into the official mythology
of the state. Even with these the artists had an 'artistic vocabu-
lary' imposed upon them in that they depicted those select images
in idealized, classical lines to evoke an intellectualized and idealized paradigm.[85]

Yet Ovid would have observed that where the artist did have
free rein was in the area of ornamentation, that the richness of
that ornamentation had never been seen before and was not con-
strained by any specific code. This was true not only for the orna-
mental borders of architectural members (geison, cornices, and
simas), but for every part of the figural decoration (bases of statues and votive dedications).[86]

The poet must have realized that the non-narrative Roman calendar provided an admirable, unifying framework for exploiting
the same 'episodic' and decorative approach of Augustan art, unified by the overall design of the building in question. The 'iconography' of Augustus and members of the ruling family, studded
throughout the year as their anniversaries decreed, could be
depicted in simple, direct language in solemn register to convey an
unambiguous, straightforward message.[87] Those portraits could
be highlighted and set in relief by a 'decorative programme' comprising the ancient, non-Julian anniversaries and the numerous

[84] Zanker (1987) 209. For symbolism in the temple of Palatine Apollo, see
Lefèvre (1989) 23–4.

[85] Zanker (1987) 117–18, 209.

[86] Ibid. 118. See fig. 203 p. 258 for an example of the great elaboration and
eclectic style of Augustan temple decoration on the Temple of Concord, dedicated
in AD 10. For a description of the extravagant sculptural decoration on the temple
of Mars in the Forum of Augustus, see p. 112.

[87] For random examples of such passages see *F* 1. 637–50; 2. 119–44; 3. 415–28; 4.
377–88.

other categories of unconnected, calendrical information to give the artist scope in three important areas: to juxtapose simple with ornate to provide variety and contrast in genre and style; to contrast the past with the present so as to reflect within the context of the unique medium of the poem the ideology of the Augustan Forum; and to give the poet, as it did the sculptors, free rein to exploit his artistic imagination and express himself according to his own individual style and temperament which was inseparable from the process of artistic composition and an essential ingredient for the success of a creative work.

Even the most cursory glance at the *Fasti* reveals that the above model correlates with the techniques employed in shaping the overall design of Ovid's elegiac epic. The Julian anniversaries provide the central focus of the *Fasti* as the poet's 'militia' in honour of the ruler. The 'filigree' in which those anniversaries are embedded is the area where the poet has given himself freer rein. It comprises calendrical entries for the older festal days in a language of a contrasting, lighter vein, and in passages more lengthy and eclectic in style and content, more heavily embroidered with extravagant detail of Greek and Roman ritual, etymology, mythology, legend, and astronomy. Where a Julian anniversary coincides with older *feriae* on the same day, the contrast is especially marked.[88]

A clear idea of practical as well as artistic success for his new work must have also played a significant part in influencing Ovid's choice of a decorative programme. For the *Fasti* to be a success as a tribute to Augustus, it would surely have to be in demand, to have wide appeal. A scheme accommodating the exercise of Ovidian wit and burlesque, and stories of divine eroticism would appeal to an audience already in thrall to his amatory poetry. A scheme accommodating the fashionable Callimachaean-style *aitia* and antiquarianism, and a subject as topical as festivals of the Roman calendar itself, would guarantee interest on an even larger scale. Ovid could have had no further doubts about the suitability of his projected enterprise from almost any aspect.

---

[88] e.g. 15 March, the festal day of Anna Perenna and the anniversary of Caesar's assassination: *F* 3. 523–710; 11 June, the festal day of the Matralia and the anniversary of Livia's dedication in the Porticus Liviae: *F* 6. 473–648.

To revert now to the quotation cited at the beginning of this chapter: Fränkel's verdict on Ovid's decision to versify the calendar, made within a disembodied context of literary criticism with no reference to the cultural scene of the day, has been shown to be misguided. It is time that verdict was revoked. The background to the creation of the *Fasti* reconstructed in this chapter is to be an essential guide to my subsequent interpretation of the work. It is only within that context that the poem itself can render to the modern scholar valuable historical information about the period in which it was written.

2

AUGUSTUS

THE present study of Augustus begins with book 2 of the *Fasti*. After the death of the Princeps in AD 14, Ovid redesigned the proem and Julian entries to book 1 for the purpose of incorporating into the calendar the poem's new dedicatee, Caesar Germanicus. Ovid's Augustan anniversaries for January, written in exile, contain themes and ideas more reflective of the early Principate of Tiberius, so these have been reserved for study in the section on Germanicus (Ch. 5).

Ovid ceased his overhaul of the *Fasti* in favour of Germanicus after book 1 (except for an isolated allusion to Sulmo at 4. 81), with the result that the original Augustan passages for the subsequent books remain as they were while Augustus was still alive. It is these passages which provide a unique documentation of how a contemporary interpreted and publicized the function of Augustus in the last decade of the Princeps' long life. The proem of book 2 (lines 3–18), paired with the excised original exordium to book 1 and fortunately evoking echoes from the original dedication to Augustus,[1] provides Ovid's given programme for Augustus' place in the *Fasti*. For example (2. 15–18):

> at tua prosequimur studioso pectore, Caesar,
> nomina, per titulos ingredimurque tuos.
> ergo ades et placido paulum mea munera voltu
> respice, pacando siquid ab hoste vacat.

Nevertheless with zealous heart we pay court to your honours, Caesar, and proceed through your titles. Lend your presence, therefore, and consider for a while with gentle mien my tribute, if you find time to spare from pacifying the enemy.

[1] The proem of bk. 2 (ll. 3–18) has commonly been regarded as the original dedication to the *Fasti*, transferred from bk. 1; see Frazer (1929) ii. 227; Bömer (1957–8) i. 19; Syme (1978) 21. But Braun (1981) 2351 n. 33, and Fantham (1985) 257–8, have demonstrated that it in fact belongs to and is needed in its present position.

As we proceed, we shall find that the titles of Augustus which adorn Ovid's 'munera' to the Princeps embrace both official and unofficial categories. The reason for this is undoubtedly to be found in the poet's intention of eulogizing the Princeps more often than the number of official anniversaries in the calendar itself allowed. We find, for instance, that Ovid celebrates Augustus' achievement of restoring temples on 1 February, an act which merited him no official title, on a date which celebrated no Augustan anniversary. Ovid's Augustus is therefore to be studied here in the various guises which the poet ascribes to the ruler in association with specific dates, as the nature of a calendrical work demanded. For simplification, titles have been contrived for the present purposes even where no official one existed: the Restorer of Temples; the Descendant of Venus; the Avenger of Caesar and Crassus. These, with the Princeps' official titles of Pater Patriae and Pontifex Maximus, are what claim our attention in this chapter. They will be treated in the order to which Ovid assigned them in his calendar.

Restorer of Temples

The first tribute to Augustus in Ovid's poem as we have it appears on 1 February (2. 55–66):

> Principio mensis Phrygiae contermina Matri
>   Sospita delubris dicitur aucta novis.
> nunc ubi sunt, illis quae sunt sacrata Kalendis
>   templa deae? longa procubuere die.
> cetera ne simili caderent labefacta ruina
>   cavit sacrati provida cura ducis,
> sub quo delubris sentitur nulla senectus;
>   nec satis est homines, obligat ille deos.
> templorum positor, templorum sancte repostor,
>   sit superis opto mutua cura tui.
> dent tibi caelestes, quos tu caelestibus, annos,
>   proque tua maneant in statione domo.

At the beginning of the month, Sospita, neighbour of the Phrygian Mother, is said to have been enriched with new shrines. Where are they now, the temples which were consecrated to the goddess on those kalends? They have fallen flat over the course of time. That the other temples might not collapse and sink into similar ruin has been taken care

of by our sacred commander; under him temples are not touched by
time. He is not satisfied with placing mortals under obligation to him;
the gods are indebted as well. You builder of temples, you holy restorer
of temples, may the celestial beings have, I pray, a reciprocal regard for
you. May the heavenly deities grant you the years that you grant them,
and may they remain at their post before your house.

The central message of this entry is quite unambiguous. It is an
encomium of the *pietas* of the Princeps towards the gods in his
role of restorer of temples. Yet the meaning of the passage in
other respects is not so clear-cut. We shall go through it step by
step to try and sort out anomalies.

The entry for the kalends of February begins with a tribute to
Sospita, well-known epithet of Juno, the goddess to whom all
kalends belong (as he had said at 1. 55). The poet records that
today is the anniversary upon which Sospita, neighbour of the
Phrygian Mother, is said to have been enriched with new shrines.
But subsequent to that assertion, we hear no more of the Palatine
goddess. Instead, Ovid focuses on the fate of her temples, dedicated to her on the kalends, which he says had been razed by the
ravages of time: 'nunc ubi sunt, templa deae? longa procubuere
die.' A like fate would have been shared by all other temples, he
says, had it not been for 'cura sacrati ducis', that is, Augustus.

Some confusion is apparent already. What temples to Sospita is
Ovid talking about? Or is he in fact referring to one temple only?
Has he used the plural of the neuter nouns 'delubrum' and 'templum' in the singular sense as he has so often elsewhere whenever
it suits the metre to do so?[2] If so, does he mean that it is the temple of Sospita on the Palatine next to the Magna Mater which no
longer exists in his day? Or does 'procubuere' mean that the ruins
are still visible? Either way, why is he making special reference to
that cult and celebrating the anniversary of a temple of no further
practical use? Especially when the whole entry is praising the
work of the great temple restorer who himself promised that he
had neglected no temple that had required restoration when he
took on that task in 28 BC. (*RG* 20. 4; cf Suet. *Aug.* 30. 2).

Answers to these questions cannot be elicited from further
scrutiny of the text at this point. Ovid's contemporaries no doubt
understood what he meant, but from this distance we must look

[2] Frazer (1929) ii. 295, and iv. 2 gives examples.

outside it to arrive at an understanding. To proceed with the enquiry we shall begin by eliminating a common theory long held by modern scholars.

Many historians have insisted that, in locating a temple to Juno Sospita on the Palatine, Ovid has confused his facts. Warde Fowler believed that he was really referring to a temple of Juno Sospita in the Forum Holitorium vowed in 197 BC, which had, on Ovid's evidence, fallen into decay in the poet's day.[3] He offered no thoughts on why Augustus might have excluded it from his restoration programme. Wissowa thought along the same lines, and suggested that Ovid confused the Magna Mater with the Mater Matuta, which accounts for the fact that Juno is described as her 'contermina'.[4] He did not mention in this context that the temple of Mater Matuta stood not in the forum Holitorium but in the Forum Boarium. The two *Fora*, while close to each other, were separated from each other by the wall of Servius.[5] This location therefore, still hardly fits the 'contermina' description even of the Holitorium Sospita, whose closest neighbours were in fact Janus and Spes.[6]

Bömer adheres without question to the idea that Ovid meant the temple in the Forum Holitorium. His verdict on Ovid's indication that it stood on the Palatine reads thus: 'Durch die Nachbarschaft der Magna Mater bringt Ovid eine völlig neue und mit den anderen nicht zu vereinigende Ortsangabe. Offensichtlich geht er mit der Apostrophe an den Kaiser über sein unzureichendes Wissen hinweg.'[7] Frazer and Platner–Ashby on the other hand applied a little more thought to the matter. While considering the possibility that Ovid confused the Magna Mater with the Mater Matuta and so does indeed refer to the temple of Sospita in the Holitorium, both sensibly expressed doubts that this was the case, given that considerable remains of the Republican temple of Juno Sospita in the Holitorium are evident to this day—incorporated into the church of S. Nicola in Carcere—and so can hardly have ceased to exist in Ovid's time.[8] Frazer concluded that 'we must reckon with the possibility that Ovid had access to a tradition,

---

[3] Warde Fowler (1899) 302.   [4] Wissowa (1912) 188 n. 9.
[5] Frazer (1929) ii. 298; Coarelli (1985) 318.
[6] Platner–Ashby (1929) 291; Coarelli (1985) 319.
[7] Bömer (1957–8) ii. 86.   [8] Frazer (1929) ii. 299; Platner–Ashby (1929) 291.

otherwise lost to us, of a temple of Saviour Juno on the Palatine
side by side with that of the Phrygian Mother Goddess'.[9]

Of the views cited above, I believe Frazer's comes closest to the
truth: it could be taken even further. First and foremost, the
notion that Ovid was unclear in his own mind about two major
cults in Rome must be dispensed with. He treats the Magna
Mater (4. 179–372) and the Mater Matuta (6. 473–568) at length in
the *Fasti*, yet there is no hint whatever that he has confused the
identity of one with the other. (He in fact syncretizes the Mater
Matuta with the Theban goddess Ino.) Moreover, he is clear
about the details of the temple of each goddess: the Mater Matuta
was founded by Servius Tullius, located in the Forum Boarium
(6. 477–80),[10] was dedicated on 11 June, and shared its founder,
location and dedication day with the temple of Fortuna (6. 569).[11]
Ovid claims that the name of the founder of the temple of the
Magna Mater, on the other hand, had not survived, but demonstrates his awareness that it had been twice burnt down in saying
that it had been restored first by Metellus, then by Augustus (4.
347–8).[12] Augustus himself confirms the latter detail: 'Aedem
Matris Magnae in Palatio feci' (*RG* 19. 2). Ovid's entry for the
Magna Mater and his mention of her temple occurs under 4 April
(4. 347–8), while the *Fasti Praenestini* and *Quirinales* record its
dedication day as 10 April.[13] Yet the six-day Ludi in honour of
the goddess began on 4 April and finished on 10 April,[14] so it is
quite clear that he has merely conflated events under the one
heading.[15] There is no doubt that the temple cults of the Magna
Mater and the Mater Matuta are quite distinct in the poet's mind.

The theory postulating confusion between the Magna Mater

---

[9]   Frazer (1929) ii. 300.   [10]   Confirmed by Livy, 5. 19. 6, 23. 7.
[11]   This association is affirmed by Dionysius of Halicarnassus, 4. 27. 7 and
Pliny, *NH* 8. 194; the propinquity in location is also affirmed by Livy, 24. 47. 15;
25. 7. 5.
[12]   The temple was burnt down in 111 BC and in AD 3. For sources see Frazer
(1929) iii. 250.
[13]   'M(atri) d(eum) M(agnae) I(daeae) in Palatio, quod eo die aedis ei dedicata
est' (*Praen.*); 'Matri deum Magnae in palatio' (*Quir.*); see Degrassi (1963) 438.
[14]   *Fasti Maffeiani, Praenestini*, etc.; Degrassi (1963) 435.
[15]   Which is entirely compatible with the entry that day of the *Fasti Praenestini*:
'Nobilium mutitationes cenarum solitae sunt frequenter fieri, quod Mater Magna
ex libris Sibullinis arcessita locum mutavit ex Phrygia Romam' (Degrassi (1963)
435).

and the Mater Matuta in the passage under discussion contradicts the poet's distinguishing of the two cults elsewhere in his poem. The notion that Ovid is really referring to the temple of Juno Sospita in the Holitorium must therefore be rejected. So, to revert to the Palatine. What is the historical feasibility of Ovid's claim that a temple to Juno Sospita existed on the site of Rome's earliest beginnings?

Juno Sospita, represented on coins of the Republican period as attired in a goatskin and armed with spear and shield, was the most important divinity at Lanuvium and the most famous Juno in Latium.[16] In 338 BC, following the last conflict between Rome and the Latins, Roman citizenship was granted the Lanuvini with the proviso that they admit the Romans to share in the worship of Juno Sospita.[17] Juno Sospita thus became incorporated into the Roman state worship. But Livy implies that the goddess retained her cult at Lanuvium and makes many later references to it.[18] He makes no mention of the fact that the goddess was also given a sanctuary at Rome.

It has been assumed from the evidence of Livy that the incorporation of Sospita's cult into Roman worship was not, unlike other cults of Juno, an instance of *evocatio*, and that her worship was maintained at Lanuvium without any shrine having been erected to her in Rome.[19] To support this assumption, both Wissowa and Gordon cited inscriptions pertaining to a priestly college of Roman knights, the Sacerdotes Lanuvini, and a reference in Cicero (*Mur.* 41. 90) to show that the Roman consuls sacrificed annually to Juno Sospita (although Cicero does not say where).[20] Silius Italicus (8. 360–1) who calls Lanuvium 'Iunonia sedes' is then cited to show that Livy was correct, and that the Roman worship of Juno Sospita was retained at the ancient Latin town.

What has not been considered by the scholars cited is that the

---

[16] Wissowa (1912) 188–9; Gordon (1938) 24. Frazer (1929) ii. 295; Palmer (1974) 31. Crawford (1974) i. 323, 396f. For a photo of Sospita's statue see Frazer (1929) v, pl. 35.

[17] Livy, 8. 12. 7, 13. 5, 14. 2; Livy actually says: 'ut aedes lucusque Sospitae Iunonis communis Lanuvinis municipibus cum populo Romano esset.'

[18] Listed by Gordon (1938) 32 n. 61.

[19] Gordon (1938) 24–5. Many other cults of Juno from territories conquered by Rome, on the other hand, were transferred to or duplicated in the city, e.g. from Veii, Falerii, Samnium, and Tusculum. See Wissowa (1912) 188; Palmer (1974) 21.

[20] Wissowa (1912) 188, 521. Gordon (1938) 241–5.

evidence they evoke is of late Republic and Imperial date, that is, it shows that the centre of worship for Juno Sospita was retained at Lanuvium—even *after* the construction of a temple to the goddess in the Forum Holitorium in 194 BC. In other words the fact that the seat of worship to Juno Sospita was retained at Lanuvium as Livy says does not preclude the existence of a sanctuary to the goddess in Rome. It is not inconceivable, therefore, that a sanctuary to Sospita was at some earlier date (338 BC?) erected in Rome, one which indeed remained inferior to the original seat of worship at Lanuvium just as the later one in the Holitorium did, but which was perhaps dedicated to symbolize the fact that the goddess was now included in the official religion of the city. Ovid's word 'aucta' in the second line of the passage lends itself to such an interpretation, suggesting that the Lanuvian cult increased in importance by having a new temple built for it on the Palatine. The site itself was perhaps chosen as appropriately imitative of the site of the seat of the cult: on the slope of the acropolis of Lanuvium.[21]

It is unfortunate, however, that there is virtually nothing in the way of more tangible evidence to support the historical feasibility of a temple to Sospita on the Palatine. An entry in the *Fasti Antiates Maiores*, dated 84–55 BC, reads 'Iunon(i) Sosp(itae) Matr(i) Reg(inae)',[22] but this probably refers to the cult in the Holitorium. If Sospita's temple on the Palatine no longer existed in Ovid's day, it is most unlikely to have been functioning as recently as the middle years of the first century BC. Ovid's testimony must also rule out the possibility that it was the temple on the Palatine which L. Julius, consul 90 BC, restored for Juno Sospita (Cic. *Div*. 1. 499; Obseq. 75).

Archaeology has little to contribute at this stage. In the late 1970s P. Pensabene, following up a theory postulated by M. Guarducci, came to the conclusion that remains of two earlier phases found beneath the so-called Auguratorium (second century AD) next to the temple of the Magna Mater on the Palatine were those of the temple of Sospita described by Ovid. He sug-

---

[21] This, at least, is the alleged site. See Gordon (1938) 26–30. Degrassi (1963) 406 does not share Gordon's reluctance to accept that a temple to Sospita could have been erected within the pomerium.

[22] Degrassi (1963) 405. The epithets on inscriptions and coins occur with the initials 'I S M R'. See Gordon (1938) 24. Crawford (1974) 323.

gested that the earlier structure was perhaps destroyed ('un incendio od altra causa') about the time of the construction of the temple of the Magna Mater, and that the second (late Republican) phase dated from that time. Amongst the earlier remains were, according to Pensabene, a fragment of an antefix showing Sospita on it, which assisted in the identification. He does not indicate any approximate foundation period for the earlier temple, or how he identified Sospita. However, in 1985 F. Coarelli, in summarizing (and accepting) Pensabene's conclusion, indicated that both Sospita, and the earlier phase of the temple, belonged to the archaic period.[23] Yet in a publication of 1988, Pensabene identified the late Republican remains beneath the so-called Auguratorium as being those of the temple of Victoria Virgo, dedicated on 1 August 193 BC by M. Porcius Cato. According to Livy (35. 9. 6) Cato dedicated an 'aediculam Victoriae Virginis prope aedem Victoriae' two years after he had vowed it. Pensabene has identified the remains of a very large temple 'subito accanto' to the Auguratorium as being those of the temple of Victoria, and it seems that, on those grounds, he has now changed his mind. Sospita, her antefix and the earlier remains receive no further mention.[24]

Could those earlier remains have been the temple of Sospita, destroyed around the time when the Magna Mater temple was built? We must wait for the archaeologists to decide. Meanwhile, a tentative step will be taken now to exploit, on the present evidence, the possibility that her cult did indeed exist on the Palatine at an earlier stage, but was relocated and so no longer existed at that site in Ovid's day. What Sospita symbolized to the Romans at any given time is difficult to ascertain without the aid of contemporary sources. However, Livy, although not contemporary, does provide a clue for the period of the very early second century BC. He says that in 197 BC the consul C. Cornelius, in a battle with the Insubrian Gauls, vowed to build a temple for Juno Sospita if he were victorious (Livy, 32. 30. 10). Cornelius was victorious, and three years later, in 194 BC, the temple was dedicated in the Forum Holitorium (Livy, 34. 53. 3). From this we might

[23] Guarducci (1971) 112–13. Pensabene (1979) 68–70. Coarelli (1985) 129.

[24] See Pensabene (1988) 57; cf. (1985) 198. I am indebted to A. Ziolkowski (Warsaw) for pointing out Pensabene's later views on the identity of the Auguratorium. Perhaps Pensabene changed his mind following Wiseman's study of 1981.

gather that Sospita was both of a militant and of a maternal, pro-
tective nature, a conjecture which would seem to be confirmed by
the numismatic representation of the spear and shield-bearing
Mater Regina on her coins of the late Republic.

Yet if a sanctuary of this militant Sospita Mater Regina was on
the Palatine when the Mater Deum Magna Idaea was called to
Rome on the advice of the Sibylline books for the purpose of
achieving victory over Hannibal, what would the effect on her
cult be? There would hardly be room for two militant mothers
representing supremacy and victory on the most antique and pre-
eminent hill of the city without one being diminished in the comparison. The Idaean Mother arrived on 4 April 204 BC and resided
in the temple of Victory on the Palatine until the temple then
contracted for her was complete and dedicated thirteen years
later, on 10 April 191 BC (Livy, 29. 14. 4, 37. 2; 36. 36. 3–4). The
Romans in the meantime had achieved their desired victory in
202/1 BC.

Why the precise location on the Palatine was chosen for the
Great Mother can only be guessed at. But if we assume that
Sospita was there before the Great Mother, surely Sospita's
importance, and her attribute, could only have paled into
insignificance beside the new arrival, her new neighbour, the
Great Mother, Mother of gods and men, creator of the world,
and now the triumphant saviour of Rome. As Sospita's central
cult was at Lanuvium, would it have been feasible for those most
concerned with her worship to consider founding another sanctuary for her in Rome and so separate her from the foreign usurper,
the new and victorious Mother on the Palatine?

Two coincidences encourage this notion: first, the close temporal connection between the arrival of the Magna Mater in 204, the
Roman victory over Hannibal in 202/1, the vowing in 197 and
dedication (presumably on 1 February) in 194 of Juno Sospita in
the Holitorium, the vowing in 195 and dedication in 193 of Cato's
Victoria Virgo, and the dedication of the temple of the Great
Mother in 191, certainly excites curiosity. Second, Livy reports
that, at the same time that the Senate vowed a day of prayer for
expiation and nine days of rites for extraordinary portents which
were being reported from Sospita's temple at Lanuvium in 204
BC, it also deliberated on the reception of the Idaean Mother
(Livy, 29. 14. 3–6). Livy merely juxtaposes the two events pertain-

ing to the two goddesses without making any connection. Warde
Fowler, however, postulated an interesting association. He suggested that the object of the foundation of Sospita's temple in the
Holitorium in 194 may have been to diminish the portents which
continued at Lanuvium.[25] I would go further than this and suggest that the portents coming from Lanuvium at this time were
emanating from priests of the goddess who were concerned about
the potential diminishing of her importance by the location of the
Great Mother on the Palatine. Another temple for Sospita, whose
foundation could be associated with another victory (Cornelius'
was indeed timely!), would, on the other hand, permit her to
maintain her status.

The hypothesis then, is this: Juno Sospita once had a sanctuary
on the Palatine, next to the site later chosen for the Magna Mater.
The proximity of the Phrygian Mother was too great a threat to
the status of her Lanuvian counterpart, and at the insistence of
Sospita's priests at the seat of her cult, it was decided to provide
her Roman sanctuary with another location, the Holitorium, and
preserve February 1st as the new dedication day. Her sanctuary
on the Palatine was then transformed and converted into Cato's
Victoria Virgo, snug in the shadow of the huge temple of Victoria,[26] and dedicated the year after Sospita was safely consecrated
in the Holitorium. The Magna Mater was then dedicated two
years after that, all precautions having been taken to ensure that
her presence might cause no offence to any resident deity.

Such a conjecture at least accounts for the possibility, as Frazer
had postulated, that Ovid had access to a tradition, otherwise lost
to us, which informed of a temple of Sospita once located next to
the Phrygian Mother. It also accounts for the possibility that the
earliest remains beneath the Auguratorium which included the
antefix with Sospita on it, mentioned by Pensabene in his 1979
publication, was the temple to which Ovid was referring. Finally,
it indicates that 'procubuere' means that the temple no longer
existed, rather than simply tumbled down and in ruins.[27] It is in

[25] Warde Fowler (1899) 354 n. 7.

[26] For the relative scale of the three temples, Magna Mater, Victoria Virgo, and
Victoria, see Pensabene (1988) 55, and 55 figs. 1 and 2.

[27] Interpretations vary. Gordon (1938) 25 n. 32 suggests that 'procubuere' may
not mean more than 'tumbled down', which is how Frazer translated it. Palmer
(1974) 31 interprets the word as implying that Sospita's temple on the Palatine no
longer existed.

any case very unlikely that Augustus would have allowed a temple situated on the venerable Palatine, so close to his own home, to remain in a state of disrepair. Such a sight would have been a highly visible mockery of his proud role as restorer of temples.

The most pressing question now is: why would Ovid choose the anniversary of a defunct temple of Sospita's to celebrate the 'restitutor templorum omnium' (Livy, 4. 20. 7), a day with which Augustus had no known connection, and when there were so many famous temples restored by him whose anniversaries he could have chosen? (*RG* 19. 2). As far as is known, Lanuvian Sospita had no direct association with the imperial house at all, and her Roman anniversary on 1 February is even ignored by the only extant Julian calendars preserving that day, the *Fasti Venusini, Fasti Maffeiani,* and *Fasti Viae Graziosa.* So why did Ovid choose to associate Palatine Sospita (not even Holitorium Sospita), of all the gods, with Augustus in his role of restorer of temples?

For an answer to this we must revert to the text. The genre is didactic. It is the very non-survival of Sospita's Palatine temple which is important to the theme of the Princeps in this particular role and the consequences to Roman religion had he not assumed it. The pivotal lines which convey the didactic vein, and which create the transition from Juno to Augustus are:

> cetera ne simili caderent labefacta ruina
> cavit sacrati provida cura ducis,

that other temples might not collapse and sink into similar ruin has been taken care of by our sacred commander,

Thenceforth the celebration of the anniversary of Sospita is modulated by assonance into an encomiastic apostrophe to the 'templorum positor, templorum repostor' (2. 63). The unusual words 'positor' and 'repostor', I believe, provide the key to the answer. It is these words, the usage of which is elsewhere unknown,[28] which have apparently been invented by Ovid not solely for metrical considerations, but also as a play on 'Sospita' for the pur-

---

[28] Lewis and Short, *A Latin Dictionary*, and the *Oxford Latin Dictionary* cite no other examples. Only at *Met.* 9. 448 does Ovid use 'positor'. The *Thesaurus* cites Itala Iac. 4. 12 (= James' Epistle): 'unus est legum positor et iudex' which of course post-dates Ovid. (The translator has translated 'positor' from the Greek 'nomothetes'.)

pose of heightening an auditory affect through assonance and association of meaning. By such a technique the motif of 'preserver' introduced with Juno's epithet is transposed and developed by cleverly transforming the subject of the encomium from the goddess to Augustus. It is the potential which the word 'Sospita' provided, in other words, which led the ingenious poet to select Juno's day on 1 February to eulogize Augustus as 'restorer of temples'.

The apostrophe to Augustus constitutes the climax of the passage. It also comprises a prayer that the gods might care for the restorer of their temples as much as he does for them, and to afford him the protection and (an oblique reference to future apotheosis) the length of years that he grants them. Ovid sustains the didactic genre by then providing a glimpse of a number of sites within and without Rome where worship of and sacrifice to various deities were being carried out on that day (lines 67–72 not quoted). The overall impression is that the example of the *pietas* of Augustus towards the gods is being emulated by the city populace at large.

To sum up: Ovid has exploited the potential for assonance and association in meaning in the epithet 'Sospita' for the purpose of introducing Augustus as restorer of temples. He has exploited the anniversary of a defunct temple to introduce the didactic genre. The goddess, in other words, served only as a catalyst for a poet's purpose of incorporating a self-appointed role of the princeps into a non-narrative calendar which was unable to accommodate an anniversary for such a role. We thus find Augustus celebrated on a day with which he had no official connection. In Ovid's calendar 1 February is important evidence of how a calendrical entry could be shaped according to the way he wished to portray Augustus. It also demonstrates that the poet was concerned above all to insert Augustus whenever he could reasonably do so, while still remaining true to the daily entries of the calendar as the year unfolded.

Pater Patriae

Unlike the kalends, the nones of February gives Ovid a valid, calendrical justification for according fulsome praise to the dedicatee of the *Fasti* (2. 119–48). This date was the anniversary of the day in 2 BC on which the Senate had conferred upon Augustus the title Pater Patriae, and it was henceforth celebrated in the calendar as *feriae* or NP day.[29]

Ovid exploits the opportunity to the full. Yet it is his eulogy of Augustus as Pater Patriae that has recently been selected by A. Wallace-Hadrill to demonstrate that the *Fasti* as a whole was an unsuitable vehicle for publicizing Augustus. He claims that the charge can be made against Ovid that, although he takes Augustus seriously, he does not take Romulus and Roman legend seriously and so contributes to a general impression of Romulan Rome that commands scant respect. Augustus would not benefit much from the company he is keeping, he adds, and his majesty risked being dragged down in the process. He concludes that this is not the sort of propaganda that Augustus welcomed, and that, as a consequence, Ovid was a failure as an Augustan panegyrist.[30]

Wallace-Hadrill's verdict on Ovid has found its adherents, most notably S. Hinds, who argues that Ovid's image of Romulus is at a subversive variance with the ideological rhetoric of Augustus Caesar and with Romulus as the ruler's own role model. A straightforward panegyrist, he concludes, would have taken the opportunity to hail Augustus as the new Romulus, a worthy successor to the original Father of the Fatherland.[31]

The question of whether Ovid was a success or failure as an Augustan panegyrist is very important for an historian of Augustan Rome. The *Fasti* is the last extant poem by a free poet of the regime, the only independent contemporary witness we have for the period. The author's success or failure is a subject that touches not only on the unique genre of the poem and the literary techniques employed by him to create his desired effect; it also brings into question the contemporary validity of the poem as a whole, that is, the validity of Ovid's work as 'munera' to the all-powerful ruler to whom the work was dedicated (2. 17). And from the question of contemporary validity arises the subject of historical validity, that is, the extent to which Ovid, through his work,

---

[29] The anniversary is celebrated as an NP day in the *Fasti Praenestini*. For this and other references to Augustus as Pater Patriae see Degrassi (1963) 407.

[30] Wallace-Hadrill (1987) 228–9.

[31] S. E. Hinds presented a paper on the subject to the Philological Society in Oxford in November 1989 (Hinds (1992)). It is in §2 of the paper, entitled 'Genre, Romulean Rome and Augustan ideology' that these views are to be found.

reveals himself to be in touch with the currents of the day, both ideological and cultural. It is only when such questions have been examined and an assessment made can the modern reader better understand the nature of the historical contribution that the work has to make as a reflection of its own times.

If the conclusions of Wallace-Hadrill and Hinds are correct, then Ovid was either subversive, or innocently out of touch with his times. There is nothing extraordinary about that, perhaps. What is extraordinary is that Ovid continued to be subversive or innocently ignorant, even after the catastrophe of his banishment. The desperate exile was still able to commend his *Fasti* with pride to Augustus from Tomis (*T* 2. 547–52), and later took on the difficult task of rededicating it to Germanicus, seriously believing it could still enhance his chances of being recalled.[32] The implication on those grounds is that Ovid did not share Wallace-Hadrill's opinion of his *Fasti* as a vehicle for panegyric in his day. Ovid's contemporary audience, even Augustus himself, may not have regarded the work as a failure for publicizing the regime either.

In order to decide who is right, Ovid or his critics, an investigation into a number of areas must be made: (1) the genre and literary techniques employed by the poet in the Pater Patriae passage; (2) the tradition of Romulus in Roman history up to Ovid's time; (3) the new mythology created by the poet with his unique treatment of Augustus; (4) the conjectured demands of a Roman audience at the time; (5) the significance of Augustus' long delayed acceptance of the title Pater Patriae and the symbolism in the Forum Augustum; (6) the significance of the time lapse between the writing of Virgil's epic and Ovid's; (7) Augustus' own ambivalent attitude towards Romulus; (8) similar techniques applied by later, successful imperial panegyrists.

1. At the outset of the Pater Patriae entry, the elegist is at pains to stress that what is to follow is adapted to the poetical persona he has made his own for the *Fasti*. He does this by spending the first four couplets in mock anguish and self-reproach for having chosen elegiac verse for the epic nature of the task at hand: the

---

[32] For the difficulties inherent in that task, see Ch. 5.

greatest honour to grace the calendar, the celebration of Augustus as Pater Patriae (119–26):

> Nunc mihi mille sonos quoque est memoratus Achilles
> vellem, Maeonide, pectus inesse tuum,
> dum canimus sacras alterno carmine Nonas.
> maximus hic fastis accumulatur honor.
> deficit ingenium, maioraque viribus urgent:
> haec mihi praecipuo est ore canenda dies.
> quid volui demens elegis imponere tantum
> ponderis? heroi res erat ista pedis.

Now would I wish that a thousand voices were within me, and your inspiration, Homer, by which Achilles was commemorated, as I extol with alternating verse the sacred Nones. This is the highest honour that crowns my calendar. My talent fails, the burden weighs more heavily than my strength can bear. This day demands the greatest eloquence from my poem. What did I mean in my folly by imposing so great a weight on elegiacs? This subject was one for the heroic hexameter.

At this stage already, the associations conveyed to a Roman literary audience would be several. First, by wanting to treat an heroic theme in elegiac couplets, Ovid is turning inside out Virgil's humorous technique, evident in the *Georgics*, of wanting to endow dignity upon everyday farming matters by treating them in heroic hexameters; perhaps he could even be inverting Virgil's lament of how great a task it was, when introducing sheep and goats, to invest such humble things with dignity (*Georg.* 3. 289–90, 294:)

> nec sum animi dubius verbis ea vincere magnum
> quam sit et angustis hunc addere rebus honorem;
> nunc, veneranda Pales, magno nunc ore sonandum.

Nor does my mind hold any doubt as to how great a thing it is to master these things in words, and to attach this distinction to such humble topics.
Now, venerable Pales, now the theme must be made to resound with mighty voice.

Second, Ovid could also be ostentatiously reminding himself that he is defying the precept laid down by Horace that the metre chosen must accord with the weight and content of the prospective poem and its poetical purpose (AP73–98). This defiance is undoubtedly a reminder that he is rejecting the *recusatio* tradition

in Roman poetry and is making an advance into new territory by
setting loftier themes to elegiac verse: in short, is inventing the
new genre discussed in Chapter 1. The proem to this second book
was the most recent reminder of the fact (2. 3–8), and the present
passage is a very strategic reiteration of his claim to the new identity he has adopted for his present work. In sum, the most important overall impression to be derived from the introductory
couplets is that Ovid has prepared a literary audience to expect an
inversion of the familiar, to anticipate a different kind of treatment of a lofty theme than has hitherto been known in Roman
poetry.

It is with Ovid's introduction in mind that we now proceed.
The tone of mock humour then undergoes a transition to one of
deference and veneration (despite the elegist's inability to resist
injecting an autobiographical touch), as the subject itself is now
introduced in the form of apostrophe:

> sancte pater patriae, tibi plebs, tibi curia nomen
> hoc dedit, hoc dedimus nos tibi nomen, eques.

Venerable Father of the Fatherland, on you the people, on you the senate, conferred this title; this title we, the knights, conferred on you.

The solemn register is sustained over the next two couplets, culminating in the highest possible praise for a mortal: Augustus as
Pater Patriae is the human counterpart to Jupiter, father of the
gods:

> hoc tu per terras, quod in aethere Iuppiter alto,
> nomen habes: hominum tu pater, ille deum.

You bear on earth the name which Jupiter bears in high heaven, you the
father of men, he of the gods.

Ovid's lines thus far confirm his critic's claim that the poet knows
how to treat Augustus seriously. Augustus himself considered the
conferment of the title Pater Patriae by the Senate, the Equites,
and the populus Romanus in 2 BC (Suet. *Aug.* 58) as the greatest
of his ceremonial honours and chose to record the event as the
climax to his own memorial, the *Res Gestae* (*RG* 35). In the same
passage he also boasts that the Senate erected, in the Forum of
Augustus dedicated in the same year, a triumphal quadriga upon
which was proclaimed his new honorific title. The day was created an NP day and all that it implied, to celebrate the occasion,

as noted above.[33] Ovid's passage thus far reflects Augustus' own
sentiments and those expressed by the Senate.

There is also nothing radical about the way Augustus is presented. The concept of the Princeps as Pater and Jupiter's counterpart on earth was already to be found long ago in Horace (*Od.*
1. 12 49 ff.; 3. 5. 1 ff.), as indeed in the final lines of Ovid's own
Metamorphoses (15. 858–60). But now comes the shock (133–44):

> Romule, concedes: facit hic tua magna tuendo
>   moenia, tu dederas transilienda Remo.
> te Tatius parvique Cures Caeninaque sensit,
>   hoc duce Romanum est solis utrumque latus;
> tu breve nescioquid victae telluris habebas,
>   quodcumque est alto sub Iove, Caesar habet.
> tu rapis, hic castas duce se iubet esse maritas;
>   tu recipis luco, reppulit ille nefas;
> vis tibi grata fuit, florent sub Caesare leges;
>   tu domini nomen, principis ille tenet;
> te Remus incusat, veniam dedit hostibus ille;
>   caelestem fecit te pater, ille patrem.

Romulus, you must stand aside. He makes your walls great by vigilant
defence: the walls you had bestowed were leapt over by Remus. Your
power was felt by Tatius, and humble Cures and Caenina: under this
commander either side of the sun is Roman. You possessed a scant
something of conquered territory: all that lies beneath supreme Jove,
Caesar owns. You raped brides: he orders them be chaste under his rule.
You gave asylum to criminals: he has repelled crime. Violence was agree-
able to you: under Caesar the laws flourish. You bore the name of
Master: he bears that of First Citizen. Remus accused you of murder: he
has granted pardon to his enemies. Your father raised you to heaven: he
raised his father.

What is startling in Ovid's passage is the manner in which Romulus is set up as the antithesis to Augustus. It is in this section that
the poet's warning that a different treatment was to be expected is
well founded. The founder of Rome emerges almost as a character of burlesque: Romulus' walls were jumped over, his battles
fought against puny opponents, the extent of his conquered territory was tiny, he aided and abetted rape, harboured criminals,
murdered his brother, ruled by force, and took the title of *domi-*

---

[33] See n. 29. For the significance of an NP day, see Ch. 1, 'History and Contemporary Significance of the Calendar'.

nus. The present-day ruler, by contrast, is the complete opposite:
Caesar has made Romulus' walls great, has made everything
under the sun Roman, enjoins women to be chaste, repels criminals, governs by laws, pardons his enemies and bears the title of
princeps. Finally, Romulus was made a god by his father; it was
Caesar who made his father a god.

2. The figure of Romulus in Roman tradition is ambiguous in
the extreme, but when the original founder is examined in relation to Augustus by authors both ancient and modern, it is only
the heroic side which is focused upon. The theme of Romulus as
the founder of the line and prototype of Augustus in Augustan
literature for the purposes of justifying the Princeps' political
ascendancy is a well-worn one.[34] Much less attention has been
paid to the fact that there was a darker side to Romulus, that the
fratricide and other deeds of the 'conditor urbis' had been turned
to his discredit by Roman writers as early as the second century;[35] the early first century shows that not all comparisons with
him could be deemed positive. Sallust, in the oration of Lepidus,
denounced the tyrannical Sulla as 'the sinister Romulus' ('scaevos
iste Romulus', *Hist.* i. 55. 5 M), and in derision of Cicero's pre-
tensions of being 'parens patriae', styled him 'the Romulus from
Arpinum' ('Romule Arpinas', *In Ciceronem*, 4. 7). It was probably
Licinius Macer, wishfully thinking of Sulla, who was the origina-
tor of the tradition that had Romulus not translated to heaven but
torn to pieces by enraged enemies.[36] It was no doubt this style of
demise that prompted a consular adversary of Pompey to warn
him that if he wished to live like Romulus, the senators might be
tempted to make him die like Romulus (Plut. *Pomp.* 25. 9). Cicero
accused Romulus of having tossed moral rectitude to the winds
by committing fratricide for the sake of expediency. Whether
Romulus was a god or not did not exonerate Rome's first king,
claims the orator (*Off.* 3. 41): 'Peccavit igitur, pace vel Quirini vel
Romuli dixerim.' And the name of Romulus had been applied by
Catullus in a bitter invective to Julius Caesar as a catamite Romulus ('cinaede Romule', 29. 5.).

Evidence of the conflicting traditions continues in the age of

[34] See Scott (1925) 82–105. Gagé (1930) 138–87; Alföldi (1951) 190–215. In art and
architecture, Zanker (1987) 204 ff.
[35] Classen (1962) 178–9. [36] Ibid. 183–4; Ogilvie (1965) 85.

Augustus. The first example is Livy, even though the historian generally follows a pre-Caesarian source which favours Romulus,[37] and hints, in the additions to his first pentad, at parallels between the 'founders' Romulus and Augustus.[38] Livy does not seem to be sure that Mars was the true father of Romulus and leaves the question open (1. 4), admits that the commoner of the two stories about the death of Remus had it that Romulus murdered him (1. 7), calls the rape of the Sabine women an act of violence (1. 9) and passes on the two versions of the founder's death: the apotheosis, and the assassination by enraged senators (1. 16).[39] Dionysius of Halicarnassus, writing twenty years later in 7 BC,[40] also reflects the existence of the 'good' and 'bad' traditions, even though he presents Romulus from 2. 7 ff. with Augustan anticipations.[41] Like Livy, he casts doubt upon the divine paternity of Romulus (2. 56. 6) and declares that the most plausible accounts about his death say that he was killed by his own people because he exercised his power more like a tyrant than a king (2. 56. 3).

In the poets, too, Romulus does not escape censure. In the 30s BC, Horace (*Epod.* 7. 17–20) saw the evils of the civil wars as a legacy of Romulus' murder of his brother at the foundation of Rome,[42] and in the 20s Virgil was unable to accept the rape of the Sabine women as lawful ('raptas sine more Sabinas', *Aen.* 8. 635). Propertius went further and pointed to the rape of the Sabine women by Romulus as the example which was responsible for the corruption of morals in the city in his own day (2. 6. 19–20).

Yet, like the historians, the same poets were equally capable of praising the founder in the most glowing terms, as for example Horace at *Od.* 1. 12. 33 and 2. 15. 10, Virgil at *Aen.* 6. 778, and Propertius at 4. 10. This same ambiguity in attitudes towards Romulus is also reflected by Ovid himself. In the passage under discussion the original founder is a figure of ridicule; in others he merits apotheosis, was not murdered by enraged senators (2.

---

[37] Ogilvie (1965) 85 suggests Valerius Antias as the source.

[38] e.g. by his use of the adjective 'augustus' with Romulus. Ogilvie (1965) 2 dates the first five books between 27 and 25 BC, but Luce (1965) 238 argues that they were written in the years before 27 BC.

[39] Ogilvie (1965) 85: now modelled on the murder of Caesar.

[40] The author himself dates his *Roman Antiquities* (1. 3. 4) to the consulship of Nero and Piso, i.e. 7 BC.

[41] Syme (1939) 306 n. 2 following Premerstein.

[42] Fraenkel (1957) 56 n. 3 dates Epode 7 between 38 and 36 BC.

475–512), and is totally exonerated from the murder of Remus (4. 840 ff.).[43]

3. To castigate Romulus, then, or to show 'scant respect for Romulan Rome', as Wallace-Hadrill puts it, is no innovation of Ovid's. But if criticizing Romulus was nothing new, what is unique about Ovid's presentation of Romulus in the Pater Patriae passage? The common denominator in the cases where the deeds of Romulus are condemned by extant writers in the time of Octavian/Augustus is the fact that the founder is never explicitly juxtaposed with the contemporary ruler. The fratricide and the kidnapper/rapist, for example, is carefully dissociated from Augustus. An understandable dissociation in the earlier part of the reign, one might suppose, in view of the possibility of finding parallels for Romulus' deeds in some of Octavian's own, such as the proscriptions, and the unseemly haste of his appropriation of Livia Drusilla while she was blatantly pregnant with her husband's second child. Instances where the legendary founder is compared with the present-day ruler, on the other hand, portray him as the deified hero and prototype of his present-day 'heir', a device to create a concept of a continuation between the revered past and the Augustan present to justify his political ascendancy and future apotheosis.[44]

Ovid's innovation lies in the fact that, unlike his literary predecessors, he has juxtaposed the inglorious Romulus with Augustus. He has done this by selecting and fusing already familiar techniques and motifs into a new combination in order to eulogize Augustus in a novel and original way. He has utilized a panegyrical technique already found in Cicero's *Pro Lege Manilia* (13, 37–8), where the subject of the encomium owes his greatness not only to his own merits but also to the demerits of others;[45]

[43] Bömer (1957–8) i. 27–8 has noted 'ein durchaus zwiespältiges Romulus-Bild' in the 1st cent., but curiously fails to accept that it was alive and well in the Augustan period.

[44] To cite a few instances: Virg. *Georg.* 1. 498 ff.; *Aen.* 1. 276–96; 6. 777–93, 875–7; 8. 342; Hor. *Od.* 1. 12. 32 ff.

[45] This device is notably different from the panegyric in Cic. *Marcell.* 1. 4, Virg. *Aen.* 6. 801–5, and Hor. *Od.* 4. 4, 14, where the subject being praised is equal or superior to other great worthies. See Maguinnes (1932) 42–61; Galinsky (1990) 281. It is also different from Propertius' panegyric at 4. 6, which is based on Callimachean lines. See Sweet (1972) 169–75.

Cicero's panegyrical comparison was restrained in that he shrank from naming the persons meant: 'ego autem nomino neminem' (13. 37). Ovid develops Cicero's technique by being less restrained, by actually naming the person whose demerits contrast with and so bring into sharp relief the merits of his subject. To find the ideal candidate for vilification he has exploited the disreputable side of the double-edged tradition of Romulus, and pithily highlighted the worst features of the founder of Rome to create the effect of elegiac caricature (Ovid had already represented Romulus as the erotic founder of Rome, see *AA* 1. 129–34). He has availed himself of the technique of antithesis between the good and the bad leader, previously used to good effect by both Cicero and Caesar.[46] He has constructed the antithetical theme around specifically Augustan virtues (*virtus*, *clementia*, and *pietas* inscribed on the golden shield in the Curia Julia since 27 BC: *RG* 34.2) and Augustan moral legislation. He has then retrojected those values on to the legendary ruler and applied the juxtaposition of past and present. The result? A brand new treatment: pride in the present Roman state, greater than its legendary past because of the unique stamp of Augustus' rule.

In measuring Romulus and Augustus against each other in this fresh, unhackneyed way, Ovid is creating a new mythology in literature in the latter part of Augustus' reign. In this new mythology Romulus is not the exemplary model of virtue, but the contrast—a complete reversal of expectation for an audience long used to being force-fed on a diet of serious treatment of the Romulan past when associated with the present regime. Augustus has not modelled his own on the less admirable behaviour of Romulus and it is precisely this, the poet is saying, that is Augustus' virtue. Augustus as Pater Patriae is now the paradigm for the future, not the original founder. By celebrating the fact that the present founder has ignored the disreputable *exempla* of the original founder, Ovid is saying that Augustus is the greatest 'conditor urbis' and Pater Patriae of them all.[47]

---

[46] See Syme (1986) 450. Cicero used this antithesis in the assessment of his own consulate: 'me non ut crudelem tyrannum, sed ut mitissimum parentem . . . vident' (*Dom.* 94), and Caesar is reported to have used it upon his return to Rome in 46 BC (Dio, 43. 17. 2); See Weinstock (1971) 201.

[47] Scott (1930) 52 has already noted that Ovid's passage could 'scarcely have built up a better case for the apotheosis of Augustus than by showing that the

4. By the time Ovid was writing the *Fasti* Augustus had been totally dominating Roman politics and society for thirty-five years. All the justifications for his dominance had been thoroughly exploited and imbued into the Roman consciousness by Virgil's epic twenty-five years before. The Golden Age, the return of which had been prophesied by Jupiter and Anchises in the same great epic (*Aen.* 1. 289–96; 6. 791 ff.), had been inaugurated with the Secular Games and celebrated in verse by Horace as long ago as 17 BC.[48] Horace had continued in the didactic vein with straightforward glorifications of the ruler in his fourth book of Odes (4; 5; 14; 15). The unrelenting edification both in poetry and in the visual arts could, with the passing of time, eventually generate tedium, as P. Zanker has recognized, and an audience might demand a respite. Ovid's copious love poetry clearly found a response, which suggests that it provided such a respite. There was apparently a demand in art as well, if we take as an example a fresco in a villa near Stabiae which caricatured the Aeneas group in the Forum of Augustus.[49] This caricature of a sacrosanct mythological image (depicted with dogs' heads and huge phalloi) displays a daring never attempted by Ovid in his portrayals of Aeneas. Indeed, it goes far beyond his caricature of Romulus in the passage under discussion. The kind of burlesque applied in the private sphere to Augustan mythological figures might well reflect a more relaxed trend of the times in viewing the past.

In this context the place of humour in Roman religion should not be ignored. Romans had traditionally been able to enjoy humour at the expense of their gods without any sense of sullying their religion. Cicero had proved it that it was no sacrilege for an individual to be compared with a diety, even to the latter's disadvantage (Roscius with Aurora: *ND* 1. 28).[50] Ovid's comparison of

Princeps surpasses on every count Romulus, the example par excellence of the Roman demigod'. A valid point, but he has not recognized the uniqueness of Ovid's approach which creates an entirely new mythology.

[48] For the significance of the Golden Age in literature, see Wallace-Hadrill (1982) 19.

[49] Depicted in Zanker (1987) 212. Zanker, who points out the need for respite, says however that this fresco is a minority voice. I do not share his confidence in that respect, as this kind of evidence, by virtue of its being in private possession, and of its being a painting, is by its very nature far less likely to survive.

[50] For other examples of humorous irreverence, see Cic. *Red. in Sen.* 4 (8), Pliny, *NH* 33 (24) 83. Also Liebeschuetz (1979) 21.

Augustus with Romulus to the latter's disadvantage no doubt struck an appreciative chord of recognition, and excited the realization that the achievements of the Princeps could be read with enjoyment as well as with enlightenment. Humour continued to flourish in religion in the imperial age without in any way undermining its institutions, as we see from the jokes at the expense of the deified emperors. S. R. F. Price has shown that Seneca's mockery of Claudius' deification in the *Apocolocyntosis* undermined the belief in the concept of deification not at all.[51] Nero was still able, in all seriousness, to call himself 'divi filius'. An emperor himself was even able to quip on his death-bed: 'Vae, puto deus fio' (Suet. *Vesp.* 23).

In view of the way in which Roman religion could accommodate humour, therefore, I suggest that Ovid's elegiac treatment of Romulus was by no means viewed by a contemporary audience as a serious and subversive attack on the institution that was the Romulan past. And the humorous contrast drawn between the caricature of Romulus and the present-day ruler could, by its very novelty, have been regarded as a very successful vehicle for publicizing Augustus without in any way undermining a healthy respect for his leadership.

5.   It is time now to turn to Augustus himself. Before we deal with the tricky question as to how he might have received Ovid's treatment of himself as Pater Patriae, it is necessary to assess the significance of his acceptance of the title as late as 2 BC. That significance could have found no better expression than in the Forum Augustum, in which stood the chariot-monument celebrating the ruler in his new style of leadership as Pater Patriae. Behind the monument stood the statues and *elogia* of the great heroes of Roman history arrayed around the hemicyclical bays and porticoes on either side of the complex. The chariot itself stood in the middle of the Forum faced on either side by statues of Aeneas and Romulus.[52]

With this monument Augustus projected a dual symbolism. On the one hand the Roman past was reduced to a single, continuous process of growth to the present day, a growth that began from the smallest beginnings to its present greatness (Suet. *Aug.*

---

[51]   Price (1984) 115. Also Liebeschuetz (1979) 89.
[52]   Zanker (1968). See fold-out plan.

31. 5). On the other there is the suggestion of a focus on the present as a new beginning,[53] of a new style of rule that Augustus himself set for the imitation of posterity. Augustus was evidently aware that there could be misinterpretation concerning this, for he issued an edict instructing the public what was to be learned from it. This edict stated that there was a standard implicit in the achievements of the Romans displayed in the Forum by which he himself should be compared, and by which the *principes* of subsequent ages should be chosen (Suet. *Aug.* 31. 5).

It is clear that with this invitation to compare him with the standards set by others, Augustus meant the observer to conclude that he was the greatest of them all, just as Ovid obligingly does in a later passage describing the array of greats in the Forum (5. 563–8). The consciousness of being an innovator, and the idea that he has put a new stamp on the city of Rome and its ancient traditions, also finds a parallel in his boast that he had found a city of brick and left it in marble (Suet. *Aug.* 28. 3; Dio, 56. 30. 3). It also finds explicit expression in the words he left to posterity: 'et ipse multarum rerum exempla imitanda posteris tradidi' (*RG* 8. 5).

The Forum of Augustus, with the chariot-monument immortalizing the Princeps in his new style of leadership as Pater Patriae, is not simply a justification for Augustus' political ascendancy as a worthy heir to Rome's historical beginnings. It is also a justification for the declaration of the fact that he had acquired by 2 BC a political success hitherto unknown in Roman history, both in scale and duration. Augustus, as Pater Patriae, was at the very zenith of his *auctoritas*, a supremacy based not on formal powers but on prestige alone. The *Res Gestae* tells us, by the arrangement of its various honours, that it was this kind of supremacy that earned him the award which he regarded as the crowning achievement of his career (*RG* 34. 3–35. 1).

Most importantly, it was this type of supremacy that distinguished him from every other Pater Patriae in Roman history, legendary or historical.[54] This can be discerned by considering

[53] 'Augustus sollte als Vollender der römischen Republik und gleichzeitig als Schöpfer einer neuen Ordnung gefeiert werden': Ganzert–Kockel (1988) 155. The symbolism of the Forum Augustum was alluded to in Ch 1, 'Influence of the Contemporary Arts'. Some repetition of that discussion is necessary here for the present argument.

[54] It is difficult to prove that anyone before Cicero assumed the title: Weinstock (1971) 202.

how his predecessors had earned it. Cicero claimed to have won
the title for saving Rome from the Catilinarian conspiracy (Cic.
Pis. 6; *Sest.* 121; Plut. *Cic.* 23. 6), and considered himself a new
founder on that account. It was he who said that Marius should
have won it also for having preserved the freedom of the citizens
through his victory over the enemy (Cic. *Rab. Perd.* 27). Weinstock sees that it was Cicero's example which inspired the historians, for it was after this that Romulus and Camillus were
accorded the title of 'parens patriae', both in the context of being
a 'founder' for having saved Rome (Livy, 5. 49. 7; 7. 1. 10).[55]
Julius Caesar was accorded the title 'parens patriae' near the end
of his life for his virtue of *clementia*, so Appian records (*BC* 2. 144.
602; Dio, 44. 4. 4 and Suet. *Div. Iul* 85 do not give the reason).
The theme of saving citizens is constant. With both Cicero and
Caesar, the granting of the title became connected with the conferral of the oak crown, awarded to those who had saved citizens.[56] This connection was made explicit on inscriptions
honouring Caesar where the words 'patri patriae' were sur-
rounded by an oak wreath.[57]

Why, then, did Augustus take so long to be proclaimed Pater
Patriae? In 27 BC Octavian took the name Augustus to symbolize
his claim to be second founder of Rome and was honoured with
the oak wreath for having saved citizens. Coins from 27 BC and
later echoed the theme in bearing the words 'ob civis servatos'.[58]
Why was he not then proclaimed Pater patriae? That it had been
proposed is suggested by a hint of the title made before then by
Horace with reference to Octavian as military saviour: 'hic mag-
nos potius triumphos, / hic ames dici pater atque princeps, / neu
sinas Medos equitare inultos, / te duce, Caesar' (*Od.* 1. 2. 49–52).
Ovid, too, in the present passage, hints that the title had been in
the air long before 2 BC (2. 129–30), and Dio states that Augustus
had been addressed as Pater long before it was formally conferred
upon him (55. 10. 10). One suspects that Augustus, despite pres-

---

[55] It difficult to prove that anyone before Cicero assumed the title: Weinstock
(1971) 202.

[56] It was only proposed for Cicero, who probably did not receive it: ibid.

[57] Ibid. 203 n. 6. For the connection between founder, 'servator' and 'parens'
see also Alföldi (1954) 103–24.

[58] Sutherland (1984) i. 86 for denarii from 27 BC; pp. 43–4, 47, 65, 86 from
19–18 BC.

sure to do so earlier, wished to assume the title only after it could come to symbolize something more than the founder/military saviour (and victor in a civil war) significance which any former 'pater' had attached to it.

An important clue to what that 'something more' was is provided by Horace when he later declares that the downward trend of Roman morals would have to be reversed before anyone could claim the title Pater: whoever wishes to banish impious slaughter and insane civic strife, if he is eager to have statues inscribed 'Pater urbium', let him have the courage to curb our unrestrained licentiousness and so win fame among men of after times (*Od.* 3. 24. 5–30). In 18 BC Augustus was able, in virtue of *auctoritas* and by means of *tribunicia potestas*, to enact measures to curb licence, establish morality and encourage procreation.[59] The following year the Golden Age could be inaugurated with confidence and Horace was able to extol the return of the old morality (*CS* 57 ff.). Later again, Horace (optimistically) celebrated the fact that law and morality had overcome polluting wrong (*Od.* 4. 5. 22).

And now Ovid, in the present passage, completes the picture. The only one of the great extant poets to witness Augustus' invitation as Pater Patriae, he accepts that invitation and compares the modern-day Pater Patriae with a select example of a leader from the past in the Forum. In so doing he imposes not only modern-day standards of military conquest but also Augustan standards of legal and moral custodianship of Rome upon Romulus. From this we gather that Ovid understood that Augustus considered that it was his achievement of arresting moral degeneracy, the commonest explanation by Roman writers of the political instability of the late Republic,[60] which earned him the title Pater Patriae. That the title bore the significance of moral custodian is given emphasis by the poet at 2. 617–38, where Augustus is invoked as Pater Patriae in a prayer for moral behaviour within the family at the feast of the Caristia. That Augustus himself recognized his new role as symbolizing that of moral custodian of the state as a family receives endorsement from an anecdote passed down by Macrobius: in 2 BC Augustus had acquired, as he put it, a new and spoilt daughter whom he had to put up with, none other than *res publica* herself (*Sat.* 2. 5. 4).

[59] *RG* 6; Suet. *Aug.* 34; Dio, 54. 16. 1 ff; Syme (1939) 443.
[60] Liebeschuetz (1979) 90 cites examples.

The fact that Augustus accepted the title Pater Patriae, not in 27 BC as he might have done, but twenty-five years later, in the year of the dedication of the monument designed to define his place in Roman history,[61] gave it a meaning unassociated with any previous Roman *pater patriae*, historical or legendary.[62] It was an affirmation that his concern for Roman moral regeneration had provided a political stability which Rome had not seen for centuries, and that this was his greatest achievement in his long dominance over Roman affairs. For this reason he could confidently invite the public passing the Forum to look to the great leaders of the past there arrayed with their *elogia* and compare their achievements less favourably with his own in the present age.

Which is just what Ovid has done. And not only in the present passage. Romulus and his deeds are exploited elsewhere in the *Fasti*, less directly perhaps but nevertheless unmistakably, as a foil for the purposes of enhancing an aspect of Augustus' unique style of moral leadership. In his celebration of the Lupercalia, the rites of which had been revived by Augustus (performed by the *flamen dialis* cf. 2. 282) (*RG* 19; Suet. *Aug.* 31. 4), the poet exhorts brides to submit to the blows of the goathides to become pregnant. To explain the rites he harks back to the age of Romulus when the community was failing to increase itself. He has Romulus realize and regret that his 'iniuria' of ravishing the Sabine women had brought only war to his people, not virile strength as he had intended: 'quid mihi prodest rapuisse Sabinas si mea non vires, sed bellum iniuria fecit? utilius fuerat non habuisse nurus' (2. 431–4). Ovid then introduces Juno Lucina into the scene (although it is not 'her' day) who, by establishing the fertility rites of the Lupercalia, got the first generation of Romans underway.[63] The passage ends in praise and thanksgiving to the goddess of birth ('gratia Lucinae!') and as a celebration of motherhood and fertility (2. 449–52).

[61] Why the Forum Augustum with the temple of Mars Ultor was not dedicated long before 2 BC is discussed later in this chapter under the heading 'Avenger of Caesar and Crassus'.

[62] Gagé (1930) 178 missed this point completely.

[63] The goat-hide thongs or *februa* were called 'amiculum Iunonis' according to Verrius Flaccus (in Festus, *Gloss. Lat.* 4. 202), who calls the goddess officiating that day Iuno Februlis. The goatskin-clad goddess is reminiscent of Juno of Lanuvium who was represented in such a manner, as we have seen in the section

The theme recurs on 1 March. Ovid, echoing Horace (*Epod.* 7. 17–20), depicts Romulus as the author of the first civil war at Rome (3. 201–2), an evil that was brought to rest only with the intervention of the mothers (3. 218–26). The passage ends with another celebration of Juno Lucina (whose temple on the Esquiline was founded on that day,)[64] of marriage, motherhood, and fertility (3. 251–8). On both occasions Ovid has the social disasters issuing from Romulus' crimes of kidnap, rape, and civil war rectified by the goddess of childbirth and the fruitfulness of mothers. Ovid's selection of Lucina on both 15 February and 1 March as a foil to Romulus is not random: an informed audience would know that Lucina was the very goddess invoked to support Augustus' legislation on producing offspring (Hor. *CS*, 13–20:[65]

> rite maturos aperire partus
> lenis, Ilithyia, tuere matres,
> sive tu Lucina probas vocari
>   seu Genetyllis:
>
> diva, producas subolem patrumque
> prosperes decreta super iugandis
> feminis prolisque novae feraci
>   lege marita,

You who are gentle at inducing birth when the time is ripe, Ilithyia, or if you approve being called Lucina or Genitalis, watch over mothers. Goddess, bring forth progeny, make successful the Senate's decrees over the yoking of women and the marriage law productive of new offspring.

6. The disreputable side of Romulus, then, serves Ovid on more than one occasion to bring into relief the unique style of Augustus' leadership from 2 BC onwards. Because of the fact that he was writing late in Augustus' reign, Ovid did not have the same problem confronting Virgil, writing twenty-five years earlier. At that

---

'Restorer of Temples'. If Verrius associated Sospita with the Lupercalia, then Ovid is either not following Verrius at all, or deliberately distorting him here.

[64] Degrassi (1963) 418.

[65] Porte (1985) 416 has totally misunderstood Ovid's intentions: 'La justification donnée par Ovide est aussi embarrassée qu'embarrassante: les femmes, ayant fait cesser la guerre, honorent le dieu Mars. a la rigueur, les Sabines, étant des mères, étant intervenues pendant une bataille, pouvaient répondre aux deux conditions requises pour l'établissement d'une étymologie mal fondée. Mais surtout, elles contribuent à faire participer le dieu Mars à des fêtes dans lesquelles il semble bien n'avoir aucune place.'

stage Virgil, in trying to compose the Augustan epic, had little to glorify but the military career of Octavian/Augustus, but the difficulty was that although Actium was important, the victor's warlike role was not always glorious, and his military expertise paled by comparison with that of Caesar, Pompey, Marius, and others. The risk was that contemporary history, depicted in epic on the Homeric model, could begin to resemble burlesque, especially when the only enemy of Octavian's allowed to be identified was a mere woman! Virgil solved the problem by creating an epic 'set in the past with glimpses forward to Augustus'.[66] Ovid's 'epic' takes the reverse stance, again inverting all expectations for those familiar with the *Aeneid*. Late in Augustus' reign, it is the present Golden Age that can be celebrated without embarrassment. The past no longer measures up. For this reason the *Fasti* may be said to represent truly the spirit and political ideology (not reality!) of the times in which it was written.[67] It will not do to impose upon this work the values propagated by poets earlier in the reign, as both Wallace-Hadrill and Hinds have done.[68]

7. We now address the final question: can we guess how Augustus, as addressee of Ovid's panegyric, would have reacted to this passage? It is Augustus' attitude to Romulus that is the key. Evidence of that attitude appears as early as 27 BC. When it was decided that Octavian should take a new name to symbolize his new status as founder of the restored state and saviour of citizens, it was the ambiguity surrounding the figure of Romulus that decided him against taking Romulus' name. It was decided that the name 'Augustus' was more holy and reverend ('sanctius et reverentius') than that of Romulus (Florus 2. 34. 66), and Sueto-

---

[66] As Griffin (1984) 213 has aptly described the epic.

[67] Ovid seemed naturally to glory in the age of culture and refinement in which he lived, as he indicates elsewhere (*AA* 3. 121): 'prisca iuvent alios, ego me nunc denique natum / gratulor: haec aetas moribus apta meis.' With such a temperament, it follows that he should be receptive to Augustus' desire that Romans should see the present age, and his rule, as the best time in the history of the city. Ovid tells the ruler from exile that he had sung of a happy age under his leadership: *T* 1. 2. 103–4.

[68] Wallace-Hadrill does so not only in the article referred to, but also in his study of the Golden Age in literature (1982) 30, where he sees Ovid as flippant on the question of the Golden Age, 'at best irreverent, at worst subversive'.

nius records that Plancus deemed 'Augustus' a greater title ('amplius') than that of 'Romulus' (Suet. *Aug*. 7. 2). There can be little doubt, as Syme recognized, that it was not only the associations of Romulus with Julius the Dictator, who had set his own statue in the temple of Quirinus, but also the less edifying versions of the Romulus legend, which influenced this decision.[69]

Augustus' attitude to Romulus is also discernible in the projection of Augustan mythology. That mythology placed far more emphasis upon Aeneas' foundation than that of Romulus, thus reflecting the Princeps' deliberate preference. The entire *Aeneid*, for example, focuses upon the Trojan, while Romulus, the local founder, rates barely a mention (only at 1. 276; 6. 778, 876; 8. 342). Why this is so is not difficult to surmise. Not only was Aeneas ancestor to a number of noble families, including the Julians. The literary tradition of Aeneas did not provide the poet with discreditable deeds to be exploited. Nor did Aeneas have a record of being disparagingly associated with Roman dynasts of the past. It is no doubt that this was a vital consideration in Virgil's decision to devote his epic to Aeneas' foundation, with remarkably few references to Romulus. That decision may reflect Augustus' awareness of the potential difficulties Romulus posed in relation to himself.

Augustan mythology as depicted in art and architecture indicates the same trend. In his study of Aeneas and Romulus on the Ara Pacis, Zanker has so much more to interpret in the portraiture of Aeneas, simply because there is less to say about the panel depicting the wolf suckling the twins, the sole representation of Romulus.[70] And there is another telling clue in the Forum of Augustus itself. In Ovid's description of the arrangement of great Roman leaders there it is clear that Romulus occupied the opposite exedra from the statues and *elogia* of Augustus' ancestors who were headed by Aeneas (5. 563–6). Dio's description of the images

---

[69] Syme (1939) 313. Luce (1965) 240 at the end of his study sees Livy's history as very probably influencing the policy of Augustus, rather than the other way round. Scott (1925) 35 sees no more than that it was the connection of Julius Caesar with Romulus that put Octavian off taking the title. Allen (1922) 263 thinks that Ovid's passage is designed to justify the refusal of the title 'Romulus' by Octavian. If this is how Augustus saw it, Ovid's panegyric certainly cannot be the failure Wallace-Hadrill imagines.

[70] Zanker (1987) 206–9.

conveyed at Augustus' funeral procession makes the same distinction: first came those of his ancestors, finally those of other
great Romans of the past, beginning with Romulus himself (56.
34). The impression given from his arrangement, both in the
Forum and in his funeral procession, is that Augustus was carefully projecting the notion that the founder with the dubious
repute was in some way being separated from direct association
with him. As the eponymous hero of the city who became a god,
Romulus could not be excised from Roman tradition, yet the cau-
tion with which Augustus treated him can be traced from 27 BC to
the staging of the final ideological advertisement of his funeral
procession.

The relatively minor place allocated to Romulus in Augustan
ideology and mythology indicates that Augustus was sensitive to
the fact that a comparison between his and the original founder's
inglorious deeds could be turned to his own disadvantage, just as
it had been with Sulla and Caesar. Now Ovid is removing that
possibility. The *Fasti* concentrates on Romulus more than any
other 'historical' figure in Rome's past, and the selection of this
figure to caricature and denigrate is not random. Aeneas, for
example, is never subjected to the same kind of treatment. And in
the Pater Patriae passage, conspicuous for directly juxtaposing
Romulus and Augustus as we have seen, Ovid has declared that
Augustus' virtue lay in the very fact that he had not emulated the
disreputable *exempla* of Romulus. He is thus relieving Augustus
of any anxiety in that regard in a way that no 'official propaganda'
could do.[71] I suggest that Augustus, prepared by Ovid in the
introductory couplets to expect something different, would have
been at first apprehensive, but then would have found, with great
relief, the entire passage comprising the eulogy of him as Pater
Patriae inventive, refreshing, amusing, and—in view of his own
misgivings about Romulus—very acceptable.

8.   Perhaps the most tangible assurance, if so needed, that Ovid
was not a failure as an Augustan panegyrist comes from the fact

---

[71] Which includes that of Verrius Flaccus. Wallace-Hadrill arrived at his conclusion about Ovid as a panegyrist mainly by comparing the *Fasti* with that of a
hypothetical literary version of the inscriptional calendar of the freedman scholar
(following Mommsen). His conviction that Ovid faithfully followed Verrius Flaccus is undermined by the case of Lucina, as we have seen above.

that later imperial panegryrists emulated and developed his technique of naming, and denigrating, a past ruler in order to enhance the greatness of the present one. The most obvious example to come to mind is Seneca's *De Clementia*. The philosopher has the youthful Nero superior to his predecessors Augustus, Tiberius (1. 1. 6 and 1. 11), and in particular, Claudius. Nero himself is made to proclaim a return to legality from the harsh arbitrariness of Claudius' reign. As M. Griffin has noted, the return of 'leges' marked off the Republic from 'regnum' (Lucr. 5. 1136–44; Cic. *Clu.* 146), and the Principate from *dominatio* (Ovid *F* 2. 141).[72] The dual symbolism of cultural continuity and a new beginning is ever present. The younger Pliny, too, disparaged the intentions of Tiberius, Nero, and Titus in deifying their fathers, for the express purpose of eulogizing the nobility of mind in the present ruler, Trajan (*Pan.* 11. 1–2).

Ovid's panegyric in the Pater Patriae passage of the *Fasti* clearly set a pattern. What better yardstick could there be to assess the success of his enterprise in the eyes of contemporaries? Is it not now understandable that Ovid felt justified in commending the *Fasti* to Augustus from exile? Both poet and Princeps knew that his 'elegiac epic' was a suitable vehicle for publicizing the ideology of the late regime in the unique fashion of the new genre that he had created for the age.

Pontifex Maximus

Before turning to Ovid's text, a brief introduction on the meaning of the title itself is in order. It has often been stated by modern scholars that Augustus, upon being elected Pontifex Maximus in 12 BC, assumed the office of 'head of the Roman State religion'.[73] Such a notion is as understandable as it is misleading. Understandable because Suetonius and Dio, used to the tradition whereby every emperor became Pontifex Maximus to indicate his complete control over religious matters, give reason to believe that such a notion existed at the time when Augustus assumed the title. Suetonius (*Aug.* 31) lists virtually every religious activity of Augustus, without regard for chronology, after stating that the

[72] Griffin (1976) 138.
[73] To mention only a few: Allen (1922) 261; Hardy (1923) 65; Taylor (1931) 133; Syme (1939) 25; Brunt–Moore (1967) 52; Liebeschuetz (1979) 70.

Princeps had become chief priest. He implies (erroneously) that Augustus carried out all these activities by virtue of the fact that he had assumed the office. Dio, referring to emperors generally, states that because an emperor is also Pontifex Maximus, he exercises supreme jurisdiction in all matters both profane and sacred (53. 17).

The notion is misleading for the period in question because it is imbued with contemporary conceptions of a 'head of religion'. The Pope, head of the present-day 'Roman Religion' is Pontifex Maximus, a title which grew directly from that once held by the Roman emperors, and correctly implies complete unequivocal authority over Church affairs. It is thus misleading to retroject such a concept on to the office of Pontifex Maximus in the Republican period, a period when, and I quote John North, 'it was as unacceptable for an individual to achieve a concentration of power in religion as in politics', when 'action depended on co-operation between magistrates and priests', and when the 'most important religious action was taken by the magistrates—vows, State sacrifices, auspices, dedications—with priests as expert advisers . . . but not as the main actors'. North, assessing the work of Scheid which still, as recently as 1985, emphasized a separation of powers between priests and magistrates, demonstrates that religious authority in the Republic was 'notoriously hard to locate'. He cites several examples, notably that of 113 BC, when the *comitia* were able to overturn the decision of the *pontifices* about the disciplining of the Vestals, even though the Vestals were ostensibly within that college's authority. North indicates quite clearly that, in a system where religion and politics were inextricably interconnected, where priests were also politicians and vice versa, there could no more be a 'head of State religion' than a 'head of State'.[74]

Another assumption which has led scholars to cleave to a 'head of the State religion' mentality is that there was in Roman religion a core of ancient Italian worship distinguishable from later foreign accretions. When Augustus became Pontifex Maximus it meant that he became head of the 'real' Roman religion and so was finally able to carry out a reorganization of the old Roman cult. Up till that time he had been engaged mainly with activities

[74] North (1986) 257. For fragmentation of priestly authority in the Republic, see Beard (1990) 42–3.

involving foreign rites or *graecus ritus*. Wissowa propounded this view which was developed by Joseph Wilhelm, who examined all Augustus' activities from 12 BC to AD 14 to highlight the 'Roman' significance of the title assumed in 12 BC.[75] Gagé confuted this notion,[76] yet North again has shown that a distinction between Italian and foreign in the highly syncretistic religion is still maintained in works as recent as Scullard's *Festivals and Ceremonies* (1981).[77]

It is not the place here to give a history of the office of Pontifex Maximus. It is worth mentioning, however, that even in the late Republic, a period that produced a succession of military dynasts, the Pontifex Maximus still occupied a position which by no means could be equated with a 'head of the Roman State religion'. The abundant literary evidence of Cicero demonstrates this most adequately.[78] So too, does the fact that Caesar, already Pontifex Maximus and Dictator, still desired to become augur in 47 BC to expand his religious powers and influence. (As indeed had Sulla desired the augurate.)[79] So too does the fact that Augustus was able magnanimously to refuse the title of Pontifex Maximus offered him by the people after Lepidus went into exile in 36 BC, yet still found it desirable to belong to every priestly college. No man of the Republic had ever achieved such an accumulation of priesthoods.[80] Gagé has shown that it was by virtue of these priesthoods (the augurate in particular), all acquired by 16 BC which, added to his permanent military and civil powers, enabled Augustus to accomplish the major part of his religious programme long before he became Pontifex Maximus in 12 BC.[81]

Unfortunately, the significance which Gagé attached to Augustus' becoming Pontifex Maximus was little more than that it gave him 'une apparence plus légale'.[82] This is to err in another direction. Augustus himself gave enormous importance to the title, as evinced by the fact that in his self-identification on inscriptions after 12 BC it is the only one of all his religious offices which he

[75] Wissowa (1912) 74; Wilhelm (1915) *passim*.   [76] Gagé (1931) 76 f.
[77] North (1986) 252.
[78] Cic. *Att.* 2. 5. 2; *dom.* 53. 136; *Har. Resp.* 9. 18; *ND* 3. 2. 5; *Leg.* 2. 12. 31; these are a very few examples demonstrating the dependency of the pontificate on the Senate, and the power of the augurate—greater than the pontificate—in the late Republic.
[79] Badian (1968) 26–46.   [80] Hoffman Lewis (1955) 22; Weinstock (1971) 32.
[81] Gagé (1931) 81 ff.   [82] Ibid. 107.

parades, and it furthermore precedes every other title. Succeeding emperors followed his example. This does not help us understand what Augustus did become, however, upon assuming the office. For that we must turn at last to Ovid.

Two poetical insertions into the calendar are important for the purpose: 6 March, when Augustus became Pontifex Maximus, and 28 April, when a dedication to Vesta was made by decree of the Senate in his home on the Palatine. Both occasions were significant enough to be made NP days and so new *feriae* in the calendar.[83] First, 6 March (*F* 3. 415–28):

> Sextus ubi Oceano clivosum scandit Olympum
>   Phoebus et alatis aethera carpit equis,
> quisquis ades castaeque colis penetralia Vestae,
>   gratare, Iliacis turaque pone focis.
> Caesaris innumeris, quos maluit ille mereri,
>   accessit titulis pontificalis honor.
> ignibus aeternis aeterni numina praesunt
>   Caesaris: imperii pignora iuncta vides.
> di veteris Troiae, dignissima praeda ferenti,
>   qua gravis Aeneas tutus ab hoste fuit,
> ortus ab Aenea tangit cognata sacerdos
>   numina: cognatum, Vesta, tuere caput.
> quos sancta fovet ille manu, bene vivitis, ignes:
>   vivite inexstincti, flammaque duxque, precor.

When Phoebus for the sixth time climbs from Ocean up the slope of the sky, and with winged horses passes over the ether, everyone present who pays homage at the inner shrine of chaste Vesta, give thanks and place incense on the Trojan hearth. To Caesar's innumerable titles (which has he most wished to deserve?), was added the honour of the pontificate. Over the eternal flames presides the eternal divinity of Caesar: you see the pledges of empire united. O deities of ancient Troy, most honoured prize to your bearer Aeneas, who, when burdened with you was protected from his enemies, a priest descended from Aeneas joins his divine kin: Vesta, guard your kinsman's head. You flames, which he tends with his sacred hand, live on. May you continue unquenchable, both fire and leader, I pray.

Ovid presents Augustus, Pontifex Maximus, as a divinity presiding over the eternal flame of Vesta, goddess of the Ilian (Trojan)

---

[83] Degrassi (1963) 420, 452.

hearth. The 'numen' of Caesar itself is eulogized as one of the 'pignora imperii' or pledges of Roman sovereignty. The poet depicts the Pontifex Maximus as priest descended from Aeneas who had brought the Penates from Troy. The Penates too, implicitly including Vesta, are also described as his 'cognata numina'. He is indeed 'cognatus' of Vesta herself. The poet exhorts Vesta to guard her kindred priest whose sacred hand guards her flame. He concludes with a supplication for the eternal life of both flame and priest.

Another important aspect to the relationship between the Pontifex Maximus and Vesta is to be found on 28 April (F 4. 949–54):

> aufer, Vesta, diem: cognati Vesta recepta est
>   limine; sic iusti constituere patres.
> Phoebus habet partem: Vestae pars altera cessit:
>   quod superest illis, tertius ipse tenet.
> state Palatinae laurus, praetextaque quercu
>   stet domus: aeternos tres habet una deos.

Claim, Vesta, the day. Vesta has been received into the home of her relation: thus have the just fathers decided. Phoebus has a part, to Vesta has been assigned a second part. What they have to spare, the third one himself occupies. Endure forever, laurels of the Palatine, and the house wreathed with oak. Three eternal gods does this one contain.

This passage celebrates the new physical propinquity of Vesta and Augustus on the Palatine. That Vesta has now been absorbed into household worship of the Lares and Penates of Augustus' home is not an unrealistic interpretation,[84] especially when considered in relation to Ovid's words elsewhere (*Met*. 15. 864–5):

> Vestaque Caesareos inter sacrata Penates
> et cum Caesarea tu, Phoebe domestice, Vesta,

And Vesta, consecrated amongst the Caesarian household gods, and, with Caesarian Vesta, you, Phoebus, at home with Caesar.

But the passage in the *Fasti* implies far more than this. According to the *Fasti* Vesta is not simply a household god of Augustus; the Pontifex Maximus is on an equal footing with the Roman goddess herself. Just as importantly, Ovid's celebration of 28 April enhances by reiteration his theme of 6 March: the divine and dynastic implication inherent in the genealogical relationship

---

[84] See Wissowa (1912) 76; Liebeschuetz (1979) 70.

between Vesta and Augustus. The two passages together celebrate the intimate relationship between Pontifex Maximus and the goddess of the hearth of Rome, both conceptually and topographically.

In order to understand how far removed ideologically the Pontifex Maximus on the Palatine is from the Pontifex Maximus of the Republic in the 'domus publica' it would be best to compare it with what we know of the cult of Vesta situated since the time of Numa in the round temple in the Roman Forum.[85] First, the Pontifex Maximus is hitherto not known to have been intimately associated with the worship of any particular deity. It was priests such as the *flamines maiores* and *minores*, for example, who tended specific cults, as did indeed the Vestals: 'Divisque aliis alii sacerdotes, omnibus pontifices, singulis flamines sunto. virginesque Vestales in urbe custodiunto ignem foci publici sempiternum' (Cic. *Leg.* 2. 8. 20:). These priests belonged to the college of pontiffs, over whom the Pontifex Maximus had authority.[86] But the Pontifex Maximus' role was necessarily of a far less specialized character than that of the flamens and Vestals. Livy, for example, assigns him the task of overseeing and advising on the correct procedure for observances generally, and outlines the nature of the Pontifex Maximus' religious role without reference to his association with any specific cult. In fact he makes no historical connection between the worship of Vesta and the duties of the Pontifex Maximus at all, and claims that the cult had been founded by Numa before the establishment of the chief priesthood (Livy, 1. 20. 5–7).

It is important to note that, though the Pontifex Maximus of the Republic lived in the *domus publica* in close proximity to the Atrium Vestae or house of the Vestals,[87] had *potestas* over its occupants and selected new members for the virgin priesthood, that did not give him a direct priestly relationship with Vesta herself. A relationship of that nature belonged to Vesta's sacred virgins; it was to them alone that the primary function of attending the perpetual fire was allotted, as Ovid tells us in his celebration of the Vestalia on 9 June in the Forum (*F* 6. 283, 289–90, 294):

[85] Ovid *F* 6. 259–60; Dion. Hal. 2. 65–6; Festus, *Gloss. Lat.* 4. 369; Plut. *Num.* 11.

[86] Wissowa (1912) 504.

[87] Platner–Ashby (1929) 58; Nash (1961) i. 362, Plan 154.

cur sit virginibus, quaeris, dea culta ministris?

You ask why the goddess is venerated by virgin attendants?

quid mirum, virgo si virgine laeta ministra
admittit castas ad sua sacra manus?
. . . comites virginitatis amat.

What surprise is there if a virgin is pleased with a virgin attendant and
admits chaste hands to her rites?
. . . she loves companions of her virginity.

These words certainly imply that the Pontifex Maximus was not
traditionally one of Vesta's ministers! It is doubtful, in fact,
whether he had even been allowed into Vesta's temple at all, as
Ovid's words intimate elsewhere—'non equidem vidi . . . / te,
dea, nec fueras aspicienda viro' (6. 253–4; cf. 6. 450–1).[88] Had
Augustus chosen to reside in the *domus publica*, a building separate from the Atrium Vestae,[89] as every Pontifex Maximus before
him had done, his relationship with the goddess would have
remained no different from that of his predecessors. His decision
to make a dedication to Vesta in his own home enabled him to
bring about the significant change to greater intimacy in that relationship with all its implications. We can be reasonably certain
that the idea of Vesta having a male priest did not exist before
Augustus became Pontifex Maximus.

It is for this reason that Ovid's depiction of Augustus as Pontifex Maximus in the role of personal attendant upon Vesta is start-
lingly different from the Pontifex Maximus of the Republic. Now
a primary relationship of a sacred nature between Augustus and
the goddess of the Roman hearth has been created. That the passage is designed to reflect and enhance the newly created intimate
topographical link between Vesta's new home in the residence of
the new Pontifex Maximus on the Palatine can hardly be doubted.

So why is Augustus presented as 'sacerdos Vestae'? One reason
is clarified by a glance at other passages by Ovid which retroject
the same notion upon Julius Caesar in his priestly role. The first
is in the *Metamorphoses* (15. 776–8) where Venus foresees the
assassination and cries:

'en acui sceleratos cernitis enses?
quos prohibete, precor, facinusque repellite neve
caede sacerdotis flammas extinguite Vestae!'

[88] See also Plut. *Cam.* 20. 5, Lact. 3. 20.   [89] Nash (1961) i. 154.

'Behold! Do you not see that accursed swords are being sharpened? Hold them off, I pray, repel the outrage and let not the flames of Vesta be quenched by the gore of her priest!'

In the *Fasti* itself, Julius as Pontifex Maximus is again depicted as 'sacerdos Vestae'. On the Ides of March, the anniversary of the assassination, Ovid has Vesta herself declare that those who had murdered her priest had committed sacrilege against herself (3. 699–70):

> meus fuit ille sacerdos,
> sacrilegae telis me petiere manus.

he was my priest, the sacrilegious hands with their weapons were aimed at me.

and the poet relates that those who had committed the sacrilege were righteously exterminated by the pious deed of the avenging son (705–10). This theme is reiterated at 5. 573–6 where Ovid has Augustus himself utter the words:

> 'si mihi bellandi pater est Vestaeque sacerdos
> auctor, et ulcisci numen utrumque paro,
> Mars, ades et satia scelerato sanguine ferrum,
> stetque favor causa pro meliore tuus'.

'If my father and Vesta's priest is the cause for my waging war, and I prepare to avenge both divinities, then stand by me Mars, satiate your sword with profaned blood and may your favour be with the better cause.'

The central message in these passages is that the crime of the assassins was a crime not against Caesar but a crime against Vesta's priest and so against the goddess herself: by implication a crime against the hearth and home of the Roman people. Octavian's bloody revenge has been elevated from a personal act of piety to one of national import. Just as significantly, the concept of 'sacerdos Vestae' communicates the notion that anyone who threatens the Pontifex Maximus threatens the heart of the Roman nation itself. This concept could not have existed in the Republic where no one man represented the embodiment of the Roman people.

The idea of the Pontifex Maximus as Vesta's priest has been retrojected by Ovid not just on to Julius but even on to L. Caecilius Metellus, Pontifex Maximus from 243–221 BC, who is said to have saved the Palladium from the burning temple of Vesta in 241 BC (*F* 6. 437–54). Ovid's retrojection of an essentially Augustan concept into Republican times has deceived the later historian Florus (*c*.AD 75–140?) who describes Scaevola, who died in 82 BC, as 'Pontifex Vestalis'. So indeed does J. G. Frazer; and Wissowa's description of the Pontifex Maximus in general terms as 'männlicher Vertreter des Vestadienstes' also smacks of Augustan ideology, and so is anachronistic when applied to Republican times.[90] Yet it is important to see that Ovid's technique of retrojection was intended to convey a sense of continuity and tradition to legitimate and camouflage the new meaning of the office of Pontifex Maximus as held by Augustus.

The concept of Pontifex Maximus as Vesta's priest has been enhanced by Ovid with a strong Trojan motif. Vesta's hearth is not Roman, but Trojan ('Iliacus focus'), the gods of Troy brought by Aeneas to Rome are invoked, Vesta is associated with the penates, and the link to the present Pontifex Maximus of Rome is made through the 'cognatio' of them all. The Roman hearth has thus been incorporated into Augustus' Trojan ancestral worship; all those who worship Vesta are worshipping a collateral ancestor of the Pontifex Maximus. His welfare is her concern (as we shall also see in the Julius passages in the next chapter), and so the concern of the Roman people.

Some ideas in Ovid's passage were not wholly new. Augustus' kinship with Aeneas, son of Venus, had long ago been celebrated by Virgil. Vesta, too, had had her origins in Ilium, according to the same author (*Aen.* 2. 296, 567; 5. 744; 9. 259) and to Dionysius of Halicarnassus (2. 65. 2). Propertius had called her 'Vesta, Iliacae felix tutela favillae' (4. 4. 69), and had perhaps anticipated her annexation as a goddess of the Julian house, along with Mars and Venus (3. 4. 11).

What is entirely new, however, is that Vesta is now explicitly 'cognata' of Augustus. This has provoked some cynical reaction from scholars. Frazer, following Paley, observed that 'the relationship of Augustus to Vesta was not very close' and saw the genealogical relationship between the two simply as flattery of an Augustan poet.[91] Bömer has examined the various modern interpretations as to how, exactly, Vesta was related to Augustus. He

[90] Frazer (1929) iv. 217; Wissowa (1912) 504.   [91] Frazer (1929) iii. 97.

discusses the possibility that either a genealogical relationship through Caesar–Venus–Iuppiter–Saturnus whose daughter is Vesta, is meant (cf. *F* 6. 286), or perhaps rather a 'landschaftliche Verbundenheit' between Troy (Augustus) and Rome (Vesta). (Bömer mysteriously ignores the fact that Virgil had Aeneas bring Vesta from Troy.) He admits the feasibility of the view that both are meant, but eventually rejects it in favour of a third possibility: that the idea of the 'cognatio' occurred arbitrarily to Ovid as he worked on the theme of the unification under the one roof on the Palatine of the 'ignes aeterni' (of Vesta) and the 'aeterni numina Caesaris'. Bömer in essence agrees with Frazer's conclusion that the contrived 'cognatio' between Augustus and Vesta was mere flattery on the part of Ovid. The poet himself, says Bömer, was not at all bothered by such trifles as to how, exactly, the two were related.[92]

All this quite misses the significance of Ovid's 'cognatio' theme in the two passages under discussion. It is this theme that is the most innovative and important feature of the poetical eulogy of Augustus as Pontifex Maximus. It is precisely this which is the vital element in the new (*post* 12 BC) mythology of the office being conveyed by the poet which reflects the dynastic implications attached to it as held by the Princeps. Augustus had taken over the *penates publici* brought by Aeneas to Rome and the hearth of Rome itself as his personal, dynastic, divine right. Only Vesta's 'cognatus' could tend her hearth, could be her priest. Only a Caesar, in other words, could be Pontifex Maximus. The dynastic relationship between Vesta and the imperial house finds expression elsewhere as well. The *Feriale Cumanum* (dated after AD 4) shows that a supplication was made to Vesta and the penates of the Roman people on the anniversary of Augustus' assumption of the office: 'Eo die Caesar pontifex maximus creatus est. Supplicatio Vestae, dis publicis penatibus populi Romani Quiritium' (On this day Caesar was made Pontifex Maximus. *Supplicatio* to Vesta, to the public gods and household gods of the Roman people, the Quirites). It also shows that Vesta received supplications made on the birthdays of the imperial princes.[93]

Ovid's celebration of the 6 March 12 BC shows us how the office of Pontifex Maximus, an ancient institution of the Roman

---

[92] Bömer (1987) 525 ff.   [93] Degrassi (1963) 279.

Republic, became transformed to become an 'hereditary' institution of the Principate, no longer open even to the narrowest competition on merit. Before this time no religious or magisterial office was associated with or held by virtue of divine ancestry, no 'divine right' could be claimed by a would-be incumbent. The creation of the ideology behind Augustus' assumption of the chief pontificate and his dedication to Vesta on the Palatine thus marked a turning point in Roman religious and political history.

A brief digression must be made to deal with an apparent contradiction to this claim. Many scholars have accepted Dio's statement that in 44 BC the Senate voted that, in the event that Julius Caesar beget or adopt a son, he should be appointed high priest (Dio, 44. 5. 3). The office was thus made hereditary before the time of Augustus. I think Dio is mistaken for the following reasons.

First, it is very curious that, of all the powers wielded by Caesar, Dictator for life and endowed with royal and divine honours, only the office of Pontifex Maximus which he had held since 63 BC should be made hereditary by the Senate. An office which, as Latte concedes, never had powers equal even to that of an ordinary magistrate.[94] What sort of honour is that? Especially when Caesar had no son and had only made provision for a testamentary 'adoption' in his will, not a real adoption. It was only a real adoption which would have involved the elimination of the adoptee's family, agnatic position, and attendant cult for the conferment of Caesar's own.[95] As Caesar had no plans to adopt a son in this way, even when at the age of 56 his chances of acquiring a natural son were waning, the 'honour' of making the chief pontificate hereditary for his sake was a meaningless one. For this reason Gagé's hypothetical justification for Dio's evidence, that Caesar in his later years considered the chief pontificate to be a family inheritance of the line of Iulus and transmittable to a successor,[96] must be rejected.

Second, although the 'divi filius' made a great deal of his refusal to be made Pontifex Maximus by the people after Lepidus

[94] Latte (1960) 401.
[95] Weinrib (1967) 247 shows how Octavian made his 'adoption' an innovation and a distortion of legal forms to acquire every advantage from his great-uncle's heritage.
[96] Gagé (1931) 76.

went into exile in 36 BC (*RG* 10. 2), he does not, as Brunt and
Moore point out, treat Lepidus like a usurper of his patrimony.[97]
It is difficult to believe that Octavian, the man who was prepared
to march on Rome to acquire the consulship, to distort legalities
to make himself Caesar's 'real' adopted son, would not also have
been prepared to appropriate the chief pontificate in 36 or even
earlier had he known: (*a*) that the pontificate possessed real political clout; (*b*) that the Senate had decreed the honour of the hereditary pontificate for Julius.

Third, Dio slightly contradicts his own evidence where he
expresses surprise that Antony conferred the chief pontificate on
Lepidus instead of securing it for himself (Dio, 44. 53. 7). He
seems to have forgotten that according to his own record of the
facts it should have gone to Octavian. I suggest that Dio, like
many modern scholars, has retrojected an anachronistic importance and the hereditary aspect of the office of Pontifex Maximus
on to the time of Caesar. Perhaps he too was deceived by Ovid!

Ovid has shown us the ideology behind Augustus as Pontifex
Maximus and his dedication to Vesta on the Palatine. Now an
assessment must be made of what it was, exactly, that was dedicated to Vesta in the house of the Pontifex Maximus on 28 April
12 BC, whether the hearth of Rome was relocated on the Palatine,
whether it was merely reproduced on the Palatine, or whether in
fact a brand new cult was founded.

Ovid says in the passage for 6 March that it was the sacred fire,
symbol of Vesta, over which the Pontifex Maximus presided. In
the passage for 28 April, day of the dedication to Vesta, he reports
that 'limine cognati Vesta recepta est', and one can only assume
by association that it was the eternal flame. That assumption
receives reinforcement at 6. 455, where Ovid again celebrates the
union of Vesta and Caesar, the emphasis once more being on the
'sacrae flammae'. The overall impression is that the hearth of
Rome is now located on the Palatine.

The calendars, on the other hand, provide a different impression. The *Fasti Caeretani* states that a 'signum Vestae' was
dedicated 'in domo Palatina'.[98] The *Fasti Praenestini* is very
mutilated but has been restored by Degrassi to agree with the
Caeretani: 'Feriae ex s c quod eo die [signum] et [ara] Vestae in

---

[97] Brunt–Moore (1967) 52–3.   [98] Degrassi (1963) 66.

domu Imp. Caesaris Augusti pontificis maximi dedicatast (Holiday by decree of the senate because on this day a statue and altar of Vesta were dedicated in the house of Imperator Caesar Augustus, pontifex maximus.[99] Degrassi's 'signum' (statue) here replaces Mommsen's 'aedicula' (chapel). Guarducci, on the other hand, believes it should be restored 'quod eo die [signum] et [aedis] Vestae' (because on this day a statue and temple of Vesta) etc.[100] It is on the evidence of these two inscriptional calendars that scholars have concluded that an image of Vesta was installed in Augustus' home on 28 April 12 BC.[101]

That an image of Vesta on the Palatine so radically conflicts with the impression given by Ovid has generated no discussion; whether there was a temple or not has, however.[102] I am prepared to accept Guarducci's argument that the small round temple ('tempietto') depicted on the Pedestal of Augustus in the museum of Sorrento, on the relief in Palermo and on a coin of Tiberius' struck in memory of 'Divus Augustus Pater', represented a shrine to Vesta on the Palatine.[103] Guarducci also asserts that the image of Vesta depicted on the Pedestal and relief prove that an image ('signum') of Vesta was also dedicated there on 28 April. This, she claims, supports the evidence of the calendars. It was the statue of Vesta ('signum'), she concludes, that was 'l'elemento piu notevole, la vera e propria novità' of the cult on the Palatine.[104] As Guarducci's conclusions (and those of others cited by her on the subject) have been reached without regard both for the importance of and the contradictions posed by Ovid's testimony, analyses of the subject have been deficient. The assertion that an image of Vesta was dedicated in the home of Augustus can be undermined by the following observations.

First and foremost, Ovid consistently represents Vesta in union with Augustus either as 'ignis' or 'flamma'. Second, although Ovid testifies to the existence of images of Vesta ('simulacra Vestae', F 3. 45), and although she was depicted anthropomorphically on monuments, the poet also emphatically states that the goddess of the Roman hearth never had a cult statue (6. 291–8).[105] Yet that

---

[99] Degrassi (1963) 132.   [100] Guarducci (1971) 98 ff.
[101] Frazer (1929) iii. 97, 419; Wissowa (1912) 161 n. 3; Bömer (1957–8) ii. 172, 359–60; Latte (1960) 305; Liebeschuetz (1979) 70.
[102] See Guarducci (1971) 89–91.   [103] Ibid. 103–4.
[104] Ibid. 98.   [105] See also Wissowa (1912) 159; Frazer (1929) iv. 216 ff.

it was a cult to Vesta being established on the Palatine is indicated
by the fact that 28 April was made *feriae*. The idea of a cult statue
then contradicts both Ovid's testimony and the notion that the
hearth of Rome was being annexed to Augustus' ancestral worship on the Palatine. Third, the calendars could be interpreted to
concur with the testimony of Ovid. It is not impossible that 'sig
Vest in domo P dedic', the 'fortissime abbreviazioni' inscribed
unevenly into the very narrow space available for any addition to
28 April on to the *Fasti Caeretani*,[106] could mean something other
than an image of Vesta. It could have signified an image of the
Palladium, a small statue of the armed Athena believed to have
been brought from Troy and traditionally preserved in the temple of Vesta in the Forum. Consider the following passages for
the way in which the Palladium is described:

Cic. *Scaur*. 23. 48: illud Palladium, quod quasi pignus nostrae salutis
atque imperii custodiis Vestae continetur (that Palladium, which is the
pledge of our safety and is in the safekeeping of Vesta).

Cic. *Phil*. 11. 10. 24: illud signum, quod de caelo delapsum Vestae custodiis continetur; quo salvo salvi sumus futuri (that statue, which fell
from the sky and is in the safekeeping of Vesta, and whose preservation
ensures that we will be preserved).

Livy, 5. 52. 7: Quid de aeternis Vestae ignibus signoque, quod imperii
pignus custodia eius templi tenetur, loquar? (What shall I say about the
eternal fires of Vesta and the statue which is in safekeeping in her temple
as the pledge of empire?)

Livy, 26. 27. 14: Vestae aedem petitam et aeternos ignes et conditum in
penetrali fatale pignus imperii Romani (the temple of Vesta had been
assailed, and the eternal fires and the pledge of destiny for the Roman
empire has been set up in the innermost shrine).

Note that the Palladium is described either as the 'signum' or the
'pignus imperii' preserved by Vesta, or both. Vesta herself is
'ignes aeterni'. Now look at what Ovid says about Augustus as
Pontifex Maximus (*F* 3. 421–2):

> ignibus aeternis aeterni numina praesunt
> Caesaris : imperii pignora iuncta vides.

Over the eternal flames presides the eternal divinity of Caesar: you see
the pledges of empire united.

[106] Guarducci (1971) 99.

The eternal fire again is Vesta. One of the 'pignora imperii' associated with Vesta would surely be understood as the Palladium, one of the 'septem pignora, quae imperium Romanum tenent' recognized by Varro (Serv. *Aen.* 7. 188). Ovid elsewhere in his poem describes the Palladium as 'armiferae signum caeleste Minervae' (6. 421), the pledge of empire once preserved by (Augustus' ancestor) Ilus in the citadel of Troy and now guarded by Vesta, 'quod assiduo lumine cuncta videt' (6. 436). The poet describes the Palladium in just the same way as Cicero and Livy.

There can be no doubt that Ovid's use of the metonyms 'ignes aeterni' and 'pignus imperii' signified that the flame of Vesta and the statue of the Palladium were united with the Pontifex Maximus on 6 March. The Palladium was an essential part of Rome's claim to her Trojan past, and Augustus' inheritance of Rome's Trojan past is a major theme celebrated in the passage. Ovid's reference to 'imperii pignora iuncta' means that the Pontifex Maximus himself is now equated and united with the Palladium as the pledge of empire.[107] Vesta is now burdened with a double responsibility of guardianship. The notion is thus conveyed that the eternal flame, the Palladium, and Augustus form a very tight-knit trinity.

In view of the evidence thus far presented the calendars could have been interpreted by Romans unused to the idea of Vesta having a cult statue as meaning that the 'signum Vestae' dedicated on the Palatine was the image in Vesta's care, the Palladium. And the Palladium would not have been transferred without its guardian, the flame of Vesta. Now a fresh reconstruction of the Fasti Praenestini is possible. Degrassi has filled the lacunae with '[signum] et [ara] Vestae', Guarducci with '[signum] et [aedis] Vestae'. Guarducci, in defence of 'aedis' pointed out that an 'ara' had 'scarsissima importanza nel culto di Vesta' by comparison.[108] It might also be pointed out that an 'aedis Vestae' on the Palatine would also be meaningless unless it included both the Palladium and the 'aeterni ignes' of Vesta herself, given such prominence by Ovid in his celebration of their union with Augustus. The *Fasti Praenestini* could therefore also be reconstructed thus: Feriae ex s c quod eo die [signum] et [ignis] Vestae in domu

---

[107] This seems to be the message conveyed by Galba's coins, depicting Vesta with the Palladium. See Sutherland (1984) i. 247.

[108] Guarducci (1971) 101.

Imp. Caesaris Augusti pontif. max. dedicatast (etc.)'. (Holiday by decree of the senate because on this day a statue and fire of Vesta were dedicated in the house of Imperator Caesar Augustus pontifex maximus.)

However, despite the temptation to see a transferral of the Forum cult to the Palatine, to see the house of Augustus now as the hearth of Rome, it is evident that the new cult of Vesta did not replace the old one in the Forum. The Vestals were not transferred to the Palatine, but remained in the Atrium Vestae, and Ovid makes clear that the traditional rites associated with the round temple in the Forum continued as before on the ancient site (e.g. *F* 2. 69; 3. 141–4; 6. 227; 295; 395).[109] Furthermore the Forum temple continued to contain both the Palladium and the eternal fire, as the poet recalls from his place of exile (*T* 3. 1. 29–30):

> hic locus est Vestae, qui Pallada servat et ignem,
> haec fuit antiqui regia parva Numae

This is the shrine of Vesta which guards the Palladium and the fire; this was the little residence of the ancient Numa

It could be suggested that the cult of Vesta was reproduced on, not transferred to, the Palatine. This has in fact been done by Lily Ross Taylor, who cites Ovid's entry for 6 March as her evidence. She says: 'In that part (of his house) he erected his own altar and shrine of Vesta equipped with a palladium and an ever burning fire just as was the shrine in the Forum.'[110] But, as Guarducci has pointed out, how could there be two Palladia?[111] Like her, I find it difficult to believe that Augustus would have had a mere copy of this pledge of empire brought to Italy by his Trojan ancestor installed in his home. The Pedestal of Sorrento depicts the Palladium on the Palatine, but Guarducci believes this is simply to allude to the destiny of Rome and its emperor.[112] The very sparse later evidence generally points to the fact that it remained in the Forum. Tacitus says the temple of Vesta and the penates of the Roman People were burnt to the ground in AD 64 (Tac. *Ann.* 15. 41). Presumably the Palladium was engulfed also,

---

[109] Roscher's *Lexicon* (s.v. Vesta cols. 252–3) says that Vesta Palatina for a long time overshadowed the cult in the Forum. For the fortunes of the cult in later times, see Fink *et al.* (1940) 139–40.

[110] Taylor (1931) 184.   [111] Guarducci (1971) 109.   [112] Ibid. 110.

yet later, Herodian (1. 14. 4) reports that in the conflagration in the reign of Commodus, the Palladium was rescued from the flames by the Vestals, who carried it along the Sacred Way to the house of the Rex Sacrificulus. The *Historia Augusta* (Heliog. 3. 4) claims that the fire of Vesta and the Palladium were transferred (from where is not stated) to the temple of Heliogabalus on the Palatine.[113] The same author states shortly after though that several identical shrines to Vesta had been made to prevent anyone ever taking the real Palladium. Does this account for the reference to a Palladium on the Palatine in an inscription of the fourth century from Privernum 'praepositus palladii Palatini' (*CIL* x 6441)? Or was it in fact a reference to the Palladium situated there since the time of Augustus, as Platner–Ashby have suggested?[114]

Despite Ovid's conceptual unification of Augustus, Pontifex Maximus with the fire of Vesta and her pledge of empire, it must be conceded that that unification was not represented physically in his home on the Palatine. This, despite the fact that the poet sustains the notion of unification even where it may not be considered necessary, such as at the end of his entry for the Vestalia on 9 June, an ancient rite celebrated in the Forum and having nothing to do with the cult on the Palatine. Here he reiterates the notion by intimating that the cult in the Forum is Caesar's own cult of Vesta *F* 6. 455–6):

> nunc bene lucetis sacrae sub Caesare flammae:
> ignis in Iliacis nunc erit estque focis;

Now you shine brightly, sacred flames, under Caesar. Now the fire both is and will be on Trojan hearths.

The entire passage to the ancient Vesta of the Forum comes to a climax with Caesar's Vesta exalting the avenger who exacted punishment on the Parthians (6. 465–8). In unifying the two the poet has achieved conceptual annexation of the old cult by the new.

To conclude, the new cult of Vesta on the Palatine appears to have consisted, as Guarducci claims, merely of a small replica of her temple in the Forum and a cult statue. Yet the visual aspect of the cult alone is not enough to provide comprehension of its implications. A statue of Vesta would not in itself induce an auto-

---

[113] See Barnes (1972) 62, 68 for the *Historia Augusta* and Herodian on Vesta.

[114] Platner–Ashby (1929) 557.

matic revelation of Augustus' associations with the goddess of the Roman hearth situated below in the Forum, of his kinship with her, of their common Trojan ancestry and his new status as Pontifex Vestae and 'pignus imperii' under her guardianship. Augustus obviously felt that to transfer an ancient cult, its 'sacra' and its festivals from its hallowed location in the Forum for the purpose of providing a new meaning to the title Pontifex Maximus was risking too radical a break with tradition. To create a new cult was his only solution, yet a sense of connection with and continuation of the tradition of the old had to be established. Not a simple task when old and new were so separate topographically.

It is this sense of connection and continuation between the old and the new which is Ovid's achievement. The imagery created by him no doubt corresponds to the ideology devised by Augustus to redefine the role of Julius and so his own as Pontifex Maximus, to develop the cult of Vesta in a direction which anticipated his own apotheosis, and to pave the way for a succession of Caesarian *pontifices maximi*. Augustus had, in other words, adapted and transformed the office into one of unprecedented religious and political importance for the purpose of supporting the new monarchical regime. That this was so receives confirmation from the fact that thenceforth, the office of Pontifex Maximus was the only Roman office to be closed to all but the emperor, the only Roman office which invoked a charisma of dynasty embodied in its incumbent, the only Roman office to be inextricably connected with the religious station and authority of every succeeding Roman emperor.

I hope I have shown that the testimony of Ovid's *Fasti* is crucial to an understanding of how the Princeps as Pontifex Maximus was at the heart of giving a new meaning to the title, at the heart of the transformation towards monarchy in religious terms. The few contemporary calendars and monuments have helped ascertain the nature of the physical cult on the Palatine. But it is Ovid alone who, by re-creating and conveying the new mythology behind that cult, shows how the ancient institution of Vesta's worship in the Forum was subordinated to the new Pontifex Maximus on the Palatine, how the office of Pontifex Maximus came to be hereditary, how the identity of the Pontifex Maximus came to be as important to the state religion as the office itself. Augustus' assumption of the office of Pontifex Maximus was a vital step in the evolution of Roman religion. The way in which this vital step was effected is witnessed by no other extant source.

Descendant of Venus

In the proem to the month of April, Ovid incorporates into the calendar a celebration of the goddess Venus in order to extol her as ancestress of Caesar Augustus and the Roman nation. Venus' connection with April was not unfamiliar. Horace had sung of April as the month of sea-born Venus (*Od.* 4. 11. 15), and Ovid himself had in earlier poetry claimed the kalends of April as joining Venus to Mars (*AA* 405–6). In the proem to book one of the *Fasti*, preparation had already been made to expect Mars and Venus as tutelary deities of the successive months, March and April, and as ancestor to Romulus, 'conditor urbis' and first regulator of the calendar (1. 39–40):

> Martis erat primus mensis, Venerisque secundus:
>   haec generis princeps, ipsius ille pater.

The first month was that of Mars, the second of Venus. She was the origin of his race, and he the father of Romulus himself.

The invocation to Venus in his proem to the fourth book would thus occasion little surprise. Allen has said that the fourth book, devoted to the month of Venus, is 'naturally' rich in references to the genealogical connection between this goddess and the Julian gens.[115] As we proceed, however, it will emerge that these genealogical references are not necessarily as 'natural' as Allen supposed, nor indeed is Venus' connection with the month of April an automatic assumption on the part of all of Ovid's own contemporaries.

The context in which Ovid was writing is an important consideration. With the completion of the Forum Augustum in 2 BC, Venus was figuring strongly in the visual imagery of the national, dynastic mythology of the late Augustan Principate. On the basis of Ovid's words: 'venerit in magni templum, tua munera, Martis, stat Venus Ultori iuncta' (*T* 2. 295–6), it is thought that the cella of the great temple of Mars Ultor in the Forum, built by Augustus on his personal property (*RG* 21. 1) enshrined his divine lineage by housing statues of the ancestral gods of the Julii, Mars

[115] Allen (1922) 254.

Ultor, and Venus Genetrix.[116] The pediment of the temple also depicted Venus standing next to Mars Ultor.[117]

The allusion to the family connection between the divine pair and the Julii was doubly reinforced in the contiguity of the Forum Augustum and the Forum Iulium. The temple to Venus Genetrix, dedicated by Julius in 46 BC (Dio, 43. 22. 2) was the centrepiece of the Forum Iulium, as the temple of Mars Ultor later became of the Forum Augustum. The two *fora* were similar in design, and their setting at right-angles to each other permitted the Forum of Augustus to extend to the colonnaded precinct of that of his father, Julius.[118] The dynastic ideological associations in such an arrangement could hardly be more manifest. From AD 4 the *Feriale Cumanum*, a calendar of anniversaries of members of the imperial house, was marking a day of supplication to Mars Ultor and Venus Genetrix. The stone is too fragmentary to show which day, but it was perhaps the birthday of Julius Caesar (12 July).[119]

The task of incorporating Venus in her ancestral role into the Roman calendar in the late Augustan Principate was not without its difficulties, however. For Ovid most of all. The image of the goddess of love in Rome appears to have evolved between the first and last decades of Augustus' rule in two different directions. In the national myth she had taken on a more modest form befitting that of the progenetrix of the reigning dynasty; in the poetry of Ovid she had became more licentious and erotic. Her former role will be considered first.

Venus had long been identified as Aphrodite, famous in Greek mythology since the days of Homer for having indulged in an adulterous love affair with Ares (*Od.* 8. 266 ff.). Her identity as a love-goddess remained with her without discomfort after she had been annexed into the Roman pantheon in 217 BC.[120] It appears that this identity posed no problem even when she was identified as Genetrix, ancestress of the Julii in the time of Caesar and Augustus. Unfortunately, we lack adequate iconography for her in this role in Caesar's day.[121] A cult image was made for her

[116] Zanker (1968) 18–19.

[117] As shown by a relief of the Ara Pietatis. See Zanker (1987) 199.

[118] For the groundplan of the *Fora*, see Weinstock (1971) pl. 7 facing p. 82.

[119] Degrassi (1963) 279.   [120] See Schilling (1982) 206–7.

[121] Although not in her role as Victrix, also exploited by Caesar. See Weinstock (1971) 83–4.

temple (Pliny, *NH* 35. 156), but this has not survived, nor has any description of it.[122] Coins issued by Caesar in 47 and 46 BC, the iconography of which is thought to refer to the cult statue, depict only a bust of Venus with Cupid, so it is not possible to discern from these the extent to which Caesar conveyed her erotic imagery.[123]

However, before 29 BC, Octavian had an image of a nearly naked Venus Genetrix bearing the arms of Mars, stamped on a denarius bearing the legend 'Caesar divi f'. The semi-nudity of Venus contrasts markedly with the fully-clothed personifications of Pax and Victory, depicted on coins issued in the same period.[124] In issuing this coin Octavian was no doubt laying claim to the divine ancestry of the Julii, and the emphasis on the erotic aspect of Venus is perhaps a continuation of the imagery conveyed earlier by Julius.[125] Furthermore, Virgil had painlessly used the name of the mother of Aeneas as a synonym for 'amor' in his great epic on the destiny of Rome (*Aen.* 4. 33; 6. 26; 11. 736).[126] Propertius was able to invoke Venus both as genetrix to Caesar (4. 1. 46–7) and as the goddess of love (4. 8. 16). Horace had, as late as his last book of Odes, still felt free to exhort Venus as the goddess of love to employ the talents of Paulus Maximus to break hearts everywhere (*Od.* 4. 1. 9–16). There was apparently no contradiction in the fact that in the last lines of the last Ode of the

---

[122] Weinstock (1971) 86.   [123] Ibid. pl. 6 nos. 10–12 facing p. 49.

[124] Sutherland (1984) i. 59, and pl. 5 nos. 250*a*, 252, 255.

[125] Zanker (1987) 44 Fig. 27*c*; 45, 199. Schilling however (1982) 310–13, asserts that Julius' cult statue of Venus Genetrix was fully clothed in the 'longa vestis' of the matron and was thus the first of its type to break with traditional Greek nudity to accord the goddess a new dignity. Schilling produces no specific evidence for the (no longer extant) statue except references to discussions of earlier scholars. To support his claim he cites the evidence of Virgil, who had Venus clothed in a full-length garment when she appeared to Aeneas (*Aen.* 1. 104). But if Julius bestowed Venus Genetrix with such a novel image from the outset, why would Octavian revert to the erotic image on his coinage when his connection with Venus in her role as Julian ancestress seems to be the intention behind the imagery? Second, Virgil's Venus would perhaps not be expected to appear in the provocative nudity appropriate to the 'judgement of Paris' when appearing before her son, Aeneas. Surely it is the context which demands a more dignified pose for Venus here.

[126] Although Schilling (1982) 363 justifiably points out that in Virgil's epic her image as adulteress has been dropped and in her tutelary role her powers of seductive love turned to a more positive and dignified use.

same book, Horace also conjured up quite a different image of the same goddess in her role as genetrix (*Od.* 4. 15. 31–2):

> Troiamque et Anchisen et almae
> progeniem Veneris canemus.

We shall celebrate Troy and Anchises and the progeny of fruitful Venus.

From the evidence of the poets of the early and middle Augustan Principate, it appears that the new identity of Venus as Trojan ancestress of Rome and the Julii, and her ancient identity as the goddess of love, successfully coexisted without friction or embarrassment.

Two occurrences seem to have altered this situation by the late Principate of Augustus. Ovid went to unprecedented lengths in graphically and unreservedly depicting Venus with erotic associations in his *Amores* and *Ars Amatoria*. In the latter work he had even invoked the goddess of love at the outset of his work as his authority on the subject (*AA* 1. 7: 'Me Venus artificem tenero praefecit Amori'), and had begged her for, and received, her inspiration of his work as 'mater Amoris' (1. 30).

In direct contrast with this extended boundary of divine eroticism set by Ovid, the portrayal of Venus as love-goddess in the iconography of the national myth had been modified. Zanker has noted, for example, that the official, visual imagery of Venus Genetrix appears to have undergone a transition from the erotic (as depicted on Octavian's denarius) to the more dignified, even though she continued to be presented as a classical Aphrodite type. He arrived at this conclusion on the evidence of the relief of the Ara Pietatis and the relief from Carthage in Algiers, both of which he interprets as reflecting the cult statue group in the temple of Mars. These reliefs depict a more modest Venus in a long garment standing in a non-erotic pose next to the war-god, which, rather than encouraging a recollection of the pair's famous adulterous affair, evokes a new interpretation of their ideological role as ancestors to the Julian Gens. Zanker also interprets the bronze statue of Venus in Brescia, fully clothed and less narcissistic in contrast to her Greek prototype, as also reflecting an adaptation to suit the goddess's new role.[127]

---

[127] Zanker (1987) 199–201. Schilling (1982) 326–30 discusses the eclipse of Venus Genetrix in the national propaganda after the battle of Actium because of her associations with Cleopatra. Zanker (1987) 196 is of the opinion that from 17 BC, the

This 'new' Venus in the iconography of the national myth must
have posed an ironic challenge for the former 'praeceptor amoris'
as he attempted to versify the calendar. His own poetry had been
instrumental in widening the gap between the two formerly
compatible identities of Venus. It was he who had accorded the
goddess with associations which were now, as never before,
inconsistent with and incongruous to a eulogy of the princeps'
kinship with her. Ovid was thus confronted with the problem of
how to reconcile the outrageously libidinous image of her he himself had evoked with the new, official representation of her as a
dignified 'genetrix' to the family of the ruler. Not an easy task
when the *Fasti* itself was also an elegiac poem containing much
irreverent, lewd, mythological narrative conveyed in a character-
istically Ovidian tone so evocative of his famous amatory elegies.

Ovid had another problem. Despite Horace's, and his own,
claim that April was the month of Venus (cited above), Venus'
association with the Roman calendar seems to have been both
controversial and relatively recent. Varro (*LL* 6. 33), discussing
the etymology of the names of the months, had rejected that provided for April by his antiquarian predecessors, Fulvius and
Junius, who had derived Aprilis from Venus, 'quod ea sit
Aphrodite'. L. Cincius, as cited by Macrobius (*Sat.* 1. 12. 12) had
actually ridiculed those who associated Venus with the month of
April at all. Cincius asserted, in his treatise on the calendar, that
those who did so showed gross ignorance in claiming that the
ancients named the month after Venus because no festival or
notable sacrifice was appointed in her honour by them; nor
indeed were her praises sung, as were those of other deities, even
in the hymns of the Salii. Macrobius (*Sat.* 1. 12. 13) has Varro
agreeing with Cincius on this point. He says that Varro had
added that even in the time of the kings the name of Venus, in
either its Latin or Greek form, was unknown at Rome, so that the
month of April could not have been named after her.

Against a background of such daunting, scholarly opposition
(Verrius will be dealt with below), a calendrical poet wishing to
eulogize the ancestry of Augustus was confronted with the task of
producing a convincing 'causa' of respectable antiquity in order

year of the Secular Games and Augustus' adoption of Julia's sons, family mythology was revived in a new form to legitimate the rule of the Julian dynasty, and
dates Venus' new image from then.

to assign Venus a place of honour in the calendar. We shall now proceed through Ovid's proemium of the month of April to consider how he deals with the problems of the new ancestral image of Venus, and her dubious claim to the month of April.

Ovid devotes the first eighteen lines of his proem to the fourth book to an acknowledgement of Venus in two different roles: that of goddess of love, and that of goddess of the fourth month. He also devotes it to a reconciliation of the two apparently contradictory functions of each. This dualistic programme is admirably anticipated at the outset, as he addresses her thus:

> 'Alma, fave,' dixi 'geminorum mater Amorum!'
> ad vatem voltus rettulit illa suos.[128]

'Gracious mother of the twin loves', I said, 'be favourable to me.' She turned her face to the poet.

In keeping with the Hellenistic genre, the poet proceeds to draw her into conversation, to acknowledge unashamedly the inspirational assistance she had given him as an amatory elegist in the past, and to beg for her assistance once again now as he fulfils his own new role as calendrical poet (4. 1–12). He has the goddess herself register surprise at this, a clever technique to anticipate and forestall surprise on the part of an audience familiar with his amatory elegies at unexpectedly seeing her in this guise. Ovid's use of analogy of his own ability to wear two hats as a poet (an echo of the proem to 2. 3–8) induces credibility in a twofold function for the goddess as well. He brings together the new role of the goddess with his own (4. 13–14):

> 'venimus ad quartum, quo tu celeberrima mense:
> et vatem et mensem scis, Venus, esse tuos'

'We have come to the fourth month when you are most celebrated: you know, Venus, that both the poet and the month are yours.'

Venus' subsequent affirmation of his statement, her agreement to inspire him as to the 'causa dierum' for the month at hand (as she had once agreed to inspire him at the outset of the *Ars Amatoria*), lends an aura of divine authority and authenticity to the less familiar association of her with the calendrical scheme (4. 15–18).

---

[128] A twist on an address he had made to her earlier in *Am.* 3. 15. 1: 'Quaere novum vatem, tenerorum mater Amorum!' And in *Her.* 16. 203: 'volucrum mater Amorum.'

In light-heartedly acknowledging Venus' erotic identity from the beginning, then contriving and superimposing upon it the greater dignity of calendrical Muse, Ovid has artfully shifted the focus from her most notorious role of his own making to the more sober one of patron of the fourth month. The poet has successfully taken the first step towards reconciling her two apparently para-doxical poses in his love poetry and the national myth. That shift in focus, and in tone, has prepared the way for her representation as ancestress of the Julii, descendants of Mars and Romulus.[129]

The next section (4. 19–60) begins by introducing Caesar into the context, and claiming his interest in the month of April by virtue of his adoption into noble ancestry (4. 19–22). The first connection has now been made between Venus and Caesar through a common interest. The next five lines, linking Romulus to the two ancestral divinities of Caesar and the nation, are crucial to Ovid's recognition of, and attempt to overcome, the contro-versy surrounding Venus' claim to the month of April (4. 23–8):

> hoc pater Iliades, cum longum scriberet annum,
>   vidit et auctores rettulit ipse tuos:
> utque fero Marti primam dedit ordine sortem,
>   quod sibi nascendi proxima cause fuit,
> sic Venerem gradibus multis in gente receptam
>   alterius voluit mensis habere locum;

This our father, son of Ilia, saw when he was distributing the months of the lengthy year and himself commemorated his ancestors. Just as he gave fierce Mars the first place in the list of months because he was the most direct cause of his own birth, so he wanted Venus, whom he found amongst his ancestors of many previous generations, to have the place of the second month.

By invoking Romulus as 'pater Iliades' to stress his Trojan affilia-tion, and by claiming that it was he, in his capacity as founder of the Roman calendar, who had allocated the second month to Venus because of his descent from her through many generations, the poet lends the weight of antiquity and the authority of

---

[129] In view of the problem confronting Ovid with regard to his presentation of Venus, his proem must be recognized as having historical as well as literary signif-icance in its repetition of the *recusatio* and other themes linking it with other such passages in the *Fasti* so often recognized by critics, e.g. Braun (1981) 2347–8; Har-ries (1989) 174–5.

Rome's founder to support Venus', and his own, earlier affirmation of her right to it.

The same passage has introduced the link between the two
mythical cycles of Caesar's divine parentage to connect him to
both Mars and Venus.[130] It was the unification of the two myths
which became the central element of the state myth as evoked by
the pairing of Mars and Venus on the temple of Mars Ultor
which sought to circumvent the associations of their adulterous
affair in Greek mythology.[131] Ovid's long and detailed genealogy
that naturally follows in the sequel, fusing the divine and Trojan
progenitors of the Julian family with the maternal ancestry of
Romulus, son of Mars, dutifully circumvents it also. He culminates the section by lending a Callimachean stamp of authenticity
to the unification of the two myths, and again reiterating Venus'
right to a place in the calendar, by uniting her with Mars and
once more invoking the authority of Romulus (4. 57–60):

> ille suos semper Venerem Martemque parentes
>   dixit, et emeruit vocis habere fidem:
> neve secuturi possent nescire nepotes,
>   tempora dis generis continuata dedit.

He always declared that Venus and Mars were his ancestors, and his
merits have required that his word should be believed. And that his
descendants after him should not be ignorant of this, he consecrated con-
tiguous months to the gods of his race.

The next section (4. 61–78) reflects Ovid's recognition of his second problem: that of producing an unassailable 'causa' of the
month in the face of the opposition of the scholarly writings of
Cincius and Varro. And having just insisted that Romulus had
assigned the months of March and April to his divine parents, he
now must account for the fact that the name of the fourth month
bore no apparent connection with the name Venus. Varro had
already said that the names of the months were in general obvi-

---

[130] Genealogies linking a patron with Ilium or Olympus were well within the
Callimachean tradition of aetiological poetry, were meant to impress, and did:
Wiseman (1974a) 159. Whether these mythical cycles were connected to acquire
double divine ancestry for the Julians in the time of Julius or in the time of
Augustus is still a matter of dispute. Weinstock (1971) 17, 129, 183 argues for
Julius; Schilling (1982) 333, and Latte (1960) 302 n. 6 for Augustus. Livy was not
sure about Romulus' Martian paternity (1. 4).

[131] Zanker (1987) 199.

ous, as Mars was an obvious derivation of Martius (*LL* 6. 33);
Ovid had virtually said as much to that god in his proem to book
three (3. 4):

> a te, qui canitur, nomina mensis habet.

From you who is being celebrated, the month has its name.

So why Aprilis, not 'Veneris'? His statement that April belonged
to Venus (4. 14) now receives its etymological justification thus (4.
61–2):

> sed Veneris mensem Graio sermone notatum
> auguror : a spumis est dea dicta maris.

but I suspect, however, that the month of Venus was designated in the
Greek language; the goddess derived her name from the foam of the sea.

At first this sudden change of course looks like an undercutting of
the Trojan section that had come before. But Ovid has clearly
selected the etymology for April (from Aphrodite) of Fulvius and
Junius rejected by Varro, and is now proclaiming its accuracy to
justify Venus' place in the calendar.[132] To make such an idea
feasible—and, just as importantly, to plead the highest antiquity
for the goddess' association with the Italian nation—he provides
in the sequel a sketch of a period in its history before the Trojan
arrival, when it was inhabited by Evander, visited by Hercules,
Odysseus, and other Greeks who had left their stamp on 'Graecia
maior'. Aeneas, he says, arrived long after the Greeks had already
made their influence felt (4. 63–78), thus implying that the Tro-
jans arrived long after Aphrodite was already known in Italy.[133]
Against this background he can only account for the fact that
some still wished to deprive Venus of the honour of the month by
attributing it to envy (4. 85–6):

> quo non livor abit? sunt qui tibi mensis honorem
> eripuisse velint invideantque, Venus.

To what lengths will envy not go? There are those who begrudge you the
honour of the month, Venus, and would deprive you of it.

---

[132] Ovid had perhaps anticipated this 'Greek interlude' earlier, at l. 15, by reference to the myrtle of Cythera, the first island with which Aphrodite came into
contact after her birth in the sea (Hes., *Theog.* 190–8).

[133] Ovid is following a tradition found (not surprisingly) also in Dion. Hal. 1.
60. 3.

He then spurns with indignation those who derived 'Aprilis' from 'aperire' as base and impious in attempting to rob Venus of her due (4. 87–8). April is Venus' month, he insists yet again, she claims it, and lays her hand on it (4. 89–90).

Ovid here is attacking the work of Cincius and Varro, who had derived Aprilis from 'aperire' (Macr. *Sat.* 1. 12. 14). And surely not just for the sake of adopting the convenient etymology of their scholarly opponents, Fulvius and Junius. It will be remembered that Cincius had denied the existence of any notable festival or sacrifice to Venus in the calendar, had denied that the month of April was named after her, or that the ancients knew anything about her. Varro had concurred. Such opinions posed a grave challenge to the validity of the Julian claim of descent from Venus, central to the national myth, as well as Venus' claim to a place in the calendar which guaranteed the profound antiquity of her association with Rome. Ovid thus has good reason to place Aphrodite in pre-Roman Italy, and to rail against the works of these particular scholars to try and obliterate any doubts about the authenticity of Venus' claim on the month.

At this point we should consider the partially extant inscriptional evidence of Ovid's scholarly contemporary, Verrius Flaccus, which does not parallel Ovid's attempt to invalidate opposing views. Unfortunately, his introduction to the month of April is so mutilated that it has had to be heavily reconstructed. Degrassi's edition reads as follows:[134]

[Aprilis a] V[e]n[e]r[e], quod ea cum [Anchisa iuncta mater fuit Aene]ae regis [Latinor]um a quo p(opulus) R(omanus) ortus e[st. Alii ab ape]ri[li] q[uod]am i[n m]ense quia fruges, flores animaliaque ac maria et terrae aperiuntur.

April is named after Venus, because she, united with Anchises, was the mother of Aeneas, king of the Latins, from whom the Roman people are descended. Others claim that April comes from 'aperilis' because in that month fruits and flowers and animals and seas and lands do open.

Degrassi's reconstruction has Verrius impartially giving two versions for the *aition* of the month of April which, according to Ovid and the earlier antiquarians, were mutually exclusive: the one reflecting the contemporary Augustan political programme of the Venereal origins of Rome; the other reflecting the late Republican

[134] Degrassi (1963) 127.

etymology which deprived Venus of a place in Roman antiquity and any association with the calendar.[135] Verrius' apparent willingness to let his reader make up his own mind about how April got its name contrasts sharply with Ovid's almost feverish insistence on a correct one. And the absence of the one which Ovid did insist upon, the 'aphros' etymology, is conspicuous in Verrius. Why did he not include that as well?[136] The evidence of Horace, who had described April as the month of sea-born Venus ('mensem Veneris marinae . . . Aprilem', *Od.* 4. 11. 15), an obvious reference to the birth of Aphrodite, suggests that the Greek derivation as *aition* for the month name was certainly in circulation. I can think of no explanation for Verrius' omission of it. Unless, perhaps, that he did not omit it, but that his reference to it simply finds no trace in the surviving fragments of his calendar.[137]

As has been noted by Porte,[138] Ovid, at the end of his proem, manages to reconcile the scholars' derivation of Aprilis from *aperire* by concluding with lines that weld Venus to the season of spring, and so succeeds in alienating neither the good graces, nor Augustus, nor the grammarians: (4. 125–8):

> nec Veneri tempus, quam ver, erat aptius ullum
> (vere nitent terrae, vere remissus ager;
> nunc herbae rupta tellure cacumina tollunt,
> nunc tumido gemmas cortice palmes agit),

And no season was more appropriate to Venus than spring. In spring the earth glistens; in spring the ground is loose; then does the grass push its pointed blades through the ruptured soil, then does the shoot drive the bud from the swelling bark.

Porte's assessment is undoubtedly correct. Ovid does seem to have merged the opposing views on the true *aition* of April by the end of the passage.

[135] Mommsen's reconstruction is slightly different but not contradictory to that of Degrassi. See *CIL* 1 (2) 235.

[136] Frazer (1929) iii. 180 thinks it is because a patriotic Roman would have preferred the native Latin etymology to the derivation from the Greek. He notes that Plutarch, who cites both etymologies, prefers the derivation from Aphrodite as a Greek (*Num.* 19. 2). But as the present work is attempting to show, there was nothing unpatriotic about Ovid when praising Augustus in the *Fasti*. Frazer's view is therefore unconvincing.

[137] Table xl in Degrassi (1963), a photograph of 1–6 April of the *Fasti Praenestini* shows how very mutilated the stone is.

[138] Porte (1985) 82.

Yet it does seem to me that his energetic rejection of the 'aperire' etymology earlier in the piece arose from his attempt to abrogate the theory of the writers who threatened the validity of Venus in the Augustan origins of Rome. (Ovid is elsewhere quite willing to cite a great variety of *aitia* without bias, such as at 4. 783–806, or numerous etymologies, such as for Maius at 5. 1–110.) It is intriguing that Verrius did not, as far as we know, attempt to do this. Ovid's proem to April can be seen also as evidence that the poet did not mechanically draw on Verrius at all times as a source for the *Fasti*, as some modern critics claim.

To revert to the proem. Having categorically rejected the 'aperire' etymology (4. 85–90), Ovid is still not content. He goes to even greater lengths to stake Venus' claim on April. As additional vindication, the poet indulges in a Lucretius-like eulogy of the goddess, elevating her to a rank never attributed to her in Greek mythology by describing her as mother of gods, of creation, of fertility, as lawgiver to heaven and earth, as goddess of civilized behaviour, of eloquence, of arts, of invention.[139]

The exaggeration of her rank to justify a claim is not Ovid's only intention here. In her elevated status Venus is still depicted as goddess of love ('perque suos initus continet omne genus', 4. 94), but nevertheless one very far removed from that normally associated with the amatory poet. Her image as love-goddess in the sexual sense has been transformed into one of love as the creative force which populated the entire earth with vegetation, men, birds, cattle, sheep, fish and all living things (4. 96–114). Not only is Venus' association with the season of spring, with which he culminates the passage, anticipated here. His determination to obliterate the associations of the Venus of his love poetry is still very evident.

Then to round off this section he returns to his already oft repeated theme (4. 115–16):

> hanc quisquam titulo mensis spoliare secundi
> audeat? a nobis sit furor iste procul.

Would anyone dare deprive this goddess of the distinction of giving her name to the second month? Far from us be such madness.

Surely Ovid 'doth protest too much'. This is no less than the fifth time in the proem that he has insisted upon Venus' right to the

[139] See Lucr. 1. 1: 'Aeneadum genetrix, alma Venus' etc.

month (4. 14, 26–7, 61–2, 85–6, 115–16). His persistent defensive-
ness points to the fact that at the time, Venus' entitlement to a
place in the calendar was by no means uncontroversial.

A recapitulation of Venus' role in Rome's Trojan origins, in
Rome's predestiny and as progenitor of the Julii and Caesar,
draws the proem to April towards its conclusion (4. 117–24). Having formerly identified Venus first as Trojan (ancestress to the
'pater Iliades'), then as Greek, Ovid now addresses her as goddess of Rome, both to sustain the imagery of the universal
'Lucretian' model, as well as to emphasize now an unquestionably indigenous identity. Although Venus is worshipped everywhere, he says, it is in Rome she carries most authority ('potens'
at line 117), because of her unique relationship with the city's pre-
history and 'magnus Caesar' (at line 124). The universal theme is
followed through to the conclusion, where Venus is united with
spring, with the fertility of the earth, and once more with the god
Mars (4. 129–30):

> et formosa Venus formoso tempore digna est,
> utque solet, Marti continuata suo est.

And beautiful Venus is worthy of the beautiful seasons, and she is, as
usual, attached to her own Mars.

This culmination of the proem projecting an image of the love-
goddess Venus as universal, ancestral, Roman goddess of spring
and fertility, unified with Mars, might well convey the message
Augustus intended with his refurbished Venus and the grouping
of the divine pair in his great temple of Mars Ultor.

A dignified pose for Venus is subsequently sustained by Ovid
throughout the month that he has so strenuously argued is hers.
(He shows particular restraint in not allowing her to revert to
Ovidian type at a festival for 'volgares puellae' at 4. 865–6.) On
the kalends, the festival of Venus Verticordia, her modesty is
invoked as the *aition* for the ritual (4. 139–44), and he exhorts
women of all rank to propitiate her, as 'forma et mores et bona
fama' were in her keeping (4. 155–6). He intimates that Venus, as
Verticordia, had been known since ancient times as a goddess of
chastity (4. 157–160), and in this context he prays to her in her
unmistakable role of 'genetrix' to the Julii (4. 161–2):[140]

---

[140] It is quite possible that the festivals of Venus Verticorda and Fortuna Virilis (1 Apr.), and the Vinalia (23 Apr.), with which Venus is also associated, were

semper ad Aeneadas placido, pulcherrima, voltu
respice, totque tuas, diva, tuere nurus.

Most beautiful goddess, ever look with mild countenance upon the sons
of Aeneas, and watch over your numerous daughters-in-law.

We are again reminded that April is the month of Venus on the
fifteenth of the month, the festival of the Fordicidia (4. 629–30).
Ovid's prompt at this point is unlikely to be accidental. Not only
is it placed strategically in the middle of the month; it is also a
fertility festival where sacrifice of a fruitful cow was made to
ensure a fruitful earth in the coming season (4. 633–44). Venus'
image of love-goddess, whose power of influence the poet had
transplanted from a sexual to a procreative sphere by associating
her with fertility and spring in the proem, thus receives reinforcement here; a contrived reinforcement, because Venus is not
known to have had anything to do with the Fordicidia. And more.
The following day was the anniversary of the day Octavian had
won his first salutation as Imperator. Ovid contrives to bring
ancestress and descendant together once again by craftily over-
coming the calendrical obstacle of the relentless diurnal division.
On the same day as the Fordicidia he has Venus (Cytherea), as
patron of the month, command the fifteenth to hasten on its way
in order to give place as soon as possible to the sixteenth, the day
on which Augustus first received the title 'imperator'. The amal-
gamation of Venus as universal fertility goddess and *genetrix* of
the present-day ruler is once more in evidence.

There can be little doubt that Ovid's reason for incorporating
Venus into the fourth month, his method of doing so, and his
representation of her, have all been motivated by a desire to
divert attention from the erotic imagery he had made synony-
mous with Venus in his amatory poetry and to promote that
which he saw as being projected in the national myth by her
present-day descendant. Yet Ovid's treatment of Venus is telling
in another respect. Venus' association with April clearly had its
roots in the past, as we saw from the earlier scholars Fulvius and
Junius. But Varro, Cincius, and Ovid have shown that, in the late

entered into the state cult only in the time of Augustus, as Varro and Cincius
knew nothing of them (Mac. *Sat.* 1. 12. 12–13). For various discussions see Warde
Fowler (1899) 67–8, 85–8; Frazer (1929) iii. 394–8; Schilling (1982) 226, 389;
Degrassi (1963) 434 (1 Apr.); 446 (23 Apr.); Porte (1985) 82, 391; Champeaux (1982)
375–95; Scullard (1981) 96–7.

Republic and early Empire, it was by no means accepted in all quarters as a tradition of irrefutable antiquity.

This controversy may well be another contributing factor to Ovid's almost circumspect handling of the love-goddess as patron of the month in an ancestral role. A new concept is unlikely to have been treated by Ovid in the *Fasti* as casually and humorously as one as familiar and assured as an ancient tradition thoroughly imbued in the religious consciousness. To do so could jeopardize its likelihood of taking root, and thus threaten its very survival. Augustus, for example, who was a modern 'concept' in the calendar, is consistently treated with dignity and respect; figures from the past on the other hand, such as Romulus and Mars, could (and do) safely receive comic, irreverent treatment by the poet because of their unassailable claim on the calendar and Roman antiquity (e.g. see *F* 2. 133 ff.; 3. 1ff.). Ovid's comparatively kid-glove treatment of Venus Genetrix in April hints at his awareness of the vulnerability and newness of the association, and points to the fact that the idea of her as a 'Julian' calendrical patron reflecting glory on her present-day descendant was still in the process of being consolidated into the state cult.

Avenger of Caesar and Crassus

Ovid celebrates the dedication of the Temple of Mars Ultor in the Forum Augustum on 12 May. Until recently it was a matter beyond dispute that Ovid was mistaken as to the date, as his record conflicted with that of Dio, who placed it on 1 August (Dio, 60. 5. 3). But in 1977 the poet was vindicated by C. J. Simpson, who showed that it was the later historian who was confused, not the contemporary and probably eyewitness poet.[141] Simpson's study, regrettably overlooked or ignored by some,[142] encourages confidence in the historical credibility of Ovid's verse which has too often been passed over in favour of a later historian's record.

Ovid marks the day with a eulogy rather longer than usual for a new Augustan festival day, too long to cite in full (*F* 5. 545–98). After observing how the stars themselves were aware of the importance of the day that had dawned, he proceeds by evoking

[141] Simpson (1977) 91.
[142] Such as Sutherland (1987) 5; Siebler (1988) 161 n. 816.

expectation that it is an anniversary of martial victory about to be commemorated (5. 549–50):

> fallor, an arma sonant? non fallimur, arma sonabant:
>> Mars venit et veniens bellica signa dedit.

Am I mistaken, or is there a clash of arms? I am not mistaken, there was a clash of arms. Mars is coming, and in coming he gave the signal for war.

an expectation enhanced by a subsequent conceit of the avenging god descending from heaven to view his splendid temple in the Augustan Forum (5. 551–2):

> Ultor ad ipse suos caelo descendit honores
>> templaque in Augusto conspicienda foro.

The avenger himself descends from heaven to his own honours and to his distinguished temple in the forum of Augustus.

It is through the eyes of Mars that the reader surveys the huge temple of the war-god in the city of his own son (Augustus), taking in a detailed description of the building as a focus for Rome's ongoing military enterprise against aggressors in east and west, as a focus for military ceremonies, as well as its adornment of armoury from conquered lands, statuary and *elogia* of great Romans of the past, and the inscribed name of Augustus on the front (5. 553–68).

However, the most fulsome section which follows is devoted, not, as may be expected, to Augustus' dynastic connection with Mars to which the temple was primarily a monument, but to the *raison d'être* of the temple itself (5. 569–96). Augustus earned the cognomen 'Ultor' for Mars on two counts. First, he avenged the murder of his father, Vesta's priest, which Ovid heightens with the emotive effect of an imaginary speech of the young Caesar at Philippi vowing the temple: 5.573–8

> 'si mihi bellandi pater est Vestaeque sacerdos
>> auctor, et ulcisci numen utrumque paro,
> Mars, ades et satia scelerato sanguine ferrum,
>> stetque favor causa pro meliore tuus.
> templa feres et, me victore, vocaberis Ultor'
>> voverat, et fuso laetus ab hoste redit.

'If my father and Vesta's priest is the cause for my waging war and I prepare to avenge both divinities, then stand by me Mars, satiate your sword with profaned blood and may your favour be with the better cause. You will receive a temple and be called Avenger when I am victorious.' He vowed, and returned jubilant from the prostrate enemy.

Second, he recovered the legionary standards lost by Crassus to the Parthians in 53 BC. The poet dwells on the impregnability of the Parthian nation, its military might, its capture of the Roman standards and the annihilation of Crassus' army, to magnify the achievement of Augustus which put an end to the shame and disgrace of a generation (5. 587–90):

> isque pudor mansisset adhuc, nisi fortibus armis
>   Caesaris Ausoniae protegerentur opes.
> ille notas veteres et longi dedecus aevi
>   sustulit: agnorunt signa recepta suos.

This disgrace would have lasted until now, were not the wealth of Italy protected by Caesar's brave troops. It was he who removed the old stain and the shame of a long period. The standards, when recovered, recognized their own.

Once again the theme of the present age outshining the past, evident also in the Pater Patriae passage as we saw, is apparent. Ovid concludes with a gloating address to the Parthians, jubilation over the twice earned epithet 'Ultor' for Mars, and the double fulfilment of vengeance. The passage culminates with an exhortation to the Quirites to celebrate the Games in honour of the mighty god.

Ovid's passage on the Temple of Mars Ultor is notable for two reasons. The gallery of national portraits in the Forum of Augustus had already been foreshadowed by older poets who did not live to see the completion of the complex (Virg. *Aen.* 6. 777 ff.; 824 ff.; Hor. *Od.* 1. 12; cf. 4. 8. 13 ff.). Ovid, who did, provides a major source for the reconstruction of the layout of the statuary and their *elogia* in the precinct of the temple.[143] The contemporary poet also provides the double historical myth created for the first temple of Mars within the pomerium itself: the vow at Philippi to avenge Julius, Pontifex Vestae; and Augustus' military greatness in retrieving the legionary standards from the Parthians. It is the dual purpose of that two-pronged myth that requires scrutiny here.

---

[143] Zanker (1968) 16–17.

The first, the poet's placing of the alleged vow at Philippi in the mouth of Augustus, indicates that the myth was invented not by Ovid but by an authorized source. That the vow was invented was demonstrated by Weinstock, who showed how Octavian could not (for political survival) have vowed to build a temple to Mars Ultor in Rome to celebrate victory in a civil war.[144] He suggested that the epithet Ultor was conceived before the death of Caesar by Caesar himself, who, wanting to honour the ancestral god of the Julii, vowed a temple to him as Ultor in exchange for victory in his projected Parthian war of revenge. This meant that Mars could not earn his title Ultor until the standards had been retrieved. Caesar died before this could be achieved, and the triumvirate inherited the war of revenge. Antony was spectacularly unsuccessful in his attempt, losing even more Roman standards in the process. Augustus was constantly urged take up the vengeful cause, and it is in 19–18 BC, after the Parthian settlement, that Mars Ultor is first found on coinage. Weinstock made the point that Mars had always been intended as the avenger of Crassus and the national honour. He was not, before the dedication of his temple in the Augustan Forum, the avenger of Caesar himself. Ovid's entry for 12 May is the first witness to Mars Ultor in that capacity.[145]

Other reasons which are not mentioned by Weinstock also cause doubt about the authenticity of the vow. Before 20 BC it was Augustus in the guise of Mercury who was known as 'Caesaris ultor' (Hor. *Od.* 1. 2. 41–4). More importantly, it is impossible to believe that Augustus would let forty years pass before fulfilling his vow. Consider, for example, that the triumvirs had vowed the temple of Divus Iulius in the same year, i.e. in 42 BC, and that was

---

[144] Weinstock's analysis of the circumstances surrounding the myth has not received the attention it deserves. Alföldi (1975) 163, reviewing *Divus Julius*, dismissed his thesis as 'a queer idea' and totally misrepresents his arguments. Siebler (1988) 145 ff. has attempted to refute Weinstock's thesis, but unsatisfactorily in my view. For example, much of his argument rests on an interpretation of a portrait on a coin issued by the triumvirate. Nor does he explain how a temple could be vowed to Mars for victory in a civil war, nor why it was not completed until 2 BC. After much hypothesizing, he is forced to admit that the very first, undoubted evidence for Mars Ultor in Augustan times appeared on the Signa Recepta series of 20 BC. Other scholars, on the other hand, have overlooked Weinstock's thesis altogether, such as Liebeschuetz (1979) 86, Fishwick (1987) 87 n. 30, and others.

[145] Weinstock (1971) 130 ff.

dedicated thirteen years later, in 29. And the temple of Apollo on
the Palatine, entailing the acquisition of private land like that of
Mars Ultor, was dedicated in 36 BC and completed only eight
years later, despite the fact that it was built during the turbulent
years of civil war.

And now to enlarge on Weinstock's thesis: it is most unlikely
that Mars Ultor could have been made the avenger of Caesar in 2
BC had Caesar not been represented as Pontifex Vestae, a title
which conflated Julian with national interests. This must therefore date the vow to 12 BC or later, after Vesta had been annexed
to the Julian 'domus' by the new Pontifex Maximus. The battle-
cry upon which Octavian's ascendancy originally rested, that of
(personal) vengeance for the death of Caesar, had become rather
impolitic well before this time. An ardent supporter and constant
eulogizer of Brutus had been honoured in the upheaval over the
resignation of the consulship in 23 BC (Dio, 53. 32. 3–5). And
Virgil had daringly (or inconveniently) attached to the elder
Brutus the very epithet of Ultor itself (*Aen.* 6. 817–18):

> vis et Tarquinios reges animamque superbam
> ultoris Bruti, fascisque videre receptos?

Would you also like to see the Tarquin kings, the proud spirit of Brutus
the avenger, and the recovery of the fasces?

Virgil's avenging Brutus, founding hero of the Republic,
appeared at a time when Augustus was finally in a position to
assume the role of avenger in a form more obviously beneficial on
a national level by retrieving the standards and so restoring
Roman honour. This may have induced Caesar's heir to play
down the emphasis on personal vindication in the civil war which
destroyed the Republic, and to instigate a reinterpretation of his
cause.

The new definition of the role of Pontifex Maximus in 12 BC
and the creation of the concept 'pontifex Vestae' provided the
opportunity. This new title and role for Julius allowed Octavian's
early emphasis on personal vindication to expand to a larger
interpretation of vengeance on behalf of Vesta and thus of the
Roman nation itself. This larger interpretation is nowhere more
evident than in Ovid's entry for the ides of March, which celebrates the 'iusta arma' by which Octavian avenged the death of
Vesta's priest (*F* 3. 697–710; see Ch. 3 on Julius). The repetition of
this reconstruction of Octavian's cause in 42 BC in the present

passage meant that Philippi was now being celebrated as a
national vindication, equal in importance to vengeance on the
Parthians. The passage of forty years since Philippi, the decease
both of his triumviral colleagues and of his later supporters,
Agrippa and Maecenas, all of whose existence would have
reminded him of the spuriousness of the vow as well as his singu-
larly unheroic part in the battle,[146] allowed the myth to take hold.
Mars Ultor as the avenger of Caesar was born, after 12 BC. Perhaps even as late as AD 4 or after, as we shall see.

The second myth reflected by Ovid is Mars Ultor as the
avenger of Crassus and Roman honour. The clamour for a war of
vengeance on the Parthians is a familiar theme in poetry predat-
ing 20 BC.[147] That vengeance in any way other than by force of
arms was possible had obviously not occurred to the poets. Yet
the standards were handed back to Rome voluntarily by the
Parthians, with not an arrow shot. Dio says that Augustus took
great pride in this diplomatic triumph, boasting that he had won
back without striking a blow what had earlier been lost in battle
(Dio, 54. 8. 1–3). But a peaceful settlement was hardly a glorious
way for a god of war to earn his allegedly long-promised epithet
Ultor, or a fitting pretext for dedicating a huge temple to him in
that capacity. So why did Augustus decide to build the temple to
Mars to celebrate the occasion? (That decision was made probably in 19 BC, hence the coinage bearing the legend MARS ULT.)[148]
The personification of Pax Augusta became much vaunted as the
regime matured.[149] Why not a temple to her, for example?

We must revert to Weinstock's thesis, which states that Julius
had wanted to honour Mars as his ancestor with a temple, just as
he had done for Venus. If Julius had vowed a temple to his war-
god ancestor and invented the epithet Ultor in exchange for a victory of revenge over the Parthians as Weinstock persuasively
argues,[150] then Augustus would have been most anxious to
appropriate this familial obligation to establish and glorify his

---

[146] App. BC 4. 110–11, 463 ff.; Dio, 47. 41. 3; 45–6; Suet. Aug. 13. 1. As Syme
points out, Agrippa and Maecenas did not deny that Octavian lurked in a marsh:
Pliny, NH 7. 148.

[147] Virg. Georg. 3. 31; 4. 560; Hor. Sat. 2. 5. 62; Od. 1. 2. 21, 51: 'ne sinas Medos
equitare inultos, / te duce, Caesar'; 3. 3. 43–4; 3. 5. 3 ff.; and Propertius, 3. 4. 9–10:
'Crassos clademque piate! / ite et Romanae consulite historiae!'

[148] Simpson (1977) 93.   [149] Wissowa (1912) 334.

[150] Weinstock (1971) 130 ff.

own place in the Julian dynasty. Yet he had a problem. Julius, a general of genius, might well claim the god of war and victory as his ancestor. But it was more awkward for Augustus, whose remarkable talents in the political arena did not extend to the battlefield. He had before him also the example of Antonius, who, charged with the war of revenge against Crassus (App. *BC* 5. 65. 275), and although having adopted the plan of campaign attributed to Julius, had nevertheless suffered defeat with the loss of not less than a quarter of the entire army.[151] With the huge pressure of demand for Parthian revenge so loudly pronounced by the poets, the opportunity to recover the standards ('Signa, decus belli', 5. 585) through peaceful negotiation must have been an overwhelming relief for Augustus. But even this diplomatic coup had been achieved through the talent and agency of Tiberius (Suet. *Aug.* 21. 3; *Tib.* 9. 1: 'Recepit et signa, quae M. Crasso ademerant Parthi').[152]

The bloodless triumph of one who was not even (at that time) a member of the dynasty posed a new problem: it created the possibility for Mars to be cheated of his Julian epithet Ultor, and for Augustus to be deprived of a valid reason for establishing a martial cult to glorify his ancestry.

[151] See Syme (1939) 263–5.

[152] It is true that Velleius Paterculus, Tiberius' panegyrist, does not mention the fact that it was Tiberius who received the standards (2. 91. 1). For this reason Suetonius' statement is usually ignored or rejected—see Syme (1978) 31; Anderson (1934) 263. However, it seems to me that Suetonius' claim ought to be given more credence. The biographer mentions Tiberius' acceptance of the standards twice, in the Lives of both Augustus and Tiberius, sources for which he had at his disposal Augustus' private correspondence which he read 'with great care' (Wallace-Hadrill (1983) 62). Public, official documents, standard historical sources, or works in general circulation, interested him less than 'private, literary products' (Wallace-Hadrill (1983) 63). In official propaganda regarding something as crucial to Augustan prestige as the return of the standards, one would not expect to see their reception by the young Tiberius given a high profile, if indeed given any mention at all. To my mind this is the type of information that would have been found only in 'unofficial' source material, such as Suetonius was fond of using. Velleius' neglect in mentioning Tiberius' acceptance of the standards (he was too young to be a contemporary witness to this event), simply indicates that he did not know about it. Yet he does seem suspicious at one point. The king of the Parthians, he says, awed by Tiberius' reputation (as conqueror), sent his children as hostages to Caesar (Vell. Pat. 2. 94. 4 cf. Suet. *Aug.* 21. 3). This statement does not really make sense if it had been Augustus who had 'compelled' the Parthians to restore the standards and to seek as suppliants the friendship of the Roman people (*RG* 29).

Not one to be thwarted by a mere problem of legitimacy, the new son of Mars would have seen the necessity of applying some armoured camouflage to this vulnerable spot so that he could simulate the kind of victory envisaged by Julius and demanded by the poets. Evidence of an attempt to do just that comes from Augustus' own words where, in the section of his *Res Gestae* stressing his military successes, he advertised the return of the standards as a great military victory, making the most of the subservience of the Parthians: 'Parthos trium exercitum Romanorum spolia et signa reddere mihi supplicesque amicitiam populi Romani petere coegi' (*RG* 29. 2). The same theme is reflected on denarii issued in 19 BC which bear the legend 'Caesar Augustus Sign(is) Rece(ptis)', and depict a kneeling Parthian extending standard and vexillum.[153] Dio affirms the Princeps' efforts at effecting a military achievement by stating that he received the standards as though he had defeated the Parthians in a campaign. He does not seem to have noticed the ambiguity in Augustus' delight in the peaceful settlement on the one hand, and his determination to make it look like a military retaliation on the other (Dio, 54. 8. 2).

Publicity advertising the return of the standards as a military victory no doubt allowed for the decision to build a temple to Mars Ultor in 19 BC. Yet later events suggest that a cloud of uncertainty hung over the legitimacy of the proposed cult. The temple and its precinct, the Forum Augustum, took an unusually long time to complete, as we see from Augustus' joke to the architect reported by Macrobius (*Sat.* 2. 4. 9).[154] It was eventually opened in 2 BC, hastily, to accommodate the increase in court cases, says Suetonius, before the temple of Mars was finished (*Aug.* 29. 1). Yet we know that the temple was also dedicated that year (Dio, 55. 9. 10–10. 1) on 12 May, as Ovid says. Does this mean the temple was dedicated before it was finished? Why the sudden rush after so long? Why 2 BC? It would seem that the timing was not coincidental.

---

[153] Sutherland (1987) 13.

[154] It was not the size of the entire monumental complex that was the cause of the long delay. Augustus did not have to wait until the Forum Augustum was complete before dedicating the temple to Mars Ultor. Julius' temple to Venus Genetrix was dedicated in 46 BC, years before the Forum Iulium was completed by his heir. For references see Weinstock (1971) 82.

The prospect of a military expedition against Parthia arose when the Parthians joined Armenia in revolt in 1 BC. Augustus was now too old for active service, so chose as commander in his place the next member of the dynasty, the young and inexperienced Gaius Caesar, born in the year of the recovery of the standards (Dio, 54. 8. 5). Dio says Augustus was driven to choose the 18-year old in the absence of any other competent general (Dio, 55. 10. 18), but this justification strains credulity, particularly when the ideological link forged between Gaius' impending war and Mars Ultor is taken into consideration. It is this link, forged both in the poetry of Ovid and in coinage for the period in which Gaius left Rome, which makes it possible to understand why the temple of Mars was dedicated in 2 BC.

First, Ovid. In the *Ars Amatoria* he draws an explicit connection between the *naumachia* staged as part of the dedication ceremony for the temple to Mars (Dio, 55. 10. 7; Vell. 2. 100. 2) and the imminent departure of Gaius to wage a war of revenge on the Parthians (*AA* 1. 171–228). He begins with:

> quid, modo cum belli navalis imagine Caesar
> Persidas induxit Cecropiasque rates?

What about when Caesar recently exhibited Persian and Athenian ships in imitation of a naval battle?

and follows this up with a panegyric on Gaius' mission to the East. The ideology behind that mission is unequivocal (*AA* 1. 177–82):

> ecce, parat Caesar domito quod defuit orbi,
>   addere: nunc, Oriens ultime, noster eris.
> Parthe, dabis poenas: Crassi gaudete sepulti.
>   signaque barbaricas non bene passa manus.
> ultor adest primisque ducem profitetur in annis
>   bellaque non puero tractat agenda puer.

Look! Caesar is making preparations to add what has been missing from the vanquished globe. Now, farthest East, you will be ours. Parthian, you will pay the penalty. Be joyful, buried Crassi, and you standards that suffered ill at barbarian hands. The avenger is here and avows his leadership in his earliest years. The boy manages wars which ought not to be waged by a boy.

This eulogy to the young avenger of Crassus is the introduction to a long excursus on the devastation about to be experienced by

the Parthians at the hands of Gaius Caesar, the future Princeps
(*AA* 1. 194):

> nunc iuvenum princeps, deinde future senum;

Now leader of the youth, next you will be leader of elders.

who sets out under the auspices of Mars and Augustus (*AA* 1.
203):

> Marsque pater Caesarque pater, date numen eunti,

Father Mars and father Caesar, grant him divine power as he goes,

with the certain prospect of the most glorious triumph awaiting
him upon his return to Rome (*AA* 1. 213–28).

Evidence of a more official nature can be found to support
Ovid's association of the dedication of the temple with the departure of the young avenger. A series of coins celebrating the
mounted and armed *C.Caes Augus f* depicting an aquila between
two standards behind him, were issued to mark, as Romer has
persuasively shown, Gaius' departure for the East.[155] Romer
argues that the standards depicted on the coins are those recovered from the Parthians in 20 BC and solemnly installed into the
temple of Mars as an important part of the dedication ceremony.
However, ignoring the content of Ovid's 'vulgar apostrophe', he
goes on to interpret the coins as representing nothing more than
the transition of the standards from the Capitol to the temple of
Mars and the honour accorded Gaius by the Princeps on the
occasion of his departure, the 'climactic part of the inaugural pro-
gram'.[156] If Romer had interpreted the coins in conjunction with
Ovid's testimony, he would have seen the possibility that they
were also celebrating Gaius' forthcoming revenge on Parthia for
the standards about to be ceremonially ensconced in the temple of
Mars Ultor.

An objection to the above interpretation might be that Dio
dates the prospect of a campaign against the Parthians to 1 BC.
How is it then that Augustus could foresee a pretext for hostilities

---

[155] Sutherland (1984) 54 nos. 198 and 199 has listed the coins under 8 BC even
though they are undated. Gaius was only 12 years old in 8 BC, which makes that
year most improbable for representing him in such a manner, especially with the
Parthian standards.

[156] Romer (1978) 198–9.

against Parthia a year beforehand? The answer is that whether he could or could not foresee it, it would have made no difference, because it emerges that he had no intention that Gaius should wage war with the Parthians. The truth of this occurs in the sequel, when the opportunity arose. When Gaius finally encountered the Parthian king in AD 2, he did so in peace. The encounter had perhaps been arranged, as Syme suggested, by correspondence between Augustus and Phraataces the year before.[157] Dio makes clear that at that time Augustus feared the prospect of war with the Parthians (Dio, 55. 10. 21).

Dio testifies to the honours conferred on Gaius after Augustus had decided that the young Caesar should be in charge of the Parthian problem in 1 BC. It is possible however that the later historian has confused chronology a little here. He claims that after Augustus was driven to choose Gaius to settle the question, he:

conferred proconsular power on him, gave him a wife so that he might enjoy the additional dignity possessed by a married man, and also appointed advisers for him. Gaius then set out, and was received by everyone with the honours due to the emperor's grandson, or was even by some regarded as his son (Dio, 55. 10. 19; trans. Ian Scott-Kilvert).

The question must be asked: where was this mysterious point from which Gaius set out with such dignity and aplomb for the first time? By the time the Parthian problem had arisen, Gaius had long left Rome. Yet it is surely not feasible that Augustus, only now and from a great distance, conferred proconsular power on him, or even less, gave him a young noble girl to wife (Livia Julia, 13-year-old daughter of Drusus and Antonia) to enhance his dignity. Less feasible still is that the youth was received only now, for the first time, long after his departure for the East, with honours due to the Princeps' heir. Bowersock has produced evidence that spectacular honours were orchestrated for Gaius, the 'new Ares', defender of the Hellenes against the Orient, as he progressed eastwards after his departure from Rome in the guise of avenger. The whole show, departure and journey, was designed to endow the young heir with an incontestable authority in the East itself.[158] It is more feasible therefore that Dio has provided details pertaining to Gaius' departure from Rome in 2 BC

---

[157] Syme (1978) 11 n. 6.   [158] Bowersock (1984) 172 ff.

and confused that departure with the moment when the genuine Parthian problem presented itself the following year.

To revert once more to Rome and the dedication to Mars Ultor. Bowersock is only partially correct in seeing the propaganda mounted for Gaius' departure as being for the benefit of the Greek East. I propose that a Parthian campaign for Gaius at the inaugural ceremonies for Mars Ultor in 2 BC was primarily for the benefit of the Romans, and its purpose twofold: to advertise Gaius as the new avenger and successor to the dynasty, and to furnish a much-needed justification for the dedication of the temple. Ovid's message in the *Ars Amatoria* is blatant. His enthusiasm over the imminent destruction of the Parthians at the hands of the avenger Gaius *in payment for the defeat of Crassus* is a palpable declaration that the recovery of the standards in 20 BC had not been accepted as a proper 'revenge' on the nation that had appropriated them by superior might. A reflection therefore, of a prevailing challenge to the legitimacy of the cult to Mars Ultor, despite the military-style publicity surrounding the 'victory' eighteen years before. Hence the long delay in completing the temple. (The embarrassment of having the temple complete without an acceptable reason for dedicating it would have been insupportable.) Hence the sudden haste for the dedication at the end, timed for the moment when Gaius was old enough to lead an expedition and provide the illusion of a genuine Parthian revenge at the hands of a member of the Julian dynasty.

Gaius' war of revenge was 'intended to be advertised rather than waged'.[159] Following the fanfare of his send-off, the new Mars embarked upon a lengthy ceremonial tour of the East. That a Parthian War was not immediately forthcoming did not matter. The propaganda mounted for the prospect of one was enough to achieve the purpose. It was possible at last for the temple to Mars Ultor to be dedicated—not now in thanksgiving for, but to inaugurate, the great revenge to be exacted by a Caesar which had not been properly achieved in 20 BC.

The unexpected death of Gaius deprived the young Ares of Ovid's predicted triumph, yet there does appear to be evidence of an attempt to magnify posthumously his Parthian achievement. The decorative programme on the cuirass of an over life-sized

[159] Syme (1978) 9.

statue found in Iol-Caesarea, capital of the kingdom of Maureta-
nia (modern Cherchel in Algeria), celebrates a military victory
watched over by Mars Ultor, an image clearly derived from the
cult statue dedicated in 2 BC. Zanker interprets the victory alluded
to as that of Gaius Caesar in Parthia. If this interpretation is correct, and the statue one of several copies of a major monument
created in the capital,[160] then such evidence supports the theory
postulated here, that Gaius' expedition was indeed required as a
justification for the existence of Mars Ultor in Rome. Yet the fact
that Ovid does not mention Gaius' Parthian 'victory' in the *Fasti*
suggests that the youth's failure to return deprived Augustus of
any enduring justification for the temple of Mars to any pestering
pedant who persisted in questioning the legitimacy of the huge
martial cult glorifying Julian ancestry in the city centre.

The absence of any real justification for Mars Ultor is Ovid's
challenge as he celebrates the dedication of the temple in the
Fasti after the death of Gaius. For all his profession to stick to
peaceful themes at the outset of his work (*F* 1. 13), he is now
obliged to adopt a military tone. Yet all that he is left to work
with is the settlement of 20 BC and the memory of Augustus'
determination to celebrate the occasion as a military triumph. Or
was it after the death of Gaius, and during a possible upsurge of
popularity for the memory of Julius,[161] that the vow at Philippi
for the revenge of Julius was invented to refurbish the inadequate
camouflage of Augustus' peaceful settlement in 20 BC?[162] If this is
so, it is not surprising that Ovid, composing his calendar in the
years AD 4–8, should be the first Roman to report the vow at
Philippi.

Ovid's justification for the dedication of Mars Ultor in the
Fasti can at last be appreciated in perspective. The longest section of the poet's longest celebration of an Augustan festal day is
devoted to the two-pronged invention, for obvious reasons sustaining the decidedly military tone announced at the beginning

[160] For a more detailed description of the scene on the cuirass, see Zanker
(1987) 224 ff. For a very detailed description, see Fittschen (1975–6) 175–210.

[161] In AD 6, after trying various unsuccessful attempts, Augustus finally
appealed to the authority of Caesar's memory to justify successfully the imposition of an inheritance tax: Dio, 55. 25. 5)

[162] Suetonius, writing 100 years later, sees only the vow as the justification for
the temple and its function as the military focus of the city: *Aug.* 29. 2.

throughout. The poet makes the transition between the first and second idea with (5. 579–80):

> nec satis est meruisse semel cognomina Marti:
> persequitur Parthi signa retenta manu.

Nor does it suffice Mars to have merited the surname just once: he pursues to the end the standards detained by the hand of the Parthian.

and follows with heavy emphasis on the uselessness of the Parthian military advantage before the might of Roman arms. Indeed, the device of the gloating apostrophe to the Parthians in this passage (repeated at *F* 6. 465 ff.) is heavily reminiscent of that in the *Ars Amatoria* devoted to the glory of Gaius. In looking for inspiration for his subject, the poet no doubt turned back the pages of time to draw on the spontaneity of long-forgotten contemporary feeling. He concludes the section for 12 May by bringing together the two glorious ways in which Mars won his title Ultor and his temple, ending with a final mention of the vow at Philippi for good measure (5. 595–6):

> rite deo templumque datum nomenque bis ulto,
> et meritus voti debita solvit honor.

Properly was the temple and the name given to the god who twice took revenge, and the deserved honour annuls the obligation of the vow.

Thus ends Ovid's contribution to the creation and perpetration of a myth that has succeeded in disguising to the present day one of the greatest hoaxes of the Augustan regime. This is the myth that provided the rationale for the colossal temple to Mars Ultor, symbol of Rome's martial origins and virtues that housed the military standards, that became the setting for senatorial debates on war and peace, where commanders started out on their campaigns, where victors returned to deposit their triumphal insignia (Suet. *Aug.* 29. 2; Dio, 55. 10. 2), where all Rome's military glory was ceremonially registered in the presence of the author of the Julian *gens*. Augustus successfully annexed Mars to his personal heritage. The bellicose god himself earned his Julian epithet Ultor without having to brandish a sword.

3

JULIUS CAESAR

OVID'S portrayal of Julius Caesar in the *Fasti* will be dealt with against the background of controversy recently raised about the posthumous role assigned Caesar in the reign of his heir. Critics have long noted the low profile accorded Julius by Augustan poets, and have long suspected that the initiative for this proceeded directly from Augustus himself.[1] The critic lending greatest currency to this view is Sir Ronald Syme, who repeatedly stated that, after Actium, Caesar's heir, having become undisputed master of Rome, began to dissociate himself from his father as he sought to establish the appearance of continuity with a legitimate government, avowing Republican rather than absolutist ideals. In consequence, Julius' claims gradually began to recede and lose ground. It is for this reason that Caesar attracted so little attention in the poetry of the age, the principal record of Augustus' manipulation of opinion on the subject.[2]

In 1988, Peter White sought to challenge Syme's view (as being the most authoritative representative of standard opinion), and to offer a different assessment of Caesar's publicity during the Principate. In order to prove that the memory of Caesar was not under siege in the reign of Augustus, he provides a survey of Roman architecture of the period in the Roman Forum designed to reflect the link between Augustus and Julius, of coinage advertising Julius' apotheosis, and of Julius' military accomplishments celebrated in the calendars. Against this background he then examines how Caesar fared by comparison with Pompey and Cato as Augustan 'Republican' heroes, and with all notable living members of Augustus' family, by constructing a comparative

---

[1] Plessis (1909) 231; Pichon (1917) 193–8; Gundolf (1924) 24–6; Green (1932) 405–11; Spaeth (1933) p. lx; Ramage (1985) 223–45.

[2] Syme's view that the poets downplay Caesar spans his entire career: (1939) 317–18; (1958) i. 432–4; (1978) 190–1; (1986) 443.

table enumerating all references to Caesar in Augustan poetry. He concludes that Caesar is mentioned in poetry more often than anyone else.[3]

White's main criticism of the view represented by Syme is that it appeals implicitly to a standard of comparison which has never been scrutinized. He claims that the position amounts to an argument that Caesar is not mentioned as often as one would expect, or in the way one would expect. The question is 'expect', he says, 'in comparison with whom, or in relation to what?' White concludes that, if Augustus is the implicit term of comparison, the observation is true but trivial. That the living ruler should be more celebrated than a dead one is the norm rather than the exception; it cannot be equated with the conclusion that the predecessor's memory is under siege in Augustan poetry, or that Augustus thereby sought to veil or diminish Caesar.[4]

White's argument concerning expectation and comparison is commendable, yet in selecting Augustus as the implicit term of comparison he has failed to exploit the very evidence available which does permit identification of a positive and explicit standard of comparison: Ovid's *Fasti*, a unique testimony in that it combines both Roman calendar and Augustan poem. It is the *Fasti* which furnishes an underlying standard of comparison between the *feriae* for Julius' anniversaries decreed long before Actium, and the treatment of them by a poet in the late Augustan Principate as he systematically works his way through the Roman year. White merely touches upon Ovid's testimony, even though by a count in the table he himself constructed, Caesar is mentioned more often in the *Fasti* than in any other Augustan poem. Instead, he inexplicably restricts his major discussion to the very few mentions of Julius in Virgil and Horace.[5] His analysis is thus fundamentally flawed. Nor indeed does Syme avail himself of the *Fasti*, though it might bolster his argument. He merely registers surprise that Julius should be mentioned at all in a poem written so late in the reign.[6]

It is time for Ovid's testimony to be exploited to the full. When

---

[3] White (1988) 334–6.   [4] Ibid. 348.   [5] Ibid. 340; 349–54.

[6] Syme (1978) 191. Ramage (1985), in a study of Augustus' motives for the low visibility of Caesar in poetry, hardly touches on the *Fasti* either. Duxbury (1988), in her epilogue examining Caesar in the poetry of the Principate, neglects to mention the *Fasti* at all.

composing his poem the Roman calendar was marking six NP days, three in the first half of the year and three in the second, in commemoration of anniversaries of Julius Caesar.[7] All except 12 July, his birthday, celebrate a military victory. They are as follows:

17 March   Fer(iae), quod e(o) d(ie) C. Caes(ar) vic(it) in Hisp(ania
           ult(eriore) *Caer*; Caesar Hi[sp(ania) vicit] *Farn*.

27 March   Fer(iae), quod eo die C. Caes(ar) vicit Alexand(reae) *Caer*;
           Hoc die Caesar Alexand(ream) recepit *Maff*; Feriae, quod
           eo die C. [Caesar] Alexandriam recepit *Verul*.

 6 April   F(eriae), q(uod) e(o) d(ie) C. Caesar C. f. in Africa regem
           [Iubam devicit] *Praen*.

12 July   Fer(iae), quod [e]o die C. Caesar est natus *Amit*; Divi
           Iul(ii) natalis *Ant.Min*; Natalis Iulii Caesaris *Silv*. [IIII
           idus Iul]ias ob natalem divi Iuli divo Iulio b(ovem)
           m(arem) *Fer.Dur*.

 2 August [Feriae ex s(enatus) c(onsulto) C. Caesa]ris h(onoris)
           c(ausa) Hisp(ania) [citerior]e devicta [et quod in P]onto
           regem [Pharnace]m dev[i]cit *Arv*; Hoc die [Caesar in
           Hispan(ia)] cit(eriore) vicit *Maff*; Feriae, quod hoc die
           Imp. Caesar Hispaniam citeriorem vicit *Vall*; Feriae,
           quod eo die C. Caes(ar) C. f. in Hispan(ia) citer(iore) et
           quod in Ponto eod(em) die regem Pharnacem devicit
           Amit; Divus Iul(ius) Hisp(ania) vic(it) *Ant.Min*.

 9 August Hoc die Caesar Hispali vicit *Maff*; Fer(iae), quod e(o)
           d(ie) v[icit C. Caesar Phars(ali)] *Allif*; Fer(iae), q(uod) e(o)
           die C. Caes(ar) C. f. Pharsali devicit *Amit*; Divus Iul(ius)
           Phars(ali) vicit *Ant.Min*

In view of the evidence cited above, we might expect three of the six anniversaries of Julius Caesar to be commemorated in the six months we have of Ovid's calendar. Instead there is only one.

6 April: Battle of Thapsus, 46 BC

Ovid introduces the day by speaking in the first person, by adopting an informal tone in relating a personal experience (memini), and by contriving an ostensibly accidental encounter with a

[7] Degrassi (1963) 426, 432, 437, 481–2, 491, 493.

spectator at the Megalesian games in order to relay information to
his audience about the *feriae* in question (4. 377–82):

> Tertia lux (memini) ludis erat, ac mihi quidam
> spectanti senior continuusque loco
> 'haec' ait 'illa dies, Libycis qua Caesar in oris
> perfida magnanimi contudit arma Iubae.
> dux mihi Caesar erat, sub quo meruisse tribunus
> glorior: officio praefuit ille meo.'

It was, I remember, the third day of the games, and as I was watching, a
certain elderly man sitting next to me said: 'This was the day on which
Caesar destroyed the traitorous army of proud Juba in the Libyan land.
Caesar was my commander, I can boast of having served under him as
tribune. He supervised my duties.'

In the vividly created casual setting the reader watches Ovid
acquire his information directly from the most competent authority on the subject of Julius' victory: a patriotic veteran who had
proudly served in that very battle, and who had served under the
supervision of Caesar himself. The episode is imbued with
greater lifelike interchange between two characters by the next
couplet, which pithily evokes a contrast between the younger
generation in peacetime and an older generation in wartime. It
also reveals a topical detail, having contemporary relevance both
to poet and protagonist, in the setting (4. 383–4):

> 'hanc ego militia sedem, tu pace parasti,
> inter bis quinos usus honore viros'

'I obtained this seat through military service, and you through service in
peacetime because of your office on the Board of Ten'.

The informal exchange is then interrupted by a sudden shower of
rain, the expectation of which is another calendrical entry for 6
April,[8] utilized here in order to terminate the brief passage (4.
385–6):

> plura locuturi subito seducimur imbre:
> pendula caelestes Libra movebat aquas.

About to say more, we were separated by a sudden downpour.
Pendulous Libra was ejecting waters from the sky.

[8] The calendar of Polemius Silvius (AD 448): 'Interdum hiemat' under 6 Apr.;
cf. Col. 11. 2. 34: 'Octavo idus Aprilis Vergiliae vespere celantur. Interdum

Ovid evidently felt that enough had been said to familiarize his audience with the *aition* of the day in question.

The anecdotal style, the personal, spontaneous tone in which Ovid presents his *aition* for 6 April is in keeping with the general literary genre of the *Fasti*, that of the Hellenistic model of Callimachus. Yet the literary form and the poet's debt to tradition must not direct attention away from the information nor its significance, both of which he is conveying. The first most notable feature of the episode is its brevity. This in itself is not unusual for a 'Julian' *feriae* in the *Fasti*, yet Ovid might have devoted more space and detail to the only anniversary he has selected out of the three which commemorate Julius between January and June.

Next, the role of Julius is crucial. Caesar here is totally human, the military commander remembered with affection by a veteran who had known him personally. There is no suggestion at all that this same military commander was also Divus Iulius, the god honoured by the imposing temple in the Forum and first mortal since Romulus to have achieved the distinction of being elevated officially to the ranks of the immortals. Ovid, apparently, is keeping the divine nature of Julius quite separate.

Critical, also, is the impact created by the particular combination of setting, information imparted, and type of protagonist chosen. The setting, for example, is the Megalesian games, celebrated over six days in honour of the Magna Mater. These games had nothing whatever to do with Julius. True, this environment was probably chosen as a backdrop to the conversation by the poet as a means of linking the present short entry with what had come before: the 193 lines devoted to the *aition* for the festival of the Magna Mater (4. 179–372), the ludi for which spanned the calendar from 4 till 10 April (4. 387–92).[9] The mention of the ludi on Julius' anniversary, then, is quite realistic. Yet while these games offer the poet an aesthetically continuous and unifying thread to offset the relentless segmentation of the poem demanded by the individual diurnal entries of the calendar, the connotation evoked by this backdrop crucially influences the communication conveyed in the passage. The old man and the memories he recalls

hiemat', and Pliny, *NH* 18. 247 (8 Apr.): 'Caesari VI idus significatur imber Librae occasu.' See Degrassi (1963) 438; Frazer (1929) iii. 261 at *F* 4. 386.

[9] Degrassi (1963) 435.

at the Megalesia serve to create the impression that Julius' festal
day is remembered, not by the Roman public at large, but by a
diminishing number of an aged, war generation. and even they,
despite their reverence for their dead commander, are spending
the day watching the ludi honouring the Great Mother instead of
paying active tribute by sacrifice to their leader on the holiday
commemorating his victory.

That Ovid should have Julius' war veteran attending the
Megalesia is in itself significant as a subtle means of 'Augustan'
promotion and 'Julian' denigration. The Phrygian Mother,
brought to Rome in 204 BC and installed in a huge temple on the
Palatine in 191 BC in recognition of her grant of victory to the
Romans over Hannibal, had been transformed by Virgil into a
tutelary Trojan goddess, granter of victory to Aeneas.[10] In so
doing he had implicitly converted her into an 'Augustan' deity, so
that Romans could assimilate her into the complex of associations
with the origins of Rome, in the centre of which Augustus had
ensconced himself on the Palatine.[11] Thus did the goddess
become annexed into the Augustan pantheon.

This 'canonical Augustan theology', established by Virgil for
the Idaean Mother in the *Aeneid*,[12] is incorporated into the
Roman calendar by Ovid on her festal day of 4 April (4. 249–52,
272–4). Yet Ovid goes a step further than Virgil. Rather than con-
centrate on the goddess only, his entry for her festival also turns
attention to the features of the cult itself. The reason is clear.
Whereas Virgil had reflected tension between a pre-Augustan
interpretation of the Great Mother as a contemptible, alien goddess served by mad, castrated priests, and an 'Augustan' interpretation of her as tutelary goddess to Aeneas,[13] Ovid eradicates
that tension by contriving elaborate *aitia* to give the cult a wholly
positive image. The repellent features of the foreign orgiastic
Eastern cult are explained and thus transformed by him into a
respectable Roman worship.[14]

[10] *Aen.* 2. 693–7; 3. 111–14; 6. 781–7; 7. 135–40; 9. 77–122; 10. 156–9, 252–7.

[11] See Wiseman (1984) 117–28.   [12] Aptly put by Littlewood (1981) 381.

[13] Wiseman (1984) 117–18 discusses the passages in the *Aeneid* reflecting this
tension between the cult's reputation in the writers of the 1st cent. BC and the
image Augustus wished to project on the citizens of Rome.

[14] Details of the techniques Ovid employs to achieve this are discussed by
Littlewood (1981) 386–95.

The fact that Ovid chose to place Julius' war veteran at the Megalesia thus serves three aims: first, to reinforce the impression of the respectability and Romanness of the cult; second, to draw a contrast between a generation of war in the past under Caesar, and a generation of peace in the present under Augustus;[15] third, to insinuate artfully the primacy of this new 'Augustan' festival of the 'Ludi Matri deum Magnae Ideae' (*Fasti Praenestini* 4 April) over the celebration of the Julian NP day on 6 April.

One final feature of Ovid's passage for 6 April is conspicuous, this time by its absence. Juba is cited as Caesar's defeated foe. There is no mention of Lucius Scipio, scion of one of Rome's most noble families, who was also crushed by the victorious general. To invoke his name would have been a reminder that the battle of Thapsus was no ordinary war. It was a civil war. It was also the battle which precipitated the suicide of the fiercest defender of Roman freedom, Cato Uticensis.[16] There must have been many in Rome at the time Ovid was writing who either remembered the day with grief, or who had no wish to be reminded of it at all.

Ovid's effort to disguise the fact that Caesar's victory had been over his own countrymen provides a positive aspect to his apparent efforts to play down the significance of the Dictator's anniversary. A dual purpose of whitewashing his memory and of undermining his importance has thus been achieved by the poet in the passage for 6 April. The positive aspect of whitewashing his memory brings us to a consideration of the Dictator's anniversaries Ovid leaves out: the 17 and 27 March. The anniversary of 27 March takes chronological precedence, so will be examined first.

27 March: Battle of Alexandria, 47 BC

This anniversary is celebrated by all extant calendars preserving that date. It is most unfortunate, however, that the entry for that day is not extant in the Praenestine calendar of Verrius Flaccus, so it cannot be known whether the freedman of Augustus would

---

[15] The *militia/pace* contrast noted by Ramage (1985) 231.
[16] App. *BC* 2. 14. 96 ff.; Dio, 43. 7–11; Plut. *Caes.* 52. 54; Livy, *Per.* 114.

have ignored it, like Ovid, or faithfully accorded it the same treatment as any other day. In the absence of such evidence we shall
have to reach a conclusion on the strength of material that is
available.

The sources for the battle of Alexandria provide consistent
impressions of contemporary attitudes towards the event, which
helps to shed light on the question as to why Ovid chose to leave
it out of the calendar. Plutarch (*Caes.* 48) reports that there were
those who said that Caesar's war in Egypt should never have
taken place, that it was brought on by Caesar's passion for
Cleopatra, and that it did him little credit while involving him in
great danger. Dio (42. 32. 2, 44. 1) claims that Cleopatra had great
influence with Caesar, that Caesar did not make Egypt subject to
the Romans, but bestowed it upon Cleopatra, for whose sake he
had waged the conflict. He goes on to assert that there was nothing the Egyptian Queen could not do because she was held in
Caesar's favour. Suetonius (*Div. Iul.* 52) enhances the picture of
Caesar' infatuation with Cleopatra. He reports that his soldiers
refused to march across Egypt to indulge his passion for her, and
records that the Egyptian queen bore a son who Mark Antony
later declared to the Senate had been acknowledged by Caesar
himself as his child.

Caesar's liaison with Cleopatra came to provide a liability to his
heir who later had to exploit the Egyptian monarch as a pretext
for his own political ascendancy. When waging his own civil war
against Antony, Caesar's heir in Cleopatra's affections, Octavian
had to promote her as a foreign danger that menaced everything
that was Roman. This was essential in order to secure Roman
sanction and moral and emotional support for the war against a
fellow countryman, whose name could not even be mentioned.[17]
Antony, after all, had the consuls and the constitution on his side,
and 300 senators fled to his support (Dio, 50. 2. 7). An image of
Cleopatra as a foreign enemy and a threat to Roman freedom had
to be created and forged as a weapon to destroy Octavian's rival.
How this was done can be gleaned by what we find in post-Actian
poetry intimating the cause of the war. Virgil (*Aen.* 8. 671–713),
Horace (*Od.* 1. 37; *Epod.* 9. 11) and Propertius (3. 11. 29 ff.; 4. 6.
13 ff.) in their various ways all informed the Roman people what

---

[17] Syme (1939) 275.

terrible danger had been menacing them in the form of the Egyptian Queen. Horace declared that the death of the foreigner, the 'fatale monstrum', called forth great jubilation. The Roman calendars are more restrained in the manner of the lapidary language of inscriptions, but celebrate 1 August, the date of Octavian's capture of Alexandria, thus:

Feria[e ex s(enatus) c(onsulto)], q(uod) e(o) d(ie) Imp. Cae[sar Augustus rem] [publicam tristissimo periculo liberavit] (*Praen*).[18]

A holiday by decree of the Senate because on that day Imperator Caesar Augustus liberated the Republic from the most serious danger.

The audience of the poets at least had been educated to understand 'periculum' as the person of the foreign queen. Any studied reminder to the Roman public of Caesar's relationship with Cleopatra following Octavian's extensive propaganda campaign against her could have risked inviting an interpretation which cast aspersions on the battle of Actium and made a mockery of the claims of the *filius divi*. Particularly in view of the fact that on the rostra before the great temple to Divus Julius in the Forum were hung the prows of the ships captured from Antony and Cleopatra at the battle of Actium (Dio, 51. 19. 2). If attitudes reflected in Plutarch, Suetonius, and Dio were prevalent in Rome in the decades after Julius' victory at Alexandria, it is logical that Augustus would have been most anxious to quash them.

It appears that a poetical tribute to Julius' victory at Alexandria was a challenge too great even for one as ingenious as Ovid. His non-observance of this festal day so late in the reign points to Augustus' enduring sensitivity to the subject. It is most unfortunate that we do not have his rendering of Octavian's conquest of Alexandria on 1 August. Had he been planning a damning sketch of Cleopatra to match or excel that of his poetic predecessors, his omission of Julius' anniversary on 27 March would become even more intelligible.

17 March: Battle of Munda, 45 BC

This anniversary fell on the same day as the great ancient festivals of the Liberalia and the Agonalia (large-lettered *feriae* extant in

[18] This calendar is greatly reconstructed, but four inscriptions record the event using much the same wording. See Degrassi (1963) 489.

the *Fasti Antiates Maiores, Caeretani, Maffeiani, Verulani,* and *Farnesiani*).[19] It was therefore already an NP day, which means that the character of the day was not altered by the commemoration of Julius' anniversary. It was not a Julian festal day in its own right, despite the implication to the contrary given by the citation from the *Fasti Caeretani* at the beginning of this chapter. It is also not mentioned in the *Fasti Maffeiani, Verulani,* or *Vaticani.* In view of this the poet might not feel obliged to celebrate the victory. Yet the occurrence of several festivals and anniversaries on the one day is not an acceptable ground for Ovid's neglect, especially when, at the outset of his poem, he had asserted that his intention was to sing of Caesar's altars (or *feriae* in the calendar (1. 13–14). The poet was furthermore quite capable of inserting *aitia* for several disparate festivals in one entry, as can be seen from his treatment of the Ides of March (3. 523–710; Ovid both celebrates Anna Perenna and remembers the assassination of Julius). Another excuse must be found.

The battle of Munda, unlike the battle of Thapsus in which a foreign king was involved, was an out-and-out civil war. No pretext such as a foreign opponent like Juba or Cleopatra could be found to pretend that it was anything else. Munda was the last of a series of civil wars fought by Caesar against his peers and former colleagues, Roman aristocrats who had opposed him and threatened his political demise. At Munda, Caesar's foes were the sons of Pompey, one of the Republic's most illustrious generals whose downfall Caesar had brought about at Pharsalus only three years before. Plutarch (*Caes.* 56) reports that, at Munda, 30,000 of the enemy were killed, and 1,000 of Caesar's troops. If these figures are correct, that made a total of 31,000 Romans who perished, fighting no foreign power but each other. Dio (43. 38. 4) provides no figures, but states simply that the losses incurred were enormous. Plutarch goes on to state that Caesar's triumph for this war, the first ever held at Rome for a victory in a civil war, displeased the Romans more than anything else he had done, because it celebrated the annihilation of the children of the family of one of the greatest of Romans. The general feeling was that it was not right for Caesar to celebrate a triumph for the calamities of the country (*Caes.* 56; Dio, 43. 42. 1; Livy, *Per.* 116).

[19] For large-lettered *feriae* see Michels (1967) 69 ff. and Ch. 1, 'History and Contemporary Significance of the Calendar'.

If 30,000 Romans died opposing Caesar on 17 March 45 BC as Plutarch says, the day could still have been remembered by many as one of mourning fifty years later, when Ovid was versifying the calendar. His refusal to celebrate Julius' victory may have been out of respect for those for whom the day evoked personal grief. (Hence the omission of Munda in the *Fasti Maffeiani, Verulani,* and *Vaticani*?) It may also have been because he was conscious that Augustus had no wish to be reminded of the ugliest aspect of his father's career, so reminiscent of the military despotism he himself had employed to fulfil his own ambitions. After all, the best protection from the civil wars was to forget them.[20] In 'forgetting' to commemorate Munda, Ovid is in fact making a positive contribution to the memory of the Dictator. The genre of the *Fasti* ('Caesaris arma canant alii, nos Caesaris aras', i. 13), was not in any case conducive to an emulation of Virgil's candour concerning men such as Caesar who turned his strength against the guts of his country ('patriae validas in viscera . . . viris' *Aen.* 6. 833). And as Ovid was composing his elegiac epic for Augustus, I would suggest that the latter reasons took priority.

Ovid's omission of two important victories of Julius Caesar shows that he was not mechanically working his way through the Roman calendar.[21] On the contrary, it shows that he was keeping himself finely attuned to the political sensibilities of Augustus and shaping the *Fasti* accordingly as he proceeded through the year and encountered the *feriae* commemorating the terrestial achievements of his father.[22] Julius thus receives far less representation in Ovid's poem than he rightly deserved by the standards of the official calendar. Ovid's perception of the desires of the Princeps seem to have taken precedence over the calendar in influencing the content of his poem.

At this point in our study, Syme's view that Augustus desired to dissociate himself from Caesar the Dictator after Actium is

---

[20] So the contemporary Labienus, orator and historian, asserted: Sen. *Cont.* 10. 3. 5.

[21] This observation puts paid to Wilkinson's conclusion (1955) 268 that 'the Fasti is a convenient but prosaic rule of thumb . . . having once chosen to follow the calendar, he can leave nothing out'.

[22] It has been postulated that Ovid drew directly from Verrius Flaccus (Wallace-Hadrill (1987) 227), and although it has been said that scholars are

vindicated. White's argument, that Caesar is mentioned in
Augustan poetry as often as one would reasonably expect, cannot
be sustained when applied to the *Fasti*. The matter does not end
there, however. How much 'reality', for example, was Ovid
reflecting about the cult of Julius in his day?

If Ovid's calendar were the only evidence, the treatment the
poet accords Julius' festal day on 6 April, and his outright neglect
of Julius' two other *feriae* on 17 and 27 March (even where whitewashing his memory is the aim), could serve to create an impression that, in the late Augustan Principate, the memory of the
mortal guise of the ruler's father was fast fading from popular
consciousness. Yet Ovid's failure to imitate the calendar faithfully gives grounds for suspicion in that regard. The testimony of
the extant *Fasti Farnesiani* (end of the first century BC), and
Verulani (between AD 14 and 37), two of the four calendars cited
as commemorating Julius' *feriae* on 17 and 27 March, cannot be
ignored. It suggests that the memory of Julius was obstinately
being fostered despite Augustus' attempts to downplay the role of
his father in the civil wars. In contradiction to Ovid's testimony
then, the calendars raise the possibility that the memory of Julius
as victorious general was alive and well and operating indepen-
dently of the contrived norm as represented in our literary
source.

A reference in Dio (55. 25. 1–5) provides welcome support to
this possibility so difficult otherwise to attest. In the year AD 6
Augustus was confronted with the task of finding an acceptable
way, amidst general resentment, to fund the military budget.
Different schemes were proposed, all to no avail. At last, he was
able to impose a 5 per cent tax on all inheritances and bequests
left by people at their death, and in this way, managed to increase
the public revenues. Dio maintains that his enterprise was suc-

'unnecessarily cautious about this' (referring to Bömer (1957–8) i. 22–3), I am not
convinced that this was his only source. Both Verrius' calendar and his etymological dictionary, the *De Significatione Verborum*, in the fragments we have, adopt a
grammatical tone appropriate to a purely fact-giving medium. It would not be
possible, for example, to gauge Augustus' attitude to Julius Caesar from the fac-
tual work of Verrius as it is from the way Ovid has shaped his poem. Much of
Ovid's 'evidence' would have come from his poetic predecessors, from Augustus'
building programme, from simply living in Rome and having a nose for the current trends.

cessful because Augustus gave out that he had found the tax set down in the papers of Julius Caesar.

Augustus' success in appealing to Caesar's authority for so unpleasant a policy as an increase in tax for all but the poorest, fleetingly lifts a veil from the existence of a strong current of favour for Julius amongst senators and/or populace at the very time Ovid was composing the *Fasti*. At this critical time of war, fire, famine, and popular discontent, Julius may well have been enjoying an upsurge of popularity in comparison with the present ruler who had to impose so many unpopular measures.[23] Perhaps it was at this very time also, that the myth of Octavian's vow at Philippi to avenge Julius' murder was born in order to help justify the temple of Mars Ultor (see Ch. 2, 'Avenger of Caesar and Crassus'). Ovid does, after all, choose to commemorate Julius' assassination on the Ides of March, even though it is not a Julian holiday (see below). At any rate, the poet's impression that 6 April was remembered by only a few veterans who preferred to attend the Megalesia on Julius' day, and that his *feriae* on 17 and 27 March were not being celebrated, must be regarded with some scepticism. It is quite possible that there was a huge showing at Julius' festivals, not just by war veterans, but also by those eager to idealize and pay homage to a ruler from the past. The 'reality' of the times may have been that it was Caesar's heir who was now suffering in the comparison with Caesar.

A study of Julius Caesar in the *Fasti* would not be complete without a brief survey of the apparently gratuitous references made to him in the poem on occasions when he has no place in the *feriae* in question. This must be done to account for the relatively high profile he enjoys in comparison with every other Augustan poem, as White's table shows.[24] The *feriae* in which reference to him is made will not for themselves receive an in-depth analysis here, however; they will be reserved for the chapters pertaining to the names in whose honour the *feriae* are celebrated. The first 'gratuitous' reference we have to Julius occurs on 13 January. The entire passage is a celebration of the name 'Augustus' (1. 587–616), but, as will be shown later in the chapter on Germanicus, it was

---

[23] For details of these measures, see Wiedemann (1975) 264–71.

[24] White (1988) 348.

written by Ovid from exile for the purposes of exalting Augustus'
adoptive grandson, who he thought would one day inherit the
title.

The victorious general is the first guise of Julius to greet us in
the revised edition of the *Fasti* (1. 599–600):[25]

> si petat a victis, tot sumat nomina Caesar,
> quot numero gentes maximus orbis habet.

Were Caesar to seek his titles from the conquered, then would he have to
assume the same number as there are peoples in the entire world.

In the second couplet following shortly, Julius is not named, only
alluded to, but his identity is unmistakeable as the conqueror of
Pompey (1. 603–4):

> Magne, tuum nomen rerum est mensura tuarum:
> sed qui te vicit nomine maior erat.

Magnus, your name is the measure of your achievements, but he who
defeated you was greater in name.

These couplets have been plucked out of a long roll-call of *cognomina* won by Roman generals for conquest of various lands
(Africanus, Numidicus, Germanicus), or conferred as honours
for some personal virtue (Magnus, Maximus), which the poet utilizes in the build-up to the climax of his eulogy of the name
'Augustus'. Julius had no *cognomen*, and the first couplet implies
that the number of his conquests would preclude the suitability
of any particular one. Yet in the second couplet he is labelled
'maior' in comparison with Pompey, surnamed 'Magnus'. Ovid
uses the comparative as a way of gauging the measure (*mensura*)
of their deeds. Julius is therefore superior to Pompey, but then
the crescendo of praise is abruptly terminated. What follows
undermines Julius completely as he is put in the shade when
compared with the Fabii, whose family was called 'Maximus' (1.
605–6):

---

[25] Frazer (1929) ii. 227 at *F* 1. 599 thinks that Augustus is meant here, not
Julius. I disagree on the grounds that, as the name 'Augustus' is distinguished
from the others in the passage by its associations, not with military achievement
but with 'summo Iove' (ll. 590, 608), it would be aesthetically unsatisfactory to
refer to Augustus half-way through the register of mortal generals and call him
'Caesar'. To my mind, Julius fits the context more appropriately.

> nec gradus est ultra Fabios cognominis ullus:
> illa domus meritis Maxima dicta suis.

Yet there is no grade of surname beyond that of the Fabii; that house was called Maxima for its services.

'Magnus, maior, maximus', each general is graded according to the merit of his deeds.[26] Yet even they are categorized as merely human in comparison with the status attached to the name 'Augustus', where the distinction is heavily drawn between human and divine (1. 607–8):

> sed tamen humanis celebrantur honoribus omnes,
> hic socium summo cum Iove nomen habet.

However, all these are renowned by human honours; he has a name in common with supreme Jove.

Ovid's allocation of Julius to the human category in a passage where a contrast is drawn between human and divine is an explicit denial of any recognition of the deified status of the first Caesar. Worse still, Ovid does not rank him supreme even amongst those who had had human honours bestowed on them. It is clear that the poet has utilized Julius purely as a convenient literary device in the 'magnus, maior, maximus' scheme in the build-up to the Fabii, who happened to possess the ultimate *cognomen* in human terms. The force of circumstances of the exiled poet has therefore had an overriding affect on the manner in which Julius is depicted here: it has caused him to demote Julius to a status which he had not done before his banishment for the purpose of stylistic convenience.[27] A demotion of Julius to this

---

[26] Bömer (1957–8) ii. 68 at *F.* 1. 605: 'Ovid steigert: Magne . . . maior . . . Maxime, eine Verbeugung vor Paullus Fabius Maximus.' See n. 27.

[27] Bömer (1957–8) i. 45 below, suggests that Ovid is deliberately flattering his influential friend Paullus Fabius Maximus (consul 11 BC), the husband of Marcia, a cousin of Augustus, in the hope of a mitigation of his sentence. In Ch. 5 I argue that this entire passage was written after the death of Augustus. If this is correct, then Fabius Maximus was dead by then also, so Ovid cannot have designed this passage simply for the purpose of flattering him. I suggest that the 'magne . . . maior . . . maxime' scheme is a purely rhetorical one, a play on hereditary *cognomina ex virtute* which culminates in the hereditary title 'Augustus'. While it is true that Ovid did flatter Fabius Maximus from exile (on the Fabian allusions as later additions made in exile, see Fantham (1985) 261–2, 279 n. 57). See also the compliment Ovid pays in a letter from exile to his friend Maximus: 'Maxime, qui tanti mensuram nominis imples' (*Ex P.* 1. 2. 1), it is unwise to assume that all references

level suggests that the initiative for such a depiction no longer issued from Augustus himself.

All other contrived invocations of Julius in the *Fasti* are pre-exilic, and bear some intimation of his deified status. The first instance occurs in a single line in the entry for 5 February, the day Augustus was named Pater Patriae (2. 144):

> caelestem fecit te pater, ille patrem.

Your father raised you to heaven; he raised his father.

Ovid is addressing Romulus, and compares him very unfavourably with Augustus. The whole passage from 'Romule, concedes' (2. 144) lists the achievements of each, both of which culminate in an apotheosis.[28] But the artful poet adds an interesting twist. At the climax of his achievement, Romulus is rewarded by being raised to heaven by his father, Mars; at the climax of Augustus' achievements he is not raised, but raises another, his father, to heaven. Julius' apotheosis is transformed into a great achievement of Augustus, who, in deifying another, performs a feat equal to that of Romulus' own divine father, Mars himself.

This father/son motif, which deprives Julius of any credit for his deification, is also utilized as a technique for an implied prediction of Augustus' own apotheosis in the *Metamorphoses*. There too, Augustus deified his father, and the poet asserts that the greatest of all Julius' accomplishments was his parentage of the present ruler ('quod pater exstitit huius' 15. 750–1). Later, he has Julius himself admit ('fatetur') that his son's achievements were greater than his own ('suis maiora'), and even has him rejoicing in being 'conquered' or surpassed by him ('vinci gaudet ab illo', 15. 850–1). Then follows a list of famous sons who surpassed their fathers (15. 855–8), which, in turn, precedes a fulsome eulogy to

to the Fabii in the *Fasti* were designed to that end). The story of the slaughter of the Fabii, for example, which rightly belongs to 18 July (Frazer (1929) ii. 322–3) but is placed on 13 Feb. by Ovid (*F* 2. 193–242), was very probably inserted there, as Bömer (1957–8) ii. 96 says, to praise the family tradition of his patron Paullus as a lead into the Lupercalia on 15 Feb. However, Ovid's tribute to the Fabii on 15 Feb. as one of the two colleges of Luperci (see Wissowa (1912) 559 and Frazer (1929) ii. 329 and nn.), is less likely to have been designed as a tribute to Paullus than as a disparagement of Romulus and so composed before exile (*F* 2. 375–80). On Ovid's portrayal of Romulus see Ch. 2, 'Pater Patriae'.

[28] See Bömer (1957–8) ii. 91 at IF 2. 133 for the antithetical comparison. For a full discussion of this passage see Ch. 2, 'Pater Patriae'.

Augustus alone, who eventually is himself to be transported to heaven (15. 869–70). The similarity between the panegyrical technique employed here and that in the *Fasti* is clear.[29]

The depiction of Augustus superior to his deified father as a presumption of his own consecration is not the only reason for the invocation of Julius' name in the *Fasti*. It is invoked also for the purpose of justifying the inglorious deeds of Octavian at the beginning of his career. This Ovid does by commemorating the assassination of Julius, even though the event was not recorded in the calendar.[30] The passage in question deserves to be cited in full (3. 697–710):

> Praeteriturus eram gladios in principe fixos,
>   cum sic a castis Vesta locuta focis:
> 'ne dubita meminisse: meus fuit ille sacerdos;
>   sacrilegae telis me petiere manus.
> ipsa virum rapui simulacraque nuda reliqui:
>   quae cecidit ferro, Caesaris umbra fuit'
> ille quidem caelo positus Iovis atria vidit,
>   et tenet in magno templa dicata foro;
>
> et quicumque nefas ausi, prohibente deorum
>   numine, polluerant pontificale caput,

---

[29] Ramage (1985) 232–3 shows that the denigration of a predecessor to highlight the superiority of the person being praised was an important technique of panegyric. Ramage's analysis is central to an understanding of this passage in the *Metamorphoses* (curiously, he does not exploit the *Fasti* for instances of similar techniques at all; see the Pater Patriae passage in Ch. 2), but I think he lends too much emphasis to Ovid's alleged separation of the earth-bound Augustus from the remote Julius in heaven (esp. at 243). Ovid does, after all, envisage Augustus' apotheosis at the very end of the work, the culmination of all his unsurpassed deeds on earth. The very epithet 'divi filius' which identified Augustus as the pious establisher of his father's divinity (Scott (1930) 50) indelibly linked him to his parent in heaven and conveyed the expectation of future apotheosis which Ovid fulfils in his poem.

[30] Degrassi (1963) 424 notes that not one extant calendar of the Augustan period commemorates Julius' murder, although he suggests that a cursory note in the *Fasti Maffeiani* might have done. Suetonius (*Div. Iul* 68) records that the day was deemed the day of Parricide shortly after the death of Caesar: 'Curiam, in qua occisus est, obstrui placuit idusque Martias Parricidium nominari ac ne umquam eo die senatus ageretur'), but we have no evidence that this was officially entered into or maintained in the calendar. Dio (47. 19. 1) says simply that the day was marked unlucky. The day was already an NP day in its own right, as were all the Ides, sacred to Jupiter (*F* 1. 56).

morte iacent merita: testes estote, Philippi,
et quorum sparsis ossibus albet humus.
hoc opus, haec pietas, haec prima elementa fuerunt
Caesaris, ulcisci iusta per arma patrem.

I was about to omit mentioning the daggers that pierced the prince,
when from her chaste hearth Vesta spoke thus: 'Do not hesitate to mention them: he was my priest, the sacrilegious hands with their weapons
were aimed at me. I myself snatched the man away and left only his sem-
blance behind. That which fell by the steel was Caesar's shadow.' Indeed
he saw, when located in heaven, the halls of Jove, and he owns a temple
dedicated to him in the great forum. But everyone who, daring the impious deed against the will of the gods, has violated the pontiff's life, lies
low in a death deserved. Be the witness Philippi, and you whose scat-
tered bones whiten the ground. This was his work, this was his pious
task, and these were the first actions of Caesar, to avenge his father with
righteous weapons.

Julius is here described as 'sacerdos Vestae' in his role as Pontifex
Maximus.[31] Ovid has Vesta herself describe his apotheosis and
her part in it (Augustus' role in the elevation of his father, appropriate in the Pater Patriae passage, is not appropriate here), a
result of the fact that those who had murdered her priest had
aimed their swords against herself and so committed sacrilege
against the gods. Ovid's entry for this day is an ill-disguised justification of Octavian's rampage against the assassins and anyone
who supported them. Suetonius observes that, of Caesar's assassins, hardly one survived him for more than three years or died a
natural death. All were doomed and perished, one in one way and
another in another, some by shipwreck, others in battle; some
slew themselves with the very dagger with which they had
stabbed Caesar (Div. Iul. 89). Appian says that not one of those
who had conspired against Caesar escaped; all were brought to
condign punishment by his adopted son (BC 2. 21. 154). Plutarch
adds that the genius which had attended Caesar all his life followed him after death, to avenge his murder, chasing his murder-
ers over every land and sea and tracking them down, till not one
of them was left, punishing every one that had had any hand or
part in the business (Caes. 69. 1).

---

[31] The concept of Pontifex Vestae attached to Julius here is a retrojection
which is discussed in Ch. 2, 'Pontifex Maximus'.

It is an awesome picture presented by the ancient authors of Octavian's terrible revenge. Ovid is not just condoning that revenge here but also elevating it from a personal vendetta to an act of benevolence to the state. The point of the whole passage is that the crime of the assassins was a crime not against Caesar but Vesta, goddess of the Roman hearth, and, by implication, against the heart of the Roman state. Octavian was thus piously righting a wrong committed against the state and its gods (and so paving the way for his own apotheosis). The theme is reiterated by Ovid in his entry for 12 May, the dedication of the temple to Mars Ultor. The words are spoken by Augustus: (5. 573–6):

> si mihi bellandi pater est Vestaeque sacerdos
> auctor, et ulcisci numen utrumque paro,
> Mars, ades et satia scelerato sanguine ferrum,
> stetque favor causa pro meliore tuus.

If my father and Vesta's priest is the cause for my waging war and I prepare to avenge both divinities, then stand by me Mars, satiate your sword with profaned blood and may your favour be with the better cause.

Julius' invocation on the Ides of March is for the purpose of exonerating his heir. Julius' identification as 'sacerdos Vestae' is utilized solely for the purpose of enhancing his heir's *pietas*. Julius himself, or better said the death and apotheosis of Julius, serve only as a catalyst to bring Augustus, and his role of Pontifex Maximus, into a direct relationship with the goddess of the Roman hearth (see Ch. 2).

At this point we may note that, whenever Julius appears in a deified role in the passages thus far discussed, some early action of Octavian pertaining to his adoptive parent is being explained or justified. There is an exception to this rule however. This comes in the long introduction to book 3, where Ovid gives a lengthy excursus on the history of the Roman calendar beginning with Romulus (3. 75–166). Ovid concludes the section with a tribute to Julius, who brought about its reform in 46 BC (3. 155–66). Julius is acknowledged as 'deus tantaeque propaginis auctor' (3. 157), the highest praise accorded him in the entire poem. The section is also conspicuous as one which does not compare Julius unfavourably with Augustus. But the lofty tone adopted by the poet here is not sustained. The reason why Julius decided to

reform the calendar borders on the burlesque: it was because he
knew of his impending apotheosis and did not want to enter a
heaven with which he was unfamiliar (3. 159–60):

> promissumque sibi voluit praenoscere caelum
> nec deus ignotas hospes inire domos.

He wanted to know beforehand the heaven promised him, and not enter
as a stranger deity into unknown palaces.

Julius' great service was motivated purely by self-interest. The
poet's technique of bathos has somewhat deprived Julius of *dignitas* at the very point where Ovid might have been expected to
accord him the greatest tribute—for the reform of the religious
calendar upon which this very poem was based. Perhaps his
motive was to deflect from a truly great achievement which
Augustus could not have outdone. At any rate such treatment is
surely in keeping with the light, humorous genre of the poem; I
cannot conceive that it would be regarded by a literary audience
of the day as a serious disparagement of the father of the ruler.

This survey of references to Julius Caesar in the *Fasti* has presented the first Caesar in several guises: as military commander,
for which he is no role model for Augustus; as 'sacerdos Vestae',
and god, for which he is; as reformer of the Roman calendar, cast
in a humorous way to deprive Augustus' predecessor of too much
reverence and credit for what was a truly outstanding achievement. Ovid ignores anniversaries associating him with Cleopatra
and civil war. His purpose seems to have been to erase memory of
Julius' most embarrassing (to his heir) and inglorious deeds.

To sum up: White's thesis that the memory of Caesar was not
under siege in the reign of Augustus cannot be sustained by a
study of Julius in the *Fasti*. Ovid's poetic predecessors gave
Julius a low profile simply by according him as few references as
possible. Ovid has adopted a different approach to a different
end: he has mentioned him often to exploit his name, his (contrived) identity, his anniversary and his achievements, to enhance
by comparison the rule of his heir.

Ovid's reason for casting Julius in such a manner can only have
been for the purpose of winning the approval of the dedicatee of
his work. He perceived that Augustus was downplaying the activities of the Dictator while at the same time profiting from his
posthumous, deified status to legitimize his own prospective path

to heaven. Augustus himself reduced the human identity of his parent by relegating him to anonymity in his *Res Gestae*, and his building programme celebrating Divus Julius was designed to demonstrate how he, 'divi filius', was superseding and surpassing him.[32]

The Julian *feriae* Ovid selected for commemoration or omission, and his invocation of Julius where he did not belong, demonstrate that he was, rather than mechanically following the calendar, reflecting, in the manner permitted by the genre of the *Fasti*, an initiative proceeding from Augustus. Just as importantly, Ovid's negative reflection of Julius as constantly being overshadowed by Augustus is admirably appropriate to the panegyrical technique of the work: to denigrate a past ruler to enhance the present one. Ovid's depiction of Julius therefore does not necessarily present a realistic picture of the standing of Julius, god or man, in the minds of those who remembered, or idealized him, at the time. Calendars commemorated his anniversaries where Ovid did not. And we have seen where Augustus, as late as AD 6, fifty years after the assassination, was able to pass an unpopular measure by invoking the name of Caesar. Julius may well have been outdoing Augustus in popularity at this difficult time. Ovid's depiction of him as less than Augustus in the *Fasti*, written in this period, is perhaps designed as a response.

[32] See Ramage (1985) 226, 230, 242.

4

LIVIA

THE consort of Augustus is invoked four times in Ovid's *Fasti*, twice in the pre-exilic edition (5. 157–8; 6. 637–8) and twice in the post exilic (1. 536; 1. 649–50). Her pre-exilic image is that of 'Livia', model Roman wife and paragon of female Roman virtue. Her post-exilic image is that of Julia Augusta, mother of the new ruler, consort of Jove and herself a goddess-in-the-making.

Before the *Fasti* Livia had hardly figured in Augustan poetry. Her name is not invoked at all in the extant works of Ovid's predecessors, Virgil, Horace, Propertius, or Tibullus, although it is true that Horace had once made a move in that direction. In Ode 3. 14. 1–10 he invokes the 'mulier' and 'soror' of Caesar as public sacrificial celebrants to the gods after the victorious return of Augustus from Spain (24 BC).[1] In the quarter century that separates that Ode from Ovid's calendar, we hear of no poetic tribute to the consort of Augustus.

The inscribed calendars appear to have been even more reticent than the poets. Our extant copies never mention Livia at all until after the death of Augustus, when she had become Julia Augusta.[2] It is true that the dates upon which Ovid incorporates his first image of Livia into his calendar, 1 May and 11 June, are both infrequently and poorly represented in the surviving fragments.[3] Yet the present study will show that it is most improbable that Livia was represented on those days in the calendrical inscriptions, the very nature of which dictated a very abbreviated form. That improbability arises from the fact that Ovid's incorporation of Livia into the calendar was not as a celebration of a

---

[1] 'Horace, the personal friend of the ruler, had shown the proper tact and reserve. He nowhere names Livia' (Syme (1978) 44).

[2] *Praen*, 23 Apr.: 'Signum divo Augusto patri ad theatrum Marcelli Iulia Augusta et Ti. Augustus dedicarunt.' *Verul* 17 Jan.: 'Feriae ex s.c. quod eo die Augusta nupsit divo Augusto.' *Acta Frat. Arv.* 30 Jan.: 'Natalis Iuliae Augustae.'

[3] 1 May: *Ver, Esq*; 11 June: *Ver. Maff., Tusc.*, in Degrassi (1963).

festival in her own honour, but as a means of associating her with, and thus assigning her patronage of, an already firmly established ancient festival of the city.

It will also emerge that Augustus would have had good reason to be pleased with the associations made by Ovid between Livia and the cults in his first edition. In each case Ovid gives her a distinct image which is intended to complement his selective treatment of the calendrical subject matter of the day in question. Yet he sometimes runs into difficulties. His first portrayal of Livia reflects the dilemma of a contemporary trying to please Augustus while at the same time ever conscious of the dynastic feuds currently raging around the ageing Princeps. His second portrayal of Livia reflects what he, and others, expected from the shift in power which had taken place after the death of Augustus and Livia's assumption of the name Augusta. Yet he misread the mood of the new regime. With this new image of Livia in the *Fasti*, the new Princeps, Tiberius, would have every good reason not to be pleased.

Between the creation of the poet's first image of Livia and the second, the subject herself had, with the death of Augustus and the terms of his will, undergone a change not just of name but also of status. So too, had the poet. With his banishment in AD 8, he had undergone a metamorphosis from a financially independent, socially confident aristocrat to an exiled outcast and suppliant. The present study will examine each of Livia's images in turn, how Ovid incorporates it into the Roman calendar, and how he selects a version of the ancient religious tale to highlight or complement the image of Livia he wants to convey. It will also examine how his own status after exile influenced his second portrayal of the *princeps femina* of Rome.

1 May

Livia's first entry into Ovid's Roman calendar is on 1 May in association with the cult of the Bona Dea (5. 148–58). This cult exclusive to females is not registered in any extant calendar. The secret nature of its rites would perhaps preclude mention of it in a public document, which makes Ovid's celebration of the cult in his calendar more noticeable. Yet before studying the passage in question, a brief survey of the history of the cult up to the time

that Ovid composed his version is essential in order to place it in
context.

The oldest known source for the Bona Dea and the aetiological
traditions associated with her come from the books of the pontiffs
quoted by the third-century AD antiquarian Cornelius Labeo in
Macrobius. If we may rely on this third-hand evidence, the Earth
was invoked in the books under the titles Bona, Fauna, Ops, and
Fatua, and that the reason there given was that the four titles represented various bountiful aspects necessary for the sustinence of
life. Labeo himself is the authority for the statement that it was
on the kalends of May that a temple was dedicated to Maia as the
Earth under the name of the Bona Dea, and that the Earth and
Bona Dea were in fact identical.[4] Labeo here omits to specify a
source for the temple itself which might have revealed the era of
its foundation, but the Bona Dea's association with the Earth,
suggestive of fertility, reflects a tradition similar to that in the
books of the pontiffs, and so very probably dates back into the
second century BC.

Writers of the mid-first century BC had very different ideas
from the *pontifices* about the identity of Bona Dea. Varro makes
her the daughter of Faunus, the Roman Pan,[5] and attempts an
explanation as to why men were excluded from her rites: her
pudicitia was such that she never left the women's quarters of her
father's house, that her name was never heard in public, and that
she never saw, or was seen by, a man, which is why no man enters
her temple.[6] Varro (*apud* Macr. 1. 12. 28) adds the pejorative

---

[4] 'Auctor est Cornelius Labeo huic Maiae, id est terrae, aedem Kalendis Maiis
dedicatam sub nomine Bonae Deae, et eamdem esse Bonam Deam et terram ex
ipso ritu occultiore sacrorum doceri posse confirmat. Hanc eamdem Bonam deam
Faunamque et Opem et Fatuam pontificum libris indigitari: Bonam, quod
omnium nobis ad victum bonorum causa est; Faunam, quod omni usui animan-
tium favet; Opem, quod ipsius auxilio vita constat; Fatuam a fando, quod, ut
supra diximus, infantes partu editi non prius vocem edunt quam attigerint terram', in Macr. *Sat.* 1. 12. 21–2. The *annales maximi* or the 80 books of the pontiffs
'ab initio rerum Romanarum usque ad P. Mucium pontificem maximum' (Cic.
Or. 2. 12. 52), i.e. 130–115 BC, was 'a great collection of aetiological explanations of
Roman rites and institutions . . .' (Rawson (1971) 168).

[5] Wissowa (1912) 212: 'schon ziemlich früh ist unter dem Eindrucke des
Bocksgewandes der Luperci die Identifikation des Faunus mit dem griechischen
Pan vollzogen worden . . .', plus references.

[6] Macr. *Sat.* 1. 12. 27; Serv. *Aen.* 8. 314; Tert. *Ad. nat.* 2. 9. 22; Lact. 1. 22. 10
introduces a husband into Varro's version.

anecdote that it was the refusal by the female worshippers of Bona Dea to allow Hercules to quench his thirst with water consecrated to the goddess that prompted the hero to ban the presence of women at the rites he instituted in the Forum Boarium to himself (Ara Maxima).

Other writers of the period connect Bona Dea with Faunus also, but in these her story is even less happy. Macrobius (*Sat.* 1. 12. 24–5) cites an unknown source which has her father Faunus turn himself into a snake for the purposes of committing incest and so depriving her of her chastity.[7] A third version comes from the sixth book of a Greek treatise on the gods by Sextus Clodius, who has Faunus, king of the Latins,[8] beat his wife Fenta Fatua to death for her crime of secret drinking, then repent and confer divine honours upon her.[9] Other stories of Bona Dea do not associate her with Faunus at all, but equate her with goddesses such as Juno, Proserpine, and Hecate. No source for these is cited by Macrobius, so it cannot be certain how old those associations were *Sat.* 1. 12. 23), but Juno, at least, is certainly pre-Ovidian, as Propertius had chosen to identify Bona Dea with her. 'Aspera Iuno', as he calls her, was the traditional enemy of Hercules (4. 9. 43 and 71).[10] In fact Propertius, in his aetiological elegy devoted to the founding of the Ara Maxima, chose to ignore the tradition (found in Virgil (*Aen.* 8. 190 ff.), Livy (1. 7), Dionysius of Halicarnassus (1. 39. 4), and Ovid (*F* 1. 543 ff.) which has the Cacus struggle as the *aition* for the foundation of the Ara. He has chosen instead that found in Varro: the refusal by the worshippers of the cult of Bona Dea to quench the hero's thirst. The scholar Verrius Flaccus on the other hand, in his *Libri de significatu verborum* (epitomized by Festus), knows Bona Dea as the Greek goddess Damia, who had a priestess with the title of Damiatrix, and a secret sacrifice in her honour known as Damium.[11]

---

[7] This author may be Butas, possibly a freedman of Cato the younger (Plut. *Cat. Mi.* 70. 2–5) whom Plutarch identifies as one who wrote *aitia* of Roman customs in elegiac verse (Plut. *Rom.* 21). He is mentioned by Arnobius 5. 18. See Wiseman (1974*b*) 136.

[8] A well-known alternative identity of Faunus: Wissowa (1912) 212.

[9] Sextus Clodius, a Sicilian rhetorician of mid-1st cent. BC (Suet. *Rhet.* 5. Wiseman (1974*b*) 136–7), is quoted by Arnobius (5. 18) and Lactantius (1. 22. 11). Plut. *QR* 20 does not name Sextus but includes a version which is similar.

[10] Prop. 4. 9. 23 ff.; cf. *Aen.* 8. 288–92.

[11] Festus, *Gloss. Lat.* 4. 178: 'damium sacrificium, quod fiebat in operto in

From the confusion over the identity of Bona Dea in the male mythographers, it becomes apparent that none of them was at all sure about who or what it was exactly that the women were worshipping. The widely differing interpretations of two scholars, Varro and Verrius, is ample evidence of this, and Wissowa sensibly suggests that Fauna was probably equated with Damia simply because men were excluded from both rites.[12] In fact that one essential particular, the exclusion of men from the ceremony 'in honour of a goddess whose very name men are not permitted to know' (Cic. *Har. Resp.* 17. 37) may have incited them to derive sometimes unsympathetic aetiological rationalizations from the external features with which they were familiar.[13] Yet on the evidence available, the unsympathetic versions seem to be a feature of the first-century BC writers, as they are absent from the aetiological explanations in the *annales maximi* of the second century BC. We shall return to this apparent disparity below.

The history of the cult itself was not uneventful. In the time of Cicero, Bona Dea had suffered considerable notoriety with the scandal of P. Clodius Pulcher, descendant of Appius Caecus and so also a kinsman of Livia's (Cic. *Dom.* 105; Suet. *Tib.* 4). Clodius had, in 62 BC, desecrated the December rites prohibited to males by dressing as a woman and so gaining entry into the house of the magistrate where the Vestal Virgins were performing the sacrifice. Clodius' alleged purpose for invading the ceremony was to gratify his lust for Pompeia, wife of Julius Caesar, in whose house the secret rites were that year being performed (Cic. *Dom.* 105; *Har. Resp.* 17. 37. 38; *Att.* 1. 13. 3; Plut. *Caes.* 9).

The outrage was deemed serious enough for the Senate to set up a special court to try Clodius. Cicero himself testified for the prosecution (*Att.* 1. 16). Four years later Cicero again raked up Clodius' sacrilege for public attention in a speech delivered before the college of pontiffs (*De Domo sua*) and in one speech

---

honore Bonae Deae; dictum a contrarietate, quod minime esset δαμοσιον, id est publicum. Dea quoque ipsa Damia et sacerdos eius damiatrix appellabatur.'

[12] Wissowa (1912) 216.

[13] Listed by Macr. *Sat.* 1. 12. 23–6. Also in Plut. *QR* 20; Arn. 5. 18: a sow was sacrificed to her; it was sacrilege for a myrtle rod to be found in her temple; a vine was spread above her head; wine brought into her temple was contained in a honey jar and called milk; tame serpents lived in her temple; herbs of all kinds were brought into her temple; no man could enter the temple.

delivered to the Senate (*De haruspicum responso*) In the first he contrasted the miscreant with his noble and pious Claudian ancestors (*Dom.* 105), and in the second claimed that before Clodius the female cult had never before in history been violated or been made light of (*Har. Resp.* 37). Cicero was doing his utmost to discredit Clodius, yet the cult itself did not remain unscathed. We have seen that the first-century BC writers constructed uncomplimentary aetiologies of Bona Dea, particularly that of Sextus Clodius, which makes the deity little less than ridiculous. The possibility exists that a client or clients of Clodius set out to ridicule the cult of Bona Dea for the purpose of trivializing and so rendering more inconsequential Clodius' sacrilege, and so serve to salvage his reputation.[14] The mid-first-century BC writers perhaps reflect efforts to achieve that affect. It may be under their influence that Tibullus too reflects an attempt to make the cult disreputable, as indeed does Ovid in an early work, where both equate intentions to worship the goddess with a pretext for committing adultery (*Tib.* 1. 6. 22; Ov. *AA* 3. 638). It was in precisely that way that Clodius, dressed as a woman, had brought public disrepute to the Bona Dea.

It is against this background that we can now examine Ovid's rendering of the cult of the Bona Dea in the *Fasti* (5. 148–58). The short passage can be quoted in full:[15]

> interea Diva canenda Bona est.
> est moles nativa, loco res nomina fecit:
> appellant Saxum; pars bona montis ea est.
> huic Remus institerat frustra, quo tempore fratri
> prima Palatinae signa dedistis aves;
> templa patres illic oculos exosa viriles
> leniter adclivi constituere iugo.
> dedicat haec veteris Crassorum nominis heres,
> virgineo nullum corpore passa virum:

[14] Wiseman (1974*b*) 136–7 believes that the good and bad reputations of Bona Dea were promoted by the writings of the clients of M. Cato and P. Clodius respectively. This is a persuasive argument, but no writing of that period has survived which provides anything like a flattering aetiology of a 'good goddess'.

[15] The text of Ovid's Fasti cited is that of Alton *et al.* (1988). Other editors read 'Clausorum' in l. 155, despite the fact that it is an obviously late interpolation in the MSS. See Alton *et al.*, (1973) 150. Even Brouwer in his study of the sources for the cult (1989) 185 follows the 'Clausorum' reading with no explanation for doing so.

Livia restituit, ne non imitata maritum
esset et ex omni parte secuta virum.

Meanwhile the Good Goddess must be celebrated. There is a mass of
native rock, after which the place is named. They call it 'the Rock'; it is a
substantial part of the hill. On this spot Remus had stood in vain at the
time when you, birds of the Palatine, gave the first omens to his brother.
There, on the gently sloping ridge, the Senate founded the temple which
detests the eyes of males. The heiress of the ancient name of the Crassi
dedicated this, who with her virgin body had submitted to no man. Livia
restored it so that she might not fail to imitate her husband and in every
way follow him.

Ovid, in contrast to his predecessors, avoids associating Bona Dea
with Faunus, Juno, or any particular deity. Nor indeed does he
provide any specific indication as to her nature, nor even of the
aition or features of her cult. Despite his claim in the first line of
this passage, the poet concentrates not on Diva Bona, as he has
chosen to call her, but rather on her temple, its location, its original dedicator and its present-day restorer.

The information he has selected, however, conveys a wealth of
implications. The allusion to Remus both locates her temple on
the Aventine and links her cult with a spot sacred to the very earliest history of Rome (cf. *F* 4. 815–16; Livy, 1. 7). That the Patres
founded the temple which detested the eyes of males indicates
that the cult exclusive to females had, in the (Romulean) past,
been ratified and encouraged by the legitimate aristocratic government. That the temple was dedicated by a virgin and heir to
the ancient name of the Crassi imparts the notion that chastity
was the essential virtue in one who worshipped the deity, and that
the goddess had historical links with the illustrious branch of the
Licinian *gens*. That we are told that Livia restored the temple
directly connects the ancient cult of Bona Dea with the Augustan
present. It also implies that Livia, although a member of the
Claudian *gens*,[16] was piously emulating the original dedicator
both in virtue and in deed, and so associates the wife of Augustus
with the essential virtue of the worshipper of the deity: chastity
and piety. Livia's purpose in restoring the temple: 'ne non imitata
maritum / esset et ex omni parte secuta virum', coming as it does
at the end of the passage and constituting its climax, reflects

[16] Her father was M. Livius Drusus Claudianus, descendant of the most eminent Claudians, Appius Pulcher, and Appius Caecus (Vell. 2. 75; Suet. *Tib.* 3–4).

above all the virtue of Augustus, for it evokes here an image of the chaste spouse, submissive to her husband, and emulating him in his own actions of restoring the ancient temples of Rome.[17]

What then has the temple on the Aventine, its virginal dedicator, and its chaste present-day restorer got to do with any pre-existing tradition about Bona Dea? The first important clue to this question is that, although the nature of the deity herself is not alluded to, Ovid has chosen to highlight the virtues of chastity and piety. The stress on chastity suggests that the poet may have kept in mind the version of Varro's which ascribed *pudicitia* as inherent to the nature of Bona Dea who avoided all possible contact with men. But Ovid has left out Varro's pejorative anecdote about the confrontation between Hercules and Bona Dea's worshippers (Macr. *Sat.* 1. 12. 27–8) which Propertius chose to dwell upon with such good-humoured relish. Ovid's account elsewhere in the *Fasti* of the foundation of the Ara Maxima contains no mention of Bona Dea's worshippers and their refusal to quench Hercules' thirst after his victory over Cacus either (1. 543–86). Nor indeed do the accounts of Virgil (*Aen.* 8. 268–305), Livy (1. 7), or of Dionysius of Halicarnassus (1. 39–42).

It is clear from the varied material at his disposal and the choices he made that Ovid was anxious to present Bona Dea in only the best light, untainted by any unedifying or discreditable allusions such as incest, drunkenness, or malevolence to the god-in-the-making, Hercules. His decision not to associate Bona Dea with the second-century BC *pontifices'* bountiful attributes of an Earth-goddess, on the other hand, may be due to one of two reasons: either he did not have access to the *annales maximi* and so was unaware of the traditions therein;[18] or he did not wish to evoke an idea of fertility in Bona Dea because he desired to foster an image of Livia which corresponded with that of the chaste Vestal, founder of the cult. Livia in her role as mother is therefore not represented. The only nagging doubt about this latter option is that it was quite possible to portray a woman both as

---

[17] *RG* 19; Livy, 4. 20; Suet. *Aug.* 31; Hor. *Od.* 3. 6; Dio, 55. 10. 2.

[18] Rawson (1971) 166–8 shows how both annalists and antiquarians made little use of the *annales maximi*. She suggests the possibility that there was only one copy, or they were for some reason hard to get at.

chaste and a mother.[19] The question of this one-sided image of
Livia will be examined at length where Ovid associates her with
the Matralia.

The question of the temple and its original dedicator is not
easy. Cicero had reported that a certain Licinia, daughter of
Gaius, a Vestal Virgin of noble birth, had dedicated an 'ara,
aedicula et pulvinar sub Saxo' in 123 BC, but this dedication 'in
loco publico' had been rejected as invalid both by pontiffs and the
Senate (*Dom.* 136). Cicero does not say to what goddess Licinia
had dedicated her offering, but the location he describes as 'sub
Saxo' has been identified with Ovid's 'appellant Saxum'. On that
basis it has been assumed that Licinia's dedication had been to
the Bona Dea. On that basis also Livia's temple of Bona Dea has
been sited at the north end of the eastern part of the Aventine
directly south of the east end of the Circus Maximus.[20]

The identity of Cicero's Licinia is not hard to establish. She
can be none other than the daughter of C. Licinius Crassus, tribune in 145 BC and granddaughter of C. Licinius Crassus, consul
in 168 BC.[21] This Licinia's career as a Vestal was not uneventful.
Not only was her dedication to the unspecified deity 'sub Saxo'
declared invalid by *pontifices* and Senate, but she was also accused
of incest and tried before the *pontifices* on December 18, 114 BC.[22]
Dio passes on a tradition that had no doubt of her guilt, and even
expands her crime from incest to having had a multitude of lovers
(Dio, 26. 87. 3). This particular heiress of the ancient name of
Crassi would seem, by reputation at least, to be a most inappropriate choice to be celebrated as the model of chastity who originally dedicated the temple of the Bona Dea. Yet there seem to be
no other likely candidates to fit the model Ovid has constructed.
The earliest known member of the *gens Licinia* to give the *cognomen* Crassus to his branch of the family was the brother of
C. Licinius Varus, consul of 236. The first Crassus to attain the
consulship was P. Licinius Crassus Dives in 205 BC. The second

---

[19] Val. Max. 7. 1: the wife of Metellus Macedonicus was 'uxor pudicitia et
fecunditate conspicua'. Tac. *Ann.* 1. 41: '(Agrippina) ipsa insigni fecunditate
praeclara pudicitia.'

[20] Platner–Ashby (1929) 85; Coarelli (1985) 314.

[21] For a diagram of the family of the Licinii Crassi, see Marshall (1976) and *RE*
13 247. On Licinia see *RE* 13 497 (181).

[22] Broughton (1951) i. 515 and 534. Fenestella in Macr. *Sat.* 1. 10. 6.

was Gaius Licinius Crassus in 168 BC, grandfather of the Licinia in question.[23] So the 'heres veteris Crassorum nominis' cannot date that far back and contenders are scarce. Cicero's Licinia still beckons.

The nature of an orator's evidence can pose a problem. In his speech concerning his house before the college of pontiffs, Cicero is constructing a case against Clodius, 'tribunus plebis scelere et audacia singulari' (*Dom.* 130). Clodius had carried a decree to banish him, and in Cicero's subsequent absence had pulled down the exile's house on the Palatine, had the site consecrated and had erected thereon a monument to Liberty, hoping thereby to place it beyond the recovery of its owner. In this speech the orator is appealing to the pontiffs to have Clodius' consecration declared null and void so he could reclaim his property. Cicero's task is to persuade, to sound plausible and truthful, not spell out every fact. He expected his audience to be sophisticated enough to distinguish the 'oratorium genus' from the 'historicum'. In another speech he makes Scaevola define the great orator as one who seems to the intelligent to be speaking eloquently, and to the stupid to be speaking the truth.[24] On these terms therefore, we have to look at the problems contained in his testimony to Licinia.

The short passage on Licinia is plainly designed to present the Vestal and events related to her in a manner which impedes easy identification of her, yet lends an air of authenticity by providing the names of the consuls for the year and quoting the Pontifex Maximus and a senatorial decree. Indications of a desire to confound the true identity of the subject are plentiful: first, the orator avoids mention of the *cognomen* Crassus when identifying the Vestal's father. Second, if we may rely on Ovid, Cicero is not precisely correct in specifying the location of Licinia's dedication. He says it was made beneath the Saxum. Ovid says the temple to Bona Dea was on top of the Saxum, on the inclined surface of the summit, where Remus had watched the birds: 'templa patres illic . . . / leniter adclivi constituere iugo'. Third, Cicero does not specify that the Vestal had dedicated a structure the size of a temple. Yet the combination of 'ara, aedicula et pulvinar' could well serve a metonymical purpose for the orator who thought that mention of a temple might awaken too close a recognition of his

[23] Marshall (1976) 5.   [24] Cic. *Or.* 2. 35. Wiseman (1979) 37, 47.

subject in his audience. The fourth point is that Cicero never mentions the Bona Dea, or deity to whom Licinia made her dedication. Fifth, he avoids mention of why her dedication was subsequently disallowed and any indication of the time lapse between the accomplishment of her dedication and the declaration that that dedication was invalid. Finally, he betrays no hint of the scandal of 114–113 BC that was to result both in damaging the integrity of the pontifical college, and in Licinia's execution.[25]

The orator had a dilemma. In the case he was presenting before the college of pontiffs, Cicero needed the precedent of the case of Licinia to demonstrate that a dedication, once made, could still be revoked and declared null and void. That was what he was trying to have done in the case of Clodius' dedication of his own property. Yet a most vital weapon in his armoury against his opponent was Clodius' violation of the cult of the Bona Dea (the cult he claimed before the Senate had never before in history been violated or made light of (*Har. Resp.* 37)), and he had already used it earlier in the same speech (*Dom.* 105, 110). He could not afford to blunt that weapon by delineating the facts of the history of the cult and so render Clodius' sacrilege insignificant by comparison. To identify Licinia positively as daughter of Crassus, as original dedicator of the temple of the Bona Dea on the Saxum on the Aventine whose dedication had later been declared invalid because of the scandal and public outrage, could

---

[25] The decree cited by Cicero shows that Licinia did carry out her dedication, ratification for which she must have first acquired by submitting to the Pontifical college. cf. Cic. *Dom.* 136, where the censor Gaius Cassius submitted to the college his project for the dedication of a statue to Concord, which was refused. The Pontifex Maximus Cicero cites, Publius Scaevola, was in office at the time of Licinia's dedication in 123 BC, but he died in 115 BC. The scandal occurred in the following year, under his successor, Metellus Dalmaticus, whose integrity was called into question when his verdict of innocence of two of the Vestals was overturned when the case was retried (see Gruen (1968) 128–9). We need not suppose that Cicero was being utterly faithful to the truth in suggesting that Licinia's dedication was revoked under Scaevola. The deconsecration of the temple of Bona Dea was not listed in the books of the pontiffs which ended with Scaevola's death in 115 BC. Mention of Metellus Dalmaticus and accompanying associations of the damaging blow to the pontifical college at the time would not be pleasing to the ear of Cicero's pontifical audience. A good orator would surely avoid causing any discomfort to those he hoped to persuade.

serve to bring ridicule to the cult and seriously dampen his ammunition against his arch-rival.[26]

The technique by which Cicero casts a veil over Licinia and her reputation and obscures her association with the temple of Bona Dea makes it most probable that the pontiffs of 57 BC were not certain as to whom he was talking about. Even if they were, perhaps they did not want to be reminded of the details, as the case of Licinia had also been a damaging blow to the integrity of their own college. Either way, the orator would have achieved his aim. That technique has caused problems to the present day for scholars who take the orator's words out of context and then predictably fail to apply them as evidence for the original dedicator of the temple that Livia restored.[27] There can be no doubt that Licinia, Caii Crassi filia, was the original dedicator of the temple of the Bona Dea, just as Ovid says.

The history of the temple after its deconsecration is obscure. Varro mentions the existence of a temple of the daughter of Faunus in the first century BC and certainly implies that it was in use (Macr. *Sat.* I. 12. 27). Yet the temple founded by the Senate on the Aventine seems to have been abandoned as the venue for the state-recognized celebration of the cult. The December rite, attended by the Vestals and performed 'pro populo Romano', did not take place in the temple but in the house of a magistrate with imperium. Whether this venue was selected only since the deconsecration of Licinia's temple is possible, for the earliest source for these rites is, again, Cicero. And again, Cicero is not likely to have made any reference to events he thought might jeopardize the erstwhile reputation of the cult Clodius violated.[28] We hear of

[26] There was great public outrage at the time of the scandal, see Gruen (1968) 128. I suggest that this was the reason for Licinia's dedication being declared invalid.

[27] For example Frazer (1929) iv. 17. Cicero's technique is also no doubt responsible for the fact that nearly all editors of the *Fasti* see no sense in the word 'Crassorum' in l. 155, and so substitute 'Clausorum' which, although inserted into the MSS by much later hands, provides sense to the passage in that it suggests that the original dedicator was an ancestor of Livia's.

[28] Cic. *Att.* I. 13. 3; *Har. Resp.* 37. The possibility exists that before the temple was built the rites were held in the house of a magistrate with imperium, and that after its deconsecration that venue was again reverted to. The later sources (Plut. *Cic.* 19, and Dio, 37. 35), however, make no reference to the antiquity of these rites.

no official recognition of the temple of Bona Dea until Ovid associates it with Livia and Augustus and incorporates it into the
Fasti.

Why Augustus should take an interest in the Bona Dea and in
rehabilitating the name of the disgraced Vestal who dedicated her
temple is our next question. Clodius' violation of the sacrifice of
the Bona Dea may have proved an effective weapon for Cicero,
but the sacrilege committed in 62 BC and recorded so vividly in
the orator's writings can have been nothing but a thorn in the
flesh for Augustus many years later. The self-appointed restorer
of the old religion and moral virtue had personal, historical, political, and religious reasons for wishing to rectify the damage done
to Bona Dea, either in anticipation of, or particularly after, his
election as Pontifex Maximus. As head of the Pontifical College,
Augustus' duties now included choosing candidates for the college of the Vestal Virgins and exercising disciplinary functions
over them.[29] As it was the Vestals who performed the rites of the
Bona Dea, Augustus became, as Pontifex Maximus, vicariously
responsible for the correct celebration of those rites.[30] The
tainted history of the cult, however, potentially cast a slur on
Augustus' religious authority in more ways than one. Let us consider the interests at stake for the new incumbent in 12 BC.

Clodius, as Claudian of the Pulcher branch, was an older kinsman of Livia.[31] His action of bringing public disrepute and
ridicule to the female cult was therefore a blot on the recent
ancestry of the wife of the ruler. But more important, that same
action became a blot on Augustus' own adoptive ancestry and the
recent history of his new office. There would be those who could
remember the time when, for political expedience, P. Clodius
Pulcher, 'contemptor divum' (Cic. *Dom.* 139; *Har. Resp.* 5 etc.)
had been seen fit by Octavian to become his father-in-law (Suet.
Aug. 62; Dio, 46. 56. 3; Plut. *Ant.* 20. 1). But worse. The scandal
of Clodius had occurred in the house of a previous Pontifex
Maximus (Cic. *Har. Resp.* 3. 4), Julius Caesar, who had felt
obliged to divorce Pompeia to protect his religious office as well
as his personal reputation. He was, in view of his position, ulti-

---

[29] Suet. *Aug.* 31. 3; Wissowa (1912) 504ff.

[30] It was the verdict of both *pontifices* and the Vestals which pronounced
Clodius' escapade a sacrilege (Cic. *Att.* 1. 13. 3).

[31] Livia was born in 58 BC. Clodius died in 52 BC.

mately responsible for the descration of the cult. Caesar himself, in his capacity as Pontifex Maximus, had to address the Senate about the scandal (*Schol. Bob. Cic. Clod.* p. 85). Furthermore, Caesar's house was not a private house, but the official residence reserved for the head of the Pontificate, the 'domus publica' on the Sacra via.[32]

Clodius' crime therefore extended beyond the desecration of the Bona Dea: it violated the residence of the Pontifex Maximus and so displayed blatant disrespect and ridicule for the authority and status of the head of a state cult. Small wonder that Augustus had no wish to install himself in that residence upon assuming office (Dio, 54. 27. 3). His desire to change the location of the residence of the Pontifex Maximus to his own house on the Palatine was very probably connected with a determination to re-establish its dignity and to eradicate the ignominious stain which polluted both its recent history and his adoptive father's career in that residence. So not only Clodius, kinsman of Livia, but also Julius Caesar, as Pontifex Maximus, had been involved in the desecration of the Bona Dea. If the female cult had suffered disrepute as a result, then the dignity of the role of Supreme Pontiff cannot have remained unscathed. Augustus' task would be to ensure that the credibility and authority of the post was in no manner impaired or at risk. He would therefore have very good reason to be anxious to rehabilitate the respectability of the cult of Bona Dea and to erase the memory of Clodius as a means to this end.

But how to achieve it? Much of Augustus' religious revival, which had included a rigorous selection for retention or burning of Greek and Latin prophetic writings and of the Sibylline books, and reviving ancient rites which had gradually fallen into disuse, had taken place long before he became Pontifex Maximus, contrary to the impression given by Suentonius (*Aug.* 31).[33] It is therefore probable that he decided that the Bona Dea temple cult should be revived well before he became Pontifex Maximus, even if he waited until assuming office before he did so. Augustus' decision to edit the Sibylline books is pertinent to a revival of the temple cult of Bona Dea, for Plutarch tells us that it was these oracles which had contained predictions of the guilt of Licinia

---

[32] Suet. *Div. Iul.* 46. Not to be confused with the Regia, which was close by. Wissowa (1912) 502 n. 7.

[33] Gagé (1931) 99–101.

and the two other Vestals condemned with her (Plut. *QR.* 83).
And the reputation of the original dedicator, Licinia, had fortunately remained unimpaired, for obvious reasons, by Cicero. The
restoration of the reputation of the original dedicator was a means
of redeeming the ancient prestige and dignity of the cult, and of
vindicating the judgement of a predecessor in the office of
Pontifex Maximus, Metellus Dalmaticus, who had originally
declared her innocent (see above, n. 25).

Restoring the good name of a Vestal of the house of Crassus
would not be to the distaste of the Princeps. The name of Crassus
the triumvir, son of Licinia's second cousin,[34] was kept alive in
the Augustan poets with no reprobation or malice. The grandson
of the triumvir had been deprived of his *spolia opima* in 27 BC and
thereafter fades from view. To the ruler no longer threatened by
the name of an illustrious family, its survival could afford some
protection. Late in the reign Augustus was eager to advertise
amity with the high aristocracy, and mutual confidence.[35] The
rehabilitation of Licinia's name would be an easy recompense to a
noble family now extruded from power.

The restoration of the temple cult of Bona Dea by Livia would
serve a number of purposes. Her identity as a Claudian would
counteract the sacrilege of her older relative and so retrieve a reputation for piety for her house. Livia's identity as the consort of
the Pontifex Maximus and ruler would bring renewed dignity
both to the cult of Bona Dea and the office which Augustus had
lately assumed. The date of 1 May, preserved as the day Licinia
dedicated the temple, was suitably distant from December for the
restored cult to be celebrated, and separated, in Roman consciousness, from the contaminated associations of the winter festival. The December rites, furthermore, being held in the house
of a magistrate with imperium, were carried out on premises not
necessarily in direct control of Augustus. The cult now celebrated in the temple under the patronage of Livia made it more
controllable and would serve as a greater deterrent for any would-

[34] Licinia was daughter of C. Licinius Crassus, tribune of 145 who was cousin
to M. Lic. Crassus Agelastus, praetor of 126 and grandfather of the triumvir. See
Marshall (1976) 7.

[35] For the name of Crassus in the Augustan poets, Crassus and the *spolia
opima*, and amity with high aristocracy including the Crassi, see Syme (1986) 271,
275, 277.

be miscreant adulterer or political emulator of the impious and socially disruptive Clodius. Finally, Livia's restoration would be regarded as a religious benefaction to the *matronae* of Rome, serve to give the cult (probably unprecedented) enormous prestige, and lend force to Augustus' policy of reviving the ancient religion of Rome.

The single most important link in re-establishing the repute of the cult of the Bona Dea, of the Claudian name, and the office of Pontifex Maximus, was the person of Livia. Not just in her role as consort of Augustus, but in her individual identity as 'Livia, Drusi Claudiani filia' (Vell. 2. 75, 94), descendant of the eminent Claudii Pulchri. The emphasis upon Livia's name, as well as her role in relation to him, was essential to the purpose which Augustus had at hand.

To revert to Ovid: his task was to incorporate the restored temple cult of Bona Dea into the Roman religious calendar. For this reason his entire verse deals with the foundation and history of the contemporary monument. He sketches the most salient features which indisputably dissociate it both from the cult violated by Clodius, and the uncomplimentary traditions handed down by the first century mythographers. He presents Licinia as a paragon of *castitas* and *pietas*, the virtues he highlights to provide a thematic thread of association to link Bona Dea with Livia, to link the revered past with the Augustan present. He portrays the consort of Augustus by lauding the virtue which does honour to her husband. He presents the present-day Claudian by invoking her by name. Ovid's Bona Dea is the first Roman appearance we have of 'Livia' in the official state cult, and in Roman poetry. Even if grudgingly, Augustus must have approved.

11 June

Livia's second entry in the *Fasti* appears on 11 June, when Ovid commemorates her dedication of a shrine to Concord. This entry is both similar to and different from that of 1 May. Similar in that Livia is again presented as dedicator in a role that does honour to her husband; different in that her dedication is juxtaposed to rather than directly connected with an ancient festival. The passage is as follows (*F* 6. 637–48):

Te quoque magnifica, Concordia, dedicat aede
  Livia, quam caro praestitit ipsa viro.
disce tamen, veniens aetas: ubi Livia nunc est
  porticus, immensae tecta fuere domus;
urbis opus domus una fuit spatiumque tenebat
  quo brevius muris oppida multa tenent.
haec aequata solo est, nullo sub crimine regni,
  sed quia luxuria visa nocere sua.
sustinuit tantas operum subvertere moles
  totque suas heres perdere Caesar opes:
sic agitur censura et sic exempla parantur,
  cum vindex, alios quod monet, ipse facit.

To you, too, Concordia, Livia dedicated a magnificent shrine, you whom
she herself manifested towards her dear husband. But learn, generations
to come, that where Livia's portico now is once stood the roofed buildings of an immense palace. The single house was the structure of a city,
and occupied an area larger than that which many towns defend with
their walls. This was razed to the ground, not because of a charge of
aspiring to kingship, but because by its own extravagance it seemed
harmful. Caesar endured demolishing so many masses of buildings and
losing so much property to which he himself was heir. In this manner is
the censorship discharged and in this manner is an example furnished
when the judge does himself what he advises others to do.

The above lines are the coda of a long section which the poet has
devoted to the *aitia* of two ancient festivals, the Matralia and the
feast of Fortuna, and so should not be treated in isolation from
them (6. 473–636). The rites of these festivals were focused on
women and family life, and Ovid appropriately begins his verse
for 11 June with an invocation to mothers whose day it was: 'ite,
bonae matres (vestrum Matralia festum) / flavaque Thebanae
reddite liba deae' (6. 475–6). That Livia's shrine to Concord was
on Ovid's evidence dedicated on the same day does suggest that
its *raison d'être* was intended by its dedicator to be connected by
association with the two cults centred on marriage and the lives of
women. The poet's words, at least, make explicit allusion to marital concord: 'quam caro praestitit ipsa viro' and leave no doubt
that it is Livia in her role as wife that is being eulogized here.

Why Livia should wish her shrine to be dedicated on 11 June
has been ably demonstrated by Marlene Boudreau Flory. Flory
shows the similarities between the cults of Mater Matuta and
Fortuna, how they both emphasized traditional female roles and

marked important aspects of women's lives: marriage, motherhood, childbearing, and the care and rear of the young. 'The date
of consecration', she argues, 'in conjunction with Livia's sponsor-
ship of the shrine and Ovid's emphasis on married love "viro caro
ipsa praestit", shows Livia, by closely associating Concordia with
long-established deities of marriage and family life, honoured
Concord as a presiding goddess of married life.'[36]

Flory's study however, has left us with problems concerning
Ovid's presentation of Livia, both in itself and in connection with
the features he highlights in his history of the women's cults. To
start in chronological order: in his description of the Matralia,
Ovid enumerates its distinguishing characteristics: it is a festival
for 'bonae matres' (6. 475), the Mater Matuta excluded female
slaves from her temple (6. 481–2), she demanded that baked cakes
('liba tosta') be offered her (6. 482), and that the women pray to
her firstly for their nieces and nephews, and secondly for their
own children (6. 559–62).

Two observations are noteworthy: first, Ovid avoids mention
of a fourth peculiarity about the festival: that only the wife who
had known one husband (univira) could deck the image of the
goddess. The only authority for this feature is a late Christian
source (Tert. Monog. 17), but contemporary evidence for other
religious rites permitted to be performed by univirae only serve
to give it credence.[37] The ideal of marriage to one husband was a
concept which also found frequent expression both on Roman
epitaphs and in Roman literature of the time, the two genres
being combined and poignantly conveyed in the tombstone
address which Propertius puts into the mouth of Cornelia,
daughter of Scribonia and half-sister of Julia (4. 11). Propertius
makes her status as univira a source of the greatest pride to
Cornelia (4. 11. 36: 'in lapide hoc uni nupta fuisse legar'), and it is
the very virtue which he has her exhort her daughter to imitate
(4. 11. 68: 'fac teneas unum nos imitata virum').[38] The convention of a one-and-only marriage as a necessary virtue of the
Roman matron who performed religious rites is indicative of the

---

[36] Flory (1984) 313–14.

[37] Fortuna Muliebris and Pudicitia Plebeia. See Wissowa (1912) 257–8; Flory
(1984) 318; Rawson (1986) 53 n. 90.

[38] Examples of the concept of univira in epitaphs and literature are in Williams
(1958) 22ff.; also Rawson (1986) 53 n. 96.

importance and dignity which Romans had long attached to the institution.

Augustus, however, is most unlikely to have wished to promote that virtue, for two reasons. In the first place, Livia, Octavia, and Julia certainly could not boast of it—the several marriages of the latter two in particular having been forged by the Princeps himself to suit his own political and dynastic designs. Livia's first marriage had ended in scandal, Octavian having removed her from her husband and married her himself while she was pregnant with her husband's second child (Tac. *Ann.* 5. 1). Furthermore, Augustus introduced legislation to enforce remarriage after widowhood or divorce, requiring widows up to the age of 50 to remarry within a period of two years.[39] The necessity of the distinction of the *univira* for certain religious practices must therefore have been a doubtful advantage in the mind of Augustus, who did not wish to see aristocratic women of child-bearing age wasted as widows or divorcees.[40] It is consequently unlikely that he would wish to have that distinction advertised as desirable as a part of his programme of religious revival.

Ovid's failure to mention the necessity of being a *univira* to participate in the Matralia may be interpreted as a sensitivity to the feelings of Livia, who did not belong in that category,[41] and of a desire by Augustus to play down and perhaps to depreciate the traditional ideal which ran counter to his social organization.

The second observation is that, although it was women in their role as aunts rather than mothers who celebrated the rites, Ovid

---

[39] Augustus' *lex Iulia de maritandis ordinibus* made the period one year, but the later Papian law of AD 9 gave widows an extra year to find another husband. For sources see Riccobono (1945) 166ff.

[40] When Antonia, wife of Drusus, became a widow at the age of 27, she refused to marry again despite pressure put upon her by Augustus. Val. Max. 4. 3. 3; Josephus, *AJ* 18. 180.

[41] Horace's line 'unico gaudens mulier marito' *Od.* 3. 14. 5, commonly quoted by scholars to prove that Livia was in fact given that rank, is no proof at all. Horace would not have equated Livia's moral stature with that of a *univira* and tactlessly excluded Octavia, with whom she is bracketed in the verse. Furthermore, as Nisbet suggests, Livia's first marriage had dissolved in scandal, and it would have been tasteless of Horace to suggest that she was a kind of honorary 'univira'. Horace can surely say that Augustus was all-in-all to his wife without raising any awkward questions about her previous history. See Nisbet (1983) 108. Also, for Augustus to accord Livia the rank of honorary 'univira' would run counter to his efforts to induce widows and divorcees to marry again.

refers to the goddess as 'parens' and calls the worshippers 'matres' (6. 479, 475). Presumably one therefore had to be a mother to participate. Furthermore, it is Ino's identity as mother rather than aunt which is focused upon, even if for the purpose of explaining how it was that she and her son came to be Roman deities. Ovid devotes far greater space to the adventure-with-the-happy-ending of the mother/son (Ino/Melicertes) than to the aunt/nephew (Ino/Bacchus) relationship in the story of Ino at 6. 485–550.[42] Ovid's choice of the happy-ending version is all the more mysterious when, to explain the custom of the aunt-role of the worshippers, Ino was said to have been unlucky in her own children but fortunate in her nephew Bacchus. Yet she and her son found happiness in Italy, became gods with the names Matuta and Portunus (Leucothea and Palaemon) and all their troubles ceased (6. 541 ff.)! This does not quite parallel 'ipsa parum felix visa fuisse parens' (6. 560), 'utilior Baccho quam fuit ipsa suis' (6. 562). Motherhood then, rather than aunthood, seems to be the main theme of Ovid's rendering of the rites of the Mater Matuta. Hardly surprising if the Matralia was the peculiar celebration of mothers.[43]

Next, Fortuna. Ovid begins by citing the features that this cult shared in common with the one just celebrated: the same day, the same founder, and the same location (the Forum Boarium 6. 477–8) for their temples (6. 569). The name of Servius, revered king of ancient Rome, invoked at the beginning of the Matralia (6. 480), is again invoked at the beginning of Fortuna to establish a positive historical and thematic connection between the two. Ovid then proceeds to enumerate the various causes which are assigned for the concealment of the king's statue. He presents three conjectural *aitia*: (1) Fortuna hides the face of the man she loved through shame of having loved a mortal 579–80; (2) after the murder of Tullius, grief-stricken plebeians hid his face because their sorrow only increased when they gazed at him; (3) the statue itself requested to be covered lest it see the impious face of Servius' murderous daughter. Fortuna thereupon forbade the matrons to remove or touch the garments (6. 615–21).

[42] Another version of the story had less than a happy ending. Ino went mad and threw Melicertes into a boiling cauldron, then leapt with the dead body into the sea. (Ov. *Met.* 4. 464–542).

[43] Michels (1967) 77.

Despite the poet's claim to be doubtful as to the correct cause
(6. 572) Ovid devotes the major section of the verse describing
Fortuna to the third reason: 'tertia causa mihi spatio maiore
canenda est' (6. 585). Significantly, the theme of this third reason
comprises the perversion of the traditional female role within the
family, a strange theme to dwell upon, perhaps, in connection
with a cult which emphasized traditional female roles. It is the
story of Tullia, daughter of Servius, who instigates the murder of
her husband, sister, and father to achieve her insatiable and
unfeminine ambition for power. The traditional ideal of the
woman as protector of marriage and family is here inverted and
she becomes the agent of discord and destruction. Ovid's version
of this story concentrates primarily on Tullia to highlight the
tragedy wrought by a woman who did not fulfil her time-hon-
oured function as guardian of the family.

Ovid's version of the story of Tullia is in some contrast with
the only other versions of this story known to us which come
from Dionysius of Halicarnassus (4. 29–40) and Livy (1. 46–8).
That of the former is a very long story in which Tullia plays the
vital but nevertheless minor role of manipulating agent to the
chief protagonist, the evil Tarquin. Dionysius lays the blame
wholly on Tarquin, who, he says, was 'assisted' by Tullia (4. 79).
Livy devotes more space to the evil of Tullia and tends to level
blame at her and Tarquin equally, although he does betray a note
of uncertainty that the actual murder was at Tullia's hands
('Creditur, quia non abhorret a cetero scelere, admonitu Tulliae
id factum', 1. 48. 5) Ovid's story betrays no such doubt: she is the
evil-doer, the agent of discord, and the poet lays the blame
squarely upon her, sparing as few words as possible for her partner in crime, Tarquin (6. 587 ff.). It is Tullia's evil which caused
the statue of Servius to cover its face, and it is the matrons who
had to utter solemn prayers before it and refrain from touching it
(6. 621–2) as if to propitiate it. The focus on Tullia and her evil
serves the purpose of bringing into sharper contrast the image of
the female ideal which follows.

What a welcome relief and pleasant contrast is the introduction
of Livia after the preceding ghastly story! Concord in the context
which Ovid places it is evoked as a goddess of harmonious married life, and Livia as the wife exemplifying it. Livia, agent of
concord, is all that Ovid's Tullia was not. Yet Ovid's image of

Livia seems incomplete. A major theme in his rendering of the
Matralia is motherhood; a major theme in his rendering of the
aition for Fortuna is the (perversion of the role of) female in
the family context. Why then does Ovid restrict Livia's role to
that of wife? Why does it not also embrace her maternal role and
place in a family context? If the female cults celebrated on this
date 'emphasized traditional female roles and marked important
aspects of women's lives such as marriage, motherhood, child-
bearing and the care and rearing of children', and if Concordia
already had a long established role 'as a guardian of family and
conjugal life',[44] then Ovid's image of Livia does not neatly fit the
model. Only one aspect of the multi-faceted role is spotlighted.
This fact deserves investigation in view of the fact that Livia had
borne two children, and public recognition of her as a mother was
given expression in 9 BC when she was awarded the privileges of
mothers of three children as part of the official consolation of her
bereavement on the death of her second son Drusus.[45]

Furthermore, Ovid does not terminate the passage with the
theme of Livia as an image of marital concord. Instead he
employs it as a lynch-pin to connect the female cults founded by
Servius in the Forum Boarium with the following ten lines
devoted to the Porticus Liviae on the Esquiline in which Livia's
shrine to Concord stood,[46] and a eulogy of Augustus as censor
and judge. Yet according to Dio, the Porticus was dedicated not
in June but in January, and although it was Augustus who had it
built, it was inscribed in Livia's name and dedicated jointly by
her and her son Tiberius (Dio, 54. 23. 6; 55. 8. 2). Modern scholars have interpreted this joint dedication as a demonstration of
(family) concord between Livia and Tiberius.[47] Why Ovid has
not exploited an opportunity to celebrate the concord between
mother and son in this context is another mystery which requires
explanation.

But first, what are Augustus and the Porticus Liviae doing in
Ovid's *Fasti* under 11 June? Flory has made a good case for the

[44] Flory (1984) 312, 314.
[45] Livia was granted the 'ius trium liberorum' (Dio, 55. 2. 5).
[46] Flory (1984) 310 shows there is good archaeological evidence for a shrine in
the form of a monumental altar in the Porticus Liviae which supports Ovid's clear
implication that there was architectural unity between the two.
[47] Wissowa (1912) 328; Flory (1984) *passim*.

idea that the building erected on the site of Vedius Pollio's extravagant house was designed to be an example of Augustus' desire to restrain private luxury, and which was reflected in his sumptuary legislation; that the shrine to concord in the Porticus was a gesture in support of Augustus' marriage laws and that the architectural unity reflected Augustus' determination to revive family life and plain living.[48] But this idea does not explain why Ovid has celebrated the building under 11 June, thereby connecting it through Livia's dedication to Concord with the cults in the Forum Boarium. The problem, I believe, arises from the fact that Flory sees the propaganda value of the site and the Porticus, a telling contrast between the old values and the new, the past and the present, reflecting a 'wholly contemporary situation',[49] that is, she takes Ovid here at face value and goes back no further than Vedius Pollio, who died in 15 BC. The answer, I believe, is more likely to be found in the earlier historical associations connected with the site of the Porticus Liviae.

Ovid has been careful to provide the information that the palace of Servius was situated on the Esquiline hill (6. 601). Livy (1. 44. 3) and Dionysius of Halicarnassus (4. 13. 2) also assert that this location had been the residence of the historical king. Ovid adds that Tullia, driving in a coach to her father's home, ran over the corpse of Servius at the foot of the Esquiline in the street named after her wicked deed: the Vicus Sceleratus (6. 609). Livy, providing a little more detail, records that, returning from the Forum on her way to her father's house, Tullia reached the top of the Vicus Cyprius and turned right into the Clivus Urbius to take her to the Esquiline. It was in this street where she ran over the body of her father. In commemoration of her deed the street was renamed Sceleratus (1. 48. 6–7) (cf. Dion. Hal. 4. 39). Varro (LL 5. 159) affirms the fact that the Vicus Sceleratus, named after Tullia's crime, was hard by the Vicus Cyprius. Solinus tells us that Servius lived on the Esquiline above the Clivus Urbius (1. 25).

No connection has been made by Platner–Ashby or Coarelli[50] between the site of the Porticus Liviae on the Esquiline and the Clivus Orbius (Urbius), renamed Sceleratus, above which the

<hr />

[48] Flory (1984) 325ff., 330.   [49] Ibid. 329.
[50] Platner–Ashby (1929) 423; Coarelli (1974) 206.

ancient sources strongly imply stood the palace of Servius Tullius. Yet the map of the Esquiline provided by Coarelli[51] shows the Clivus Orbius leading directly up into the Clivus Pullius as if it were simply a continuation, terminating at the top precisely at the site of the Porticus Liviae. On these grounds the possibility must exist that the mansion of Vedius Pollio which Augustus razed in order to construct the Porticus, was thought by Augustus to have been on, or very near, the site associated with the ancient palace of Servius.

The erection of a public building by Augustus in honour of Livia, dedicated by Livia and her son, containing within it a shrine dedicated to Concord by Livia on the site associated with an ancient ruling house destroyed by internal familial discord, would provide an apt and telling contrast between the past and the present family cohesion of the contemporary ruling house. But the structure on the Esquiline needed to be associated not merely topographically with Servius, but also religio-historically. The choice of 11 June for the dedication of Livia's shrine to Concord on the Esquiline, the same day as the two female cults founded by Servius in the Forum Boarium, together with an appropriate rendition of their *aitia* adapted by Ovid, provided the necessary link.

The shrine of Concord, however, could not be treated without the Porticus, as the structure on the Esquiline in its entirety was, with its dual dedication, symbolic of the theme of dynastic cohesion and familial concord. Yet Ovid's *aition* for the Porticus with the theme of value contrast between Vedius and Augustus makes no sense in the context of rounding off the image of familial concord he has begun with Livia's dedication. Augustus' policy against luxury would only make sense under the date in January on which the Porticus was dedicated, and even then only as a subsidiary theme without Livia's shrine. Ovid's *aition* of the Porticus sits most awkwardly at the end of the passage in which the themes of discord in the house of Servius Tullius, and Concord in the house of Augustus, are paramount.

Why Ovid does not pursue the themes of Servius and Concord in his presentation of the Porticus Liviae is not hard to divine. To begin with, Dio (55. 8. 1) says it was early in January 7 BC that the

---

[51] Coarelli (1974) 192.

Porticus was dedicated jointly by Livia and Tiberius. Ovid says that Livia dedicated an altar of Concord in the Porticus on 11 June. We cannot be sure of the year of the dedication of the altar. The exclusion of a very important name from this family group could provide a clue: Julia, daughter of Augustus, wife of Tiberius, and daughter-in-law of Livia.

The absence of Julia's name is suggestive of the fact that imagery being promoted was in conflict with the reality. Julia, married to Livia's son in 11 BC had initially lived in harmony with her husband. In 9 BC she was still doing so, publicly at least. In that year Tiberius celebrated an ovation for his conquests in the north, and Julia collaborated with Livia in entertaining the women of Rome to a banquet (Dio, 55. 2. 4;). In 7 BC Julia is absent from the triumphal festivities, which Dio makes clear were conducted by Livia alone (55. 8. 2). It would appear that between 9 and 7 BC the seeds of discord within the imperial family were being made manifest. Suetonius suggests the reason as being attributed to the death in infancy of the son born to Tiberius and Julia, which caused Tiberius to cease loving and living with Julia (Suet. *Tib.* 7. 3). Levick has constructed a far more plausible hypothesis. The decline in relations between Julia and Tiberius belongs precisely to the period of Tiberius' rise to power, a threat not only to Julia's ambitions for a place for herself in a post-Augustan regime (Tiberius' Principate later proved he believed women had no place in politics), but also to that of a place for her sons, Gaius and Lucius Caesar.[52] The rift between Julia and Tiberius could then well account for the absence of her name in the dedication of the Porticus Liviae in January 7 BC.

If Livia's dedication to Concord in the Porticus occurred at any time before 2 BC, Julia would understandably have taken the public symbol of family cohesion inherent in the monument as a direct insult and threat to the position of herself and her sons, whose names are also conspicuous by their absence in the dedications. The suspicion that dynastic discord did exist within the ruling house from about 7 BC was very soon evinced by Tiberius' retirement to Rhodes in 6 BC, and the scandal and lifelong banishment of Julia in 2 BC. What better proof is needed that the imagery promoted by the structure on the Esquiline was an

[52] Levick (1972) 779ff.; (1976a) 37ff.

attempt to conceal the discord in the house of Augustus which was so reminiscent of that which destroyed the house of Servius? Julia, as daughter of the Princeps, may well have been regarded after 2 BC by Augustus or her opponents as potentially analogous to Tullia, daughter of Servius, who had destroyed both husband and father to fulfil her own ambitions. It is possible therefore, that Livia's 'ara' to Concord in the Porticus was dedicated after 2 BC to advertise that, despite the departure of both Julia and Tiberius, there was still cohesion in the ruling family.

Ovid was in a cleft stick. To please the dedicatee of his poem he wanted to celebrate the major female cults founded by Servius Tullius in the Forum Boarium and make a conceptual connection between them and the ideological role of Livia which found expression in her shrine on the Esquiline, and thus to link Servian past with Augustan present. He wanted to make the physical relationship and thematic contrast between her shrine to Concord and symbol of marital harmony with the site of discord of the palace of Servius Tullius on the Esquiline. Yet he could not ignore the physical relationship of the Aedes Concordiae to the Porticus built by Augustus, whose dedications represented the concord between Augustus, Livia, and her son Tiberius which were necessary to complete the symbolic picture.

Why Ovid should want to ignore this most likely reflects his dilemma as a contemporary uncertain of the outcome of dynastic feuds. At the time of writing the *Fasti* the discord inherent in the imperial house had made itself well apparent. To present the true *aition* for the construction of the Porticus would have entailed not only naming and eulogizing Tiberius at the risk of incurring the displeasure of his dynastic rivals, but also eulogizing a familial cohesion which the Roman public was now well aware did not exist. Even after the adoption of Tiberius by Augustus in AD 4, the intrigues of his political enemies did not cease.[53] Those intrigues very probably account for the fact that Ovid again refrained from mentioning Tiberius' name where he should have: in association with the dedication of the temple of Castor and Pollux under 27 January (1. 705–8). To a contemporary such as Ovid who had witnessed the extraordinary vicissitudes both in the career of Tiberius and in Augustus' lifelong attempts to find

---

[53] Levick (1976b) 301ff.

an heir, the identity of the next Princeps could never be a certainty. Not only was the familial concord reflected in the Porticus now inappropriate for eulogy; to introduce dynastic imagery into the scheme while writing in a period when the subject was still speculative would be downright foolish. The poet wisely desisted.

Thus, Ovid's less than satisfactory rendering of the female cults and their connection with Livia on 11 June seems to reflect his own predicament as a witness to the dynastic tensions of his time. He could not afford to evoke in his poem images or events that looked beyond the Augustan regime. That predicament accounts for his image of Livia as an exemplary wife and avoidance of her status and role as 'mater familias' which could succeed in connoting a dynastic theme. It also accounts for his inability to incorporate successfully the Porticus Liviae on 11 June. His mention of the name of the structure and the fact that it was Augustus who had it built is in accordance with the theme of concord, but the *aition* he has provided for it is a clever red herring designed to avoid potentially tactless and inadvertent adherence on the part of the poet to one side of the dynastic battle.

A Change of Status for Author and Protagonist

Between Ovid's creation of the image of Livia just examined and that of the next which he incorporated with a revision of the *Fasti* some years later, several events occurred. The poet was banished in AD 8 to Tomis, an old colony of Greek Miletus on the Black Sea (*T* 3. 9. 1). It is this event which he claims interrupted the composition of his poem (*T* 2. 549–52). The same year had seen the banishment of Augustus' granddaughter Julia, sister of Agrippa Postumus, who had already been disgraced and banished in AD 7. Julia's disgrace appears to have been the culmination of a desperate struggle by a particular clique which, after the deaths of Augustus' adopted sons Gaius and Lucius Caesar, was anxious to oust Tiberius (who threatened to be Augustus' political successor) and advance a candidate of its own choosing. Ovid's poems from exile, written as early as AD 9, clearly demonstrate that, in his mind at least, the dynastic struggle which had been going on since 7 BC and which had so much inhibited his portrayal of Livia, had at last been resolved. Examples of relevant passages will suffice to illustrate the point.[54]

Ovid's certainty that Tiberius was now, since the resolution of the crisis in dynastic politics in AD 8, the only contender to rule with and eventually succeed Augustus as the next Princeps, is made explicit. He addresses Augustus thus: 'sospite sit tecum natus quoque sospes, et olim imperium regat hoc cum seniore senex' (*T* 2. 165–6; cf. *T* 4. 2. 1–10; *Ex P.* 2. 8. 31 ff.). Yet the outcome of the crisis of AD 8 had done more than simply resolve the question as to who was to succeed to the supreme power; it had also elevated Tiberius' status from that of a possible contender to that of a *de facto* heir apparent, as well as adding to Livia's status as consort of the present Princeps by making her mother of the next. As long as Tiberius remained single, his new status guaranteed the continuation of Livia's status as 'princeps femina' (*Ex P.* 3. 1. 125) in the Roman polity through to the next Principate.

Just as importantly for our purposes, Ovid's status also changed drastically in AD 8. From the Roman aristocrat (he had renounced a senatorial career in favour of writing poetry, *T* 4. 10. 27 ff.) he became the outcast suppliant, a status to which he makes frequent reference in his exile poetry.[55] Just as significantly, the poet's new degraded status had a marked affect upon his attitude towards Augustus, Livia, and Tiberius. Yet he does not simply elevate their status to that of heir apparent and mother of heir apparent. It is from exile that we note that he now accords them honours of a divine nature, sometimes even calling all three of them 'dei' (*Ex P.* 2. 8. 1–8):

> Redditus est nobis Caesar cum Caesare nuper,
> quos mihi misisti, Maxime Cotta, deos;
> utque tuum munus numerum, quem debet, haberet,
> est ibi Caesaribus Livia iuncta suis.
> argentum felix omnique beatius auro,
> quod, fuerit pretium cum rude, numen habet.
> non mihi divitias dando maiora dedisses,
> caelitibus missis nostra sub ora tribus.

Caesar has been given back to us together with another Caesar, which gods you have sent to me, Cotta Maximus. And in order that your gift

[54] On Ovid's and Julia's banishment in AD 8, see Syme (1978) ch. 12; Levick (1976*b*).

[55] e.g. *T* 2. 201; *Ex P.* 2. 8. 23–6, 43–4; *Ex P.* 3. 3. 107–9; etc.

should have the number it deserves, there is Livia there joined with her
own Caesars. Oh happy silver, more blessed than all gold because,
though it was a crude metal, it now contains a god. Not by giving me
riches would you have given greater things than the three divinities sent
to our shores.

Before his exile, Ovid has not accorded Augustus explicit divine
status in his poetry, as had Virgil (*Ecl.* 1), for example, and
Horace (*Od.* 4. 5). Whether he was now simply emulating the
practice of the provincials used to according divine honours to
the ruling house, or whether his new status as suppliant motivated the change, cannot be known. More likely, it was a combination of the two. Augustus had never encouraged formal divine
honours for himself or for his family in the capital of the empire.

Livia had already received divine honours in her lifetime in the
provinces, especially in the East.[56] She was also used to performing the role of advocate of the causes of foreign ambassadors who
wanted to secure the favour of Augustus.[57] Ovid, in his new persona and from his new location, has combined the two aspects of
Livia and celebrated them for the first time in Roman poetry. He
makes no attempt to disguise his motive: his desire to be recalled
from exile. His representation of Livia from exile therefore cannot be considered as reflecting the 'spirit of his time' in the capital of the empire, where no cult to Livia existed, nor can it be
considered as reflecting a popular form of flattery common in
poets generally.[58] The Roman poet's situation was unique, and
cannot be isolated from his portrayal of Livia in the exile poems.
That situation might conceivably have influenced his new
portrayal of Livia in the *Fasti* which he incorporated from exile,
after the death of Augustus. It is to that portrayal that we now
turn.

---

[56] See Grether (1946) 222–42; Purcell (1986) 93.

[57] Ollendorf, 'Livia' in *RE* xiii col. 906–7; Purcell (1986) 87.

[58] Scott (1930) 64: 'Ovid, as usual, reflects the spirit of his time, and compares
Livia to Venus in beauty and to Juno in character'. Ollendorf col. 914: 'Die
Gleichsetzung der Kaiserin mit irgend einer Göttin war natürlich auch lange vor
ihrem Tode oder ihrer Konsekration eine beliebte Form der Schmeichlei bei den
Dichtern', but has only Ovid's poetry from exile to cite to illustrate her point.

11 January

The first of the two entries portraying Livia from exile is on 11 January, the great and ancient festival of the Carmentalia.[59] Ovid divides his account of the causes and manner of these rites (1. 465) into two sections. The first relates the story of the arrival of the divine prophet Carmentis and her son Evander to Rome (1. 461–542), the second the story of the combat between Hercules and Cacus which took place during Evander's reign (1. 543–85). It is towards the end of the first section that Ovid incorporates Livia into the ancient cult with an invocation which comprises the culmination of a long prophecy, uttered by Carmentis as she first sets eyes on the ancient site of Rome. The relevant lines are (1. 531–6):

> et penes Augustos patriae tutela manebit:
>   hanc fas imperii frena tenere domum.
> inde nepos natusque dei, licet ipse recuset,
>   pondera caelesti mente paterna feret;
> utque ego perpetuis olim sacrabor in aris,
>   sic Augusta novum Iulia numen erit.'

'And with the house of the Augusti the guardianship of the fatherland shall remain: it is the will of heaven that this house should hold the reins of empire. From it the grandson and son of a god, though he himself refuse it, shall bear with god-like mind the burden which his father bore. And as I shall one day be consecrated in perpetual altars, so shall Julia Augusta be a new divinity.'

The contrast between this new image of Livia and the old could scarcely be more startling. More than simply invoking her by her new name, Julia Augusta, which she was bequeathed by the terms of Augustus' will (Tac. *Ann.* 1. 8), Ovid positions her name at the climax of the eulogy of the house of Augustus and culminates the prophecy with a prediction of her apotheosis and eternal sanctification. No longer is Livia portrayed in a manner which merely does honour to the male potentate. Carmentis, mother of Evander and the eponymous goddess of the major female cult being celebrated, likens Julia Augusta to herself by promising that she will one day be worshipped just as she herself is to be.

---

[59] On the antiquity of the cult see Wissowa (1912) 220f.; Latte (1960) 136–7.

Ovid has elevated Livia's rank from the chaste, obedient wife of the ruler to incipient goddess and head of the Augustan dynasty.

As with the earlier entries of Livia in Ovid's calendar, a study must also be made here of the story of Carmentis with which it is connected to see if the poet has consciously shaped the ancient myth for the purpose of accommodating the modern image. Opinions vary as to which sections of the passage celebrating Carmentis were inserted from exile after the death of Augustus. One is that only the lines that introduce the dynasty, carrying on events after Augustus' death, are added after the succession of Tiberius.[60] Another is that 1. 529–30, which forms a natural climax, could have been the last couplet of the original version.[61] A third opinion is that 1. 481 ff., a passage where Carmentis consoles Evander for his forced departure from his homeland, and bearing a striking resemblance to Ovid's complaints from exile, must be suspected of being inserted from that standpoint.[62] I do not agree with any of these views. For reasons discussed below, I am of the opinion that the entire section of Carmentis (1. 461–542) was written after the death of Augustus, and shaped specifically for the purpose of eulogizing Julia Augusta.

The story featuring Carmentis is divisible into two sections, the arrival of the Arcadian goddess into Rome (1. 461–502), and the goddess's prophecy of the Roman history of religion (1. 503–38). The first section deals essentially with the relationship between mother and son, and the predominance and authority of the mother in that relationship. Evander had illustrious ancestry on both sides, yet was the nobler for the blood of his sacred mother (1. 471–2); Evander wept at being exiled from his homeland, but it was the mother who taught him fortitude in the face of adversity (1. 479–98). It was at Carmentis' direction that Evander steered his boat up the Tiber to the future site of Rome (1. 499–500).

Ovid's account of the balance of this relationship is unusual by comparison with others. Virgil gives Carmentis minimal notice, but when he does it is Evander, 'rex' and 'Romanae conditor arcis' (*Aen*. 8. 313), who undoubtedly takes precedence over his mother, here not a goddess, but merely a nymph (8. 333–41). It is Evander's paternal heritage which is far more illustrious, as his

---

[60] Frazer (1929) ii. 205.   [61] Fantham (1985) 261.
[62] Bömer (1957–8) ii. 55.

sire is the god Mercury, his paternal grandmother Maia, and paternal great-grand-father Atlas (8. 138–40). The versions of Dionysius of Halicarnassus (1. 31. 1), Pausanias (8. 43. 2), and pseudo-Aurelius Victor (*Orig.* 5. 1), all agree with Virgil that Evander's father was a god, his mother only a nymph,[63] and he was thus far more illustrious through his paternal lineage.[64] In none of these accounts does the mother take precedence over the son. 'Ovid would seem to have followed some other tradition as to Evander's father,' observes Frazer (1929; ii. 189). Livy hints at the existence of another such tradition. He says that Evander was revered in his new country primarily for the supposed divinity of his mother Carmentis (1. 7. 8).

Ovid seems to have elaborated upon a version of the tale known to Livy to suit his design of highlighting the theme of maternal dynastic superiority which begins the first section on Carmentis. The dynastic allusion in this mother/son relationship is directly analogous with that of Livia and Tiberius. Tiberius was a Nero Claudian through his father, but a descendant of the far more illustrious Pulcher Claudians through his mother Livia.[65] To contemporaries familiar with the more orthodox version of Evander's ancestry, Ovid's rendering must have seemed not only unconventional, but blatantly reflective of the ancestral position of the present Princeps, Tiberius. That connection, made at the outset of Evander's entry, can be followed throughout the passage on Carmentis. Carmentis' authority over her son reflected in Ovid' portrayal of their relationship establishes her as the maternal head of the dynasty, individuals of which are enumerated in her prophetic list in the next section, beginning with her grandson, Pallas (1. 521). That section is completed with Julia Augusta, the maternal head of the present-day dynasty, and made directly comparable by Carmentis to herself in the climax of her promised deification.

Ovid's version of the myth of Carmentis would have little meaning if the passage that comes to a climax in Julia Augusta were not included. The dynastic allusions in the relationship between mother and son are thematically connected with the prophetic dynasty in the next, Julia Augusta culminating as the

---

[63] Bömer (1957–8) ii. 55.

[64] Ovid seems aware of a connection between Evander and Hermes in *F* 5. 100.

[65] Levick (1976a) 11–13.

latter-day Carmentis. Why Ovid should choose Carmentis is not
difficult to understand. In looking to the past to find an ancient
counterpart to the modern-day empress-mother, the nymph who
was mother of Evander, king of the Palatine, would have been the
most immediately suitable he could find. True, Aeneas had a
divine mother in Venus, but the poet would have had to wait
until April before he could have contrived any suitable similarities. And Romulus had no known relationship with Rhea
Silvia/Ilia. He had been nurtured by a wolf and brought up by a
peasant couple. Best of all, Carmentis occupied an important
place in the Roman religious calendar, providing Ovid with an
excellent opportunity to select and rework the myths relating to
her, enabling him to upgrade her status, lay new emphasis upon
the balance in the relationship between her and Evander, and so
produce an *aition* which he saw reflecting the present-day situation in the seat of power.

The portrayal of Carmentis and the medium of her prophecy at
the hands of Ovid indicate what the contemporary poet saw, or at
least expected, from the shifts in the balance of power which had
taken place since the death of Augustus. That Ovid wished to
evoke Julia Augusta with such a powerful image, especially in
relation to her son, is confirmed most strongly in the poet's next
entry of Livia in the *Fasti*. Why he wished to evoke such an
image is a major theme in my discussion of Livia's next appearance.

16 January

The second of the two entries portraying Livia in the *Fasti* from
exile is on 16 January, the anniversary of the dedication of the
temple of Augustan Concord in AD 10. The extant calendars celebrate the imperial NP day thus:[66]

Concordiae Au[g(ustae) aedis dedicat]a est P. Dolabella, C. Silano
co[(n)s(ulibus)]. Ti Caesar ex Pan[nonia reversus dedi]cavit. (*Praen.*)

The temple of Augustan Concord was dedicated in the consulship of
P. Dolabella and C. Silanus. Tiberius Caesar dedicated it when he
returned from Pannonia.

[66] Degrassi (1963) 398.

Fer(iae) [e]x s(enatus) c(onsulto), quod eo die aedis C[o]ncordiae in Foro
dedic(ata) est. (*Verul.*)

Holiday by decree of the Senate because on that day the temple of
Concord was dedicated in the Forum.

Ovid celebrates it as (1. 637–50):

> Candida, te niveo posuit lux proxima templo,
>   qua fert sublimes alta Moneta gradus,
> nunc bene prospiciens Latiam Concordia turbam,
>   nunc te sacratae constituere manus.
> Furius antiquam populi superator Etrusci,
>   voverat et voti solverat ille fidem.
> causa, quod a patribus sumptis secesserat armis
>   volgus, et ipsa suas Roma timebat opes.
> causa recens melior: passos Germania crines
>   porrigit auspiciis, dux venerande, tuis.
> inde triumphatae libasti munera gentis
>   templaque fecisti, quam colis ipse, deae.
> hanc tua constituit genetrix et rebus et ara,
>   sola toro magni digna reperta Iovis.

White goddess, the following day consecrated you in a snow-white temple where lofty Moneta raises her steps on high. Now, Concord, you
shall have a view of the multitude of Latium, now consecrated hands
have fixed your abode. Furius, conqueror of the Etruscan people, had
vowed the ancient temple and had fulfilled his vow. The reason was that
the populace, having taken up arms, had seceded from the senators, and
Rome itself feared its own strength. The recent cause is a better one:
Germany offers its dishevelled hair under your auspices, venerated commander. It is from that place that you made an offering from the tributes
of the conquered people and have built a temple to the goddess to whom
you yourself are devoted. Your mother constituted this goddess both in
reality and with an altar, she alone who was found worthy of the bed of
great Jove.

Ovid's description of Livia here as 'genetrix' of the 'dux venerandus' confirms that the passage was added after the death of
Augustus and the succession of her son, i.e. four years at least
after the dedication of the temple. Ovid would have known long
beforehand of its intended restoration, as it must have been con-
spicuously under scaffolding in the Forum for fifteen years by the
time he was exiled. It was vowed in the joint names of Tiberius
and his deceased brother Drusus just before the former's German

triumph in 7 BC (Dio, 55. 8. 2), but completion was delayed by the dynastic strife that brought about Tiberius' long exile in 6 BC.[67] Its final dedication seventeen years later must have been a triumph indeed for Tiberius. That dedication was symbolic not only of the Concord brought about by the 'causa recens' or victory he had won over the Germans in 7 BC which Ovid is advertising, ('recens' is valid when the contrast is with the deeds of the founder, Camillus), but also of the domestic Concord he could now offer as victor to his defeated political opponents of the long-drawn-out dynastic struggle which had raged over the last two decades, and which reached a crisis in AD 8.[68] That Ovid should make no reference to the new state of domestic Concord, a theme which he could have followed through from Camillus, is explicable if he regarded such mention as an admission of its conspicuous absence in the history of the imperial family since, in the public view at least, 6 BC.

The calendrical entry that Ovid has devoted to the temple of Concord may at first be seen as complimentary to the new Princeps. His lines address, praise, and so personalize the abstract divinity Concord (1. 637, 639), emphasize her importance as a deity to Tiberius and his devotion to her (1. 648), describe the strategic position of her temple (1. 638), and the purpose of the goddess installed in her lofty home (1. 639). They look to the Roman past, to the history and *aition* of the origin of the temple, then compare it by contrast with the *aition* of its present reconstruction (1. 641–8). In comparing and contrasting the *aitia* of the dedications of Camillus and Tiberius, Ovid is emphasizing the rule of Concord at home and abroad under Tiberius. That emphasis is an undoubted compliment to the new regime, which set great store by it.[69] We may note in passing that Ovid has not commemorated the achievement of Drusus, even though he had participated in the German wars, and though his name was on the dedicatory inscription of the temple.[70] Artistic priorities could be the answer, as the device of compare and contrast of past and pre-

[67] Levick (1978) 224.

[68] Levick (1978) 217 for the different kinds of Concord.

[69] For a discussion of the temple and its significance to Tiberius see Pekáry (1966–7) 105ff.; Levick (1972) 803ff.; (1976a) 62; Syme (1978) 29.

[70] Dio, 56. 25. 1. Suet. *Tib.* 20 misdates the dedication to AD 12. See Syme (1978) 29.

sent would be rendered more difficult with an imbalance of one hero to two.

Not only Concord but also the person of the Princeps himself is accorded distinctive treatment by Ovid. Tiberius is not named, but is introduced into the passage as the dedicator of the temple with 'sacratae manus'. The epithet not only provides a tone of reverence to the verse, but is also suggestive of a religious or divine aspect of the ruler's role or nature. Not many lines before this, Ovid had declared: 'sancta vocant augusta patres, augusta vocantur / templa sacerdotum rite dicata manu' (1. 609–10). Tiberius was now Pontifex Maximus (although he was not at the time of the dedication itself), his hands which had dedicated the temple were those of a priest, the temple of Concord is therefore 'augusta'. Ovid then addresses him six lines below as 'dux venerande', thus paying homage to his supreme position in the empire (cf. 1. 613 where 'dux' was used to address Augustus), the epithet sustaining the reverend, dignified and formal tone and acknowledgement of the sacred aspect of that role.[71]

Yet the most startling feature in Ovid's celebration of Tiberius' temple of Concord is the inclusion of Livia in the final couplet. In just two lines he pays homage to her as the 'genetrix' of Tiberius, as the constitutor of the goddess Concord both in reality and by an altar she dedicated,[72] and last but not least by identifying her

---

[71] For the meanings associated with 'dux' at this time, see Bömer (1957–8) ii. 72 and Fantham (1985) n. 60.

[72] In interpreting Livia as 'constitutor of the goddess Concord' I have had to choose between two readings of the text, 'haec' or 'hanc' at 1. 649. Editors are divided in their preference. Merkel (1841), Bömer (1957–8), Le Bonniec (1965), and Pighi (1973) opt for 'haec' (from AU), which refers to 'templa' in the previous line, and means that Livia established the temple of Concord in the Roman Forum by providing it with an 'ara' and 'rebus'. Peter (1907), Frazer (1929), and Alton et al. (1988) opt for 'hanc' (from GM), which refers to 'deae' in the previous line, and means that Livia constituted the goddess Concord by an 'ara' and 'rebus' (translated as 'by her life' by Frazer).

Unfortunately the reading affects the sense considerably, and one must make a selection. I have accepted 'hanc', mainly on the grounds that I feel obliged to reject 'haec', and any alleged connection Livia might have had with the temple of Concord in the Forum at that time, i.e. 7 BC, for the following reason. Levick's very acute study of the history and the ideological associations of the temple of Concord, and the political leanings of Tiberius, make an association of Livia, or any woman, with the temple politically incongruous and unfeasible. For example, she explains the significance of Tiberius' dedication in 7 BC: 'He took upon himself the duty of restoring, in his own name and in that of his brother, the temple of

as Juno, the consort of the now deified Augustus whom Ovid
conjoins with Jove. What is an accolade to Livia doing at the
climax of a verse celebrating the dedication of Tiberius' temple of
Concord in AD 10? Her name was not included in the dedication,
and in 7 BC, when Tiberius decided that the temple should be
restored, any connection with Livia was politically quite unfeasible (see n. 72). We have seen that she had built an altar to
Concord in the Porticus Liviae as a public testimonial to her harmonious married life, celebrated by Ovid on 11 June (6. 637) Why
is he then paying homage to Livia and her altar again here, where
they do not belong?

   An examination of the several facets in the image Ovid accords
Livia here may provide an answer. For the first time in the *Fasti*
Livia is given recognition of her role as parent, a role Ovid had
carefully avoided in his celebration of her altar on 11 June.
Furthermore, he is now saying that the mother has been exem-
plary in demonstrating her devotion to Concord, selecting as a

Concord. An innocuous act, if the temple had not had such controversial associations, so clear a connexion with the more conservative type of politician. The
claim was that the temple had been founded by that godsend to optimate pam-
phleteers, M. Furius Camillus . . . and it had been restored once before, in 121 by
the reactionary consul Opimius . . . In making his first act as consul an offer to
restore it, Tiberius was taking on the mantle of Camillus and Opimius . . . he was
announcing that he wished to be known as the champion of strong senatorial government' (Levick (1972) 803–4).

   I find the idea of Livia constituting a monument to 'strong senatorial government' both contrary to her own interests as wife of the ruler (Concord was not an
Augustan virtue: Wissowa (1912) 113 n. 4; Fears (1981*b*) 827–948), and contrary to
the interests of Tiberius, who categorically abhorred the idea of women in politics. For this reason, also, I am not tempted by the possibility that Dio's reference
(55. 8. 1) to the precinct (temenisma) of Livia, dedicated by Tiberius and Livia in
the early days of January 7 BC, could mean that they were in fact dedicating the
precinct of the temple of Concord, a view put forward by C. J. Simpson (1991).
Dio after all separates Tiberius' vow to restore the temple, and his dedication with
Livia, by the celebration of a triumph. Their joint dedication of the Porticus
Liviae on the Esquiline, on the other hand, symbolized harmony within the imperial family at a time when it threatened to collapse with Julia's alienation from
Tiberius (see previous section), and so was in the interests of both mother and son
who were utterly dependent on their familial ties with Augustus for power and
status. Furthermore, Ovid's Livia in the passage under discussion is definitely
associated with Concord as a concept of marital harmony, which harks back to his
depiction of her in the Porticus Liviae (11 June) passage. On this I am in agreement with Flory (1984) 324. Why Ovid has included Livia and her special association with familial Concord to the entry for 16 Jan. is discussed below.

particular example the altar she dedicated. That 'ara' is unlikely
to be any other than that he has already celebrated in the *Fasti*
under 11 June. Having already included it in his work under that
date, he had no further need to explain it. In the final line he then
celebrates her role as consort, a role familiar from earlier portrayals of Livia in the poem. Ovid's tribute to the more rounded ideological female image of both wife and mother he now accords
Livia, associated as it is specifically with both Tiberius and her
altar to Concord, makes it difficult not to suspect that the poet is
covering his tracks for his inhibited rendering of her altar and
Porticus on 11 June. Ovid's incorporation of Livia and her association with Concord into a passage which should belong to
Tiberius (and Drusus) alone achieves the effect of creating a concord of partnership in power and ideological unity between the
two on an occasion which had some validity after the death of
Augustus (see below), but which in 7 BC had no historical foundation. It is as if the poet is self-consciously trying to compensate
for having misrepresented the concord of dynastic unity symbolized in the dedication of the structure on the Esquiline in 7 BC.[73]

That is not all: the language Ovid has chosen to describe
Livia's role elevates her image to another plane. He has selected
words and phrases to associate her with one, and identify her as
another, important Roman deity. 'Genetrix' is instantly recogniz-
able as the epithet of Venus, ancestress of the Julian *gens*; as one
worthy to share the bed of Jupiter, Livia is identified as Juno.[74]
Livia's role as mother and wife is being magnified to a superhu-
man level; in effect, she is elevated from human to divine status
and honoured as a goddess, a sharp contrast indeed with her thoroughly human image in the pre-exilic version of the *Fasti*.

As Livia was not officially deified by the state until AD 41 the
elevated language describing her here, which contrasts so vividly
with her earlier images in the *Fasti*, requires explanation. Ovid's
new degraded status as a suppliant and his elevation of Augustus,
Livia, and Tiberius to divine status from that standpoint have
already been briefly demonstrated in his poems from exile. It is
noteworthy that in one poem Ovid actually singles out Livia

---

[73] Levick (1978) for a description of concord of partners in power. Ovid's technique of incorporating Livia into a day where she did not belong finds a parallel in
his treatment of Germanicus. See Ch. 5.

[74] Scott (1930) 65.

alone and accords her a role as mediatrix for suppliants within the framework of her role as consort to Augustus. From his place of banishment he begs his wife to plead with Livia on his behalf (*Ex P.* 3. 1. 114–18).[75] The language he uses and divine associations the poet employs with regard to Livia in that role are revealing in their stunning similarity with that used in the passage of the *Fasti* under discussion:

> Caesaris est coniunx ore precanda tuo,
>   quae praestat virtute sua, ne prisca vetustas
>   laude pudicitiae saecula nostra premat:
> quae Veneris formam, mores Iunonis habendo
>   sola est caelesti digna reperta toro

The spouse of Caesar must be supplicated with your own lips; she who by her virtue ensures that venerable antiquity shall not surpass our age in praise of chastity; she who, having the beauty of Venus and the conduct of Juno, alone has been found worthy to share a heavenly couch.

The similarity of language between Ovid's petition through his wife to Livia and that at the end of the passage in the *Fasti* suggests that the poet has superimposed yet another image of Livia— that in her role as benefactress for suppliants. That role which he had acknowledged before the death of Augustus is after all unlikely to have changed with the new regime in the absence of a consort for Tiberius. The adopted persona of the poet of the *Fasti* in Rome has given way to the persona of the suppliant poet of the exile poems from Tomis.

A brief aside must anticipate an obvious question that springs to mind at this point: why is the suppliant appealing to Livia in this passage when it provided such an excellent opportunity to appeal to Tiberius himself? The answer must be that Ovid was aware that Tiberius would never, in any circumstances, respond to the exile's pleas. This seems an important factor also which prompted the poet's inclusion of his 'post-exilic Livia' when he saw an opportunity, as he knew he would have been wasting his time in appealing to Tiberius.[76]

---

[75] Perhaps belonging to the year AD 13. Syme (1978) 148.

[76] This view receives support in the fact that Ovid rededicated the *Fasti* to Germanicus, not Tiberius (see Ch. 5). I am of the opinion that it was Tiberius who was responsible for having Ovid exiled in the first place, but the reasons behind that opinion lie beyond the scope of this monograph.

Meanwhile, Ovid's image of Livia on 16 January is still not fully accounted for. From exile Ovid had accorded Tiberius divine status along with Augustus and Livia (*Ex P.* 2. 8. 1–10, 37–8). But in his celebration of Tiberius' temple, the language selected by the poet not only accords the 'dux venerandus' an inferior status to the divine rank of his mother, but also uses Livia's divine image to bring to its climax a passage ostensibly in honour of Tiberius. The overall effect is that the mother is now a political partner in power—and more. She is the dominant partner in the Concord of partnership evoked in the verse.

One interpretation of Ovid's order of rank between Livia and Tiberius here could be that, from his lowly status and far-flung location in the outskirts of the empire, he had lost all sense of reality of the balance of power in the capital. But the possibility also exists that he had good reason for believing that, after the death of Augustus, Livia did enjoy an extraordinary elevation in rank in relation to Tiberius. The will of Augustus stipulated that Livia be admitted to the Julian family with the name of Augusta. Tiberius, already adopted by Augustus in AD 4, was also to receive the title of Augustus in the terms of the will (Suet. *Aug.* 101. 2) but he refused to use it (Dio, 57. 2. 1).[77] Exactly what Augustus meant to achieve by giving Livia the name Julia Augusta can be assessed only from the various reactions to her in her new identity.

The Senate's reaction was to vote her extraordinary honours. It was voted that an altar be erected to commemorate her adoption; some senators voted that she receive the title 'parens', others that of 'mater patriae'. The majority proposed that the epithet 'filius Iuliae' be added to Tiberius' name (Tac. *Ann.* 1. 14; Dio, 57. 12. 4). There can be little doubt from the parental nature of these honours that the Senate understood Augustus' testamentary adoption of Livia to signify that she was to fulfil a public parental role in the state as 'genetrix gentis Iuliae' and so head the dynastic nexus.[78] Tiberius was voted no equivalent honours to accord

[77] Although he did employ the title in letters to kings and princes of eastern states in which it was his policy to encourage the imperial cult. For sources see Grether (1946) 233.

[78] Weinrib (1967) 259ff. on Livia's adoption shows how choice of filiation was still available after a testamentary adoption, which accounts for the fact that she was sometimes styled as 'filia Drusi', sometimes 'filia Augusti' in inscriptions.

him equal familial status, even though he had inherited the title Augustus. The Senate's honours to Livia, then, assign her a kind of 'queen mother' status in relation to her son, a higher rank of inheritance (as opposed to merit) than that which she had enjoyed in her relationship with her son before his elevation to the Principate.

The precedence Livia enjoys over Tiberius in Ovid's passage reflects the honours proposed by the Senate. His portrayal of Livia in this way surely indicates that he was attuned to the implications of Augustus' will and the reactions of the Senate towards it. He must also have been attuned to Livia's response. She seems to have understood her adoption as meaning that she should share rule equally with her son, indeed take precedence over him (Tac. *Ann.* 4. 57; Suet. *Tib.* 51. 2; Dio, 57. 12. 3–4). She would have been happy with Ovid's portraying her dynastic rank as superior to that of her son.

But the exile was not attuned to the reaction of Tiberius. The new ruler promptly vetoed all honours for his mother, regarding, as Tacitus puts it, a woman's elevation as a slight to himself (Tac. *Ann.* 1. 14; Dio, 57. 12). It is unlikely that the new ruler of Rome could find in a woman's elevation a slight to himself unless it threatened to diminish his own *auctoritas*. While it is true that Tiberius generally had strong contempt for honours (Tac. *Ann.* b. 37), his veto of his mother's honours from Romans is suggestive of the degree to which he felt inhibited by the *potentia* attached to the new rank assigned Livia by Augustus' will. Augustus' adopted son was clearly embarrassed by the fact that the honours resulting from his mother's 'adoption' were designed as a buttress to strengthen his own elegibility to follow in his father's footsteps.

Ovid was not the only one unattuned to Tiberius' attitude towards Livia's new status as 'genetrix'. Several of the western provinces styled her 'Augusta, mater patriae' and 'genetrix Orbis' on coins and inscriptions.[79] But whereas Tiberius could tolerate honours both for Livia and for himself from the provincials[80] it is

[79] Grether (1946) 234 n. 67.

[80] In a letter to the people of Gytheum in Laconia, Tiberius politely indicated that he was quite happy with honours of a more human sort, but said he would allow Livia to decide for herself whether to accept honours fit for gods. See Ehrenberg *N* Jones (1976) n. 102(*b*); also Grether (1946) 240.

most improbable that he would have found Ovid's elevation of Livia over himself in a versification of the Roman calendar acceptable. Ovid's prediction of Julia Augusta's deification was fulfilled, but not until the reign of Claudius. Tiberius vetoed it at the time of Livia's death (Tac. *Ann*. 5. 2; Suet. *Tib*. 51. 2; Dio, 58. 2). The poet's assignation to her of the title 'genetrix tua' in relation to Tiberius would have been a painful reminder of the Senate's abortive attempt to create for him the title 'filius Iuliae'.

The exile's friends in Rome evidently did not keep him informed about the sensitive attitude of the new Princeps towards Livia in her new rank as Augusta. Ovid's portrayal of Livia in the *Fasti* from exile would have pleased the powerful mediatrix for suppliants (who, despite Tiberius' veto of her honours, nevertheless enjoyed exceptional power[81]), but for that very reason would have offended the male potentate. Ovid was on the wrong track. He had misjudged the mood of the new regime.

The study of Ovid's first two portrayals of Livia in the *Fasti* has shown that the poet must have been under some constraint to incorporate her in the first place. That constraint is most likely to have come from a desire to please Augustus, who had reason to use her image for the purpose both of cleaning up the discredited cult of the Bona Dea, and of exercising control through the patronage of the 'femina princeps' of the major female cults in Rome.

Ovid's pre-exilic portrayal of Livia in connection with the Bona Dea may be deemed successful in reflecting the reinstated respectability of the temple cult. Yet the portrayal of her on 11 June reflects the dilemma of a contemporary poet witnessing the uncertainties of the dynastic struggles and frequent shifts in power which plagued the last two decades of the Principate of Augustus. Had Ovid not felt required to incorporate Livia in his poem, that dilemma would not have existed. Livia was both wife of Augustus and mother of Tiberius, but had the author portrayed her in this dual role, he risked upsetting Tiberius' opponents and possibly the future holders of power. The image of Livia, therefore, is incomplete. she is the wife of Augustus and presented in a manner that does honour only to him. But for this

[81] Grether (1946) 235.

reason Ovid has difficulty in incorporating Livia into the female cults which celebrated and sanctified the paramount roles of the Roman *matrona*, marriage and motherhood. It is for this reason also that the poet encountered problems in making the ideological connection between the female cults founded by Servius Tullius in the Forum Boarium, and Livia's altar to Concord and the Porticus Liviae, a structure built by Augustus which the dual dedications of Livia and Tiberius tell us must have symbolized selective dynastic cohesion.

Ovid's post-exilic Livia is unsuccessful for different reasons. The dilemma which inhibited him from representing her in her full ideological role as wife and mother has now been removed by the resolution of the long-running dynastic struggle and the emergence of Tiberius as sole heir. But his own exile in AD 8 induces in him not only a reaction of certainty as to who was now to succeed Augustus and a suppliant's perceptions of the new status of Livia and Tiberius, but also makes him sensitive to the deficiency in his first image of Livia. He tries to compensate by revising the *Fasti*, with unfortunate results. He demonstrates a contemporary perception of what Augustus intended in adopting Livia by reflecting her new rank as 'genetrix' and head of the dynastic nexus, also perceived by the Senate and by Livia herself. But the outcast misreads the new incumbent's reaction to it. He exacerbates his error of ranking Livia over her son by according her divine honours, honours which he had been used to according her as a suppliant in his petitions from exile. Perhaps his most fatal error was to incorporate Livia into a day sacred to Tiberius alone—the dedication of his temple to Concord. It is the only entry of Livia in the *Fasti* where she is not associated with a female cult. It is Ovid's last portrait of Livia in the *Fasti*.

5

GERMANICUS

AFTER the death of Augustus in AD 14, Ovid rededicated the *Fasti* and revised sections within it to incorporate the new dedicatee. That rededication was not, as might be expected, to the successor of Augustus, the new Princeps and Pontifex Maximus, but to Germanicus Caesar, nephew and adopted son of the new ruler. Yet Ovid's reworking of the poem to honour his new dedicatee did not last long. Except for a brief outburst in the proem to book 4 (79–82), nothing beyond book 1 reveals any revisions to incorporate Germanicus. Even in book 1, the passages honouring him are few.

The present chapter is devoted to a study of Germanicus in relation to Ovid's poem. Not only are the passages honouring him to be examined; the question of why Ovid overlooked Tiberius in favour of his youthful heir, when recall from exile was uppermost in his mind, must be considered. So too must the question of why the poet abandoned his revision of the *Fasti* in favour of its new dedicatee so soon. We begin with the most pressing problem first.

Why Germanicus?

The new proem to the *Fasti* reads thus (1. 1–26):

> Tempora cum causis Latium digesta per annum
>   lapsaque sub terras ortaque signa canam.
> excipe pacato, Caesar Germanice, voltu
>   hoc opus et timidae derige navis iter,
> officioque, levem non aversatus honorem,   5
>   en tibi devoto numine dexter ades.
> sacra recognosces annalibus eruta priscis
>   et quo sit merito quaeque notata dies.
> invenies illic et festa domestica vobis;
>   saepe tibi pater est, saepe legendus avus,   10

quaeque ferunt illi, pictos signantia fastos,
　　tu quoque cum Druso praemia fratre feres.
Caesaris arma canant alii: nos Caesaris aras
　　et quoscumque sacris addidit ille dies.
adnue conanti per laudes ire tuorum   15
　　deque meo pavidos excute corde metus.
da mihi te placidum, dederis in carmina vires:
　　ingenium voltu statque caditque tuo.
pagina iudicium docti subitura movetur
　　principis, ut Clario missa legenda deo.   20
quae sit enim culti facundia sensimus oris,
　　civica pro trepidis cum tulit arma reis.
scimus et, ad nostras cum se tulit impetus artes,
　　ingenii currant flumina quanta tui.
si licet et fas est, vates rege vatis habenas,   25
　　auspice te felix totus ut annus eat.

The seasons distributed throughout the Latin year, their causes, and the
constellations which set beneath the earth and rise, I shall celebrate.
Caesar Germanicus, welcome this work with a tranquil countenance and
guide the voyage of my timorous craft. Do not turn from a trifling honour but come, lend a god-like presence to this service here offered you.
You will recognize the sacred rites extracted from ancient chronicles,
and by what distinction each day is known. There too, you will discover
the festivals of your own family; often must your father and your grandfather be read about; the honours which they bear and which decorate
the red-lettered calendar, you too shall carry off with your brother
Drusus. Let others celebrate the wars of Caesar; we shall celebrate the
altars of Caesar and the days he has added to the sacred register. Grant
your approval as I attempt to enumerate the glories of your family, and
dispel the frightful anxiety in my heart. Show yourself gentle with me;
then you will have given me strength for my verse, for according to your
mien, my genius stands or falls. My page, about to be submitted to the
judgement of a learned prince, is awestruck, as though sent to the
Clarian god to read. For we have experienced the command of language
in your polished speech when it bore civic arms in defence of the trem-
bling accused. And we know too, when inspiration has moved you to
poetry, how powerfully the stream of your genius flows. If it is permissible by law, human and divine, guide as a poet the reins of a poet, so that
under your auspices the whole year may proceed with favour.

The first section of the proem is addressed to Germanicus as heir
to the house of Caesar (1. 3–14), the second to the orator and poet
(1. 15–26). The sections of equal length make the dual role equally

important, although it is upon Germanicus' identity as a poet
which receives the final and heavier emphasis. It is no longer
from his Muse but from Germanicus the poet, elevated to semi-
divine status, that Ovid now seeks inspiration and a favourable
verdict on his efforts. It is under the auspices of Germanicus the
poet that the year shall run favourably in its entire course.

In the new proem to the *Fasti* Ovid gives the impression that it
was the young Caesar's literary expertise that caused him to
replace Augustus with Germanicus as its dedicatee. This is not the
entire picture, however. In an epistle written to Suillius after the
death of Augustus, Ovid addresses a direct appeal to Germanicus,
entreating him to recall him from exile (*Ex P*. 4. 8. 31–6)

> nec tibi de Pario statuam, Germanice, templum
>   marmore: carpsit opes illa ruina meas.
> templa domus facient vobis urbesque beatae.
>   Naso suis opibus, carmine gratus erit.
> parva quidem fateor pro magnis munera reddi,
>   cum pro concessa verba salute damus.

I will not build a temple of Parian marble to you, Germanicus. That catastrophe has consumed my material means. Your own household and
prosperous cities will build temples for you. Naso will express gratitude
with poetry, which is his wealth. I acknowledge indeed that small service
is returned for large when I give words in return for the granting of my
deliverance.

In return for the favour he will devote all that was left of his poetic
genius to assure him the lasting fame required by gods (including
Augustus) and heroes alike that only poetry could bestow. Ovid
promises to serve Germanicus in the only way he knows how.
Germanicus, himself a poet, would have been the supreme glory of
the Muses had not his station called him to greater things, so
would not despise the tribute of a poet. He was thus in the best
position to appreciate the value of his offer (*Ex P*. 4. 8. 65–8):

> siquid adhuc igitur vivi, Germanice, nostro
>   restat in ingenio, serviet omne tibi.
> non potes officium vatis contemnere vates:
>   iudicio pretium res habet ista tuo.

If, then, there is still life left in my genius, Germanicus, it will all be at
your service. You cannot as a poet disregard the homage of a poet. By
your own conviction that pursuit has its reward.

Ovid could not be more explicit about his reasons for dedicating his work to Germanicus. The proem of book 1 of the *Fasti* demonstrates how he is now keeping his side of the bargain. It is natural that he does not request assistance for a mitigation of his sentence here, as it would be a violation of genre for the proem of a major work to request anything other than in the undertaking of the poem.[1] But the question is: was Tiberius' heir, as a poet, really in a better position than the Princeps himself to appreciate the value of Ovid's tribute?

That Germanicus had some literary talent is not in dispute. That the calibre of his talent was significant enough to merit him a eulogy as a master of verse from Ovid, however, is questionable. As an orator he was postumously voted honours by the Senate, a tribute considered exaggerated by Tiberius (Tac. *Ann.* 2. 83. 3), but Suetonius says that his powers in that sphere were considerable (*Cal.* 3. 1). Among the fruits of his literary studies the biographer singles out comedies in Greek (Suet. *Gaius*, 3. 2; cf. *Claud.* 11. 3). Pliny mentions a poem on the funeral mound for a horse ('fecit et divus Augustus equo tumulum, de quo Germanici Caesaris carmen est', *NH* 8. 155).

Yet there is nothing in the ancient evidence (apart from Ovid) to indicate true poetic merit. The only extant evidence of his poetic activity survives in a work of some 857 lines of a free translation into Latin hexameters of an astronomical poem by Aratus entitled *Phaenomena*, which describes the northern and southern fixed stars, the circles of the celestial sphere, and the risings and settings of the stars. The *Prognostica*, dealing in weather signs, are also an integral part of the poem. Yet the possibility exists that Germanicus was not even the author of this work. D. B. Gain has presented a very good case to show that it may well have been written by Tiberius. Gain concludes that the evidence does not allow one to say whether the author was Tiberius or Germanicus.[2]

---

[1] Fantham (1985) 253 also demonstrates the great similarity in theme and language between the elegy to Suillius and the proem of the *Fasti* to Germanicus, both of which pay homage to poetry and emphasize Germanicus as critic and poet.

[2] Gain (1976) 17, 20. The Budé edition of Germanicus' *Phaenomena* (Le Bœuffle, 1975) does not question the authorship of the work at all. See its introduction.

Even if Germanicus did translate the *Phaenomena* of Aratus he was by no means original in performing such a task. Aratus' poem had also been translated by P. Terentius Varro Atacinus (b. 82 BC) and by Cicero as a young man. Ovid himself translated the *Phaenomena* (Lact. 2. 5. 24). The appeal of such an exercise evidently did not wane with time. Jerome (*In Tit.* 1. 12) mentions the very many translations of it. As late as the fourth century we find Rufus Festus Avienus putting the *Phaenomena* into Latin.[3] The great popularity of the work among the Romans (Cic. *Or.* 1. 69) suggests that translating the poem into Latin may have been a common exercise for talented and untalented alike. If this is so it might explain the absence of any ancient mention of Germanicus' translation (if indeed he did it), as part of his literary achievement.

Yet it is Germanicus' putative translation of Aratus which has engaged the attention of scholars today with regard to Ovid's interest in the young Caesar as a poet. Despite the fact that the work contains serious obstacles to an Augustan dating (such as lines 558–60 which report Augustus' apotheosis), some are still ready to believe that the exiled Ovid not only knew it, but that this was the work that prompted him to rededicate the *Fasti* to its author. They have thus taken Ovid's pretext for his choice of second dedicatee at face value.[4]

But if it were merely literary gifts that Ovid was looking for in the house of Caesar, why not Tiberius? He was known to have talent significant enough to attract praise from Augustus as a warrior of the Muses (Suet. *Tib.* 21. 4). He wrote verse in both Latin and Greek, particularly favouring the learned works of the Alexandrian 'epigoni' poets as models. His passion for the latter was renowned enough for many learned men to vie with one another in issuing commentaries on their works and dedicating them to him (Suet. *Tib.* 60). Furthermore, as patron and dedicatee Tiberius also received Manilius' *Astronomica*. This last dedication clearly suited Tiberius' preoccupation with astrology (Tac. *Ann.* 6. 20. 3; Suet. *Tib.* 14. 4), as well as with poetry.[5] Moreover,

---

[3] See Ogilvie (1978) 13 for a survey of the ancient translations of the *Phaenomena* of Aratus.

[4] So Fantham (1985) 256; Syme (1978) 46; Bömer (1957–8) i. 17.

[5] Levick (1976a) 229 f.; Syme (1986) 350.

Tiberius apparently indulged in writing bawdy verse (Pliny, *Ep*. 5. 3) and was also passionately fond of mythology (Suet. *Tib* 70).

Ovid's poem, a combination of Alexandrian aetiological genre, of sequential rising and setting of constellations ('lapsaque sub terras ortaque signa'), stories of their origin in myth, of encomia in praise of astronomers for their heavenly aspirations and services to men (1. 297–310; 3. 105–14) and of bawdy tales from Greek and Roman mythology, could have had a very strong claim to appeal to Tiberius' literary tastes. Indeed, from what we know of the literary talents and tastes of the two, Tiberius would seem to have a far stronger claim than Germanicus to appreciate the value of the *Fasti* as a tribute and so be a suitable dedicatee of the poem. There is in fact a suggestion that he did appreciate Ovid's literary talent. Velleius puts Ovid on the select list of poets ranked highest in the Tiberian Principate, a list which excludes Horace 92. 36. 3).[6]

The comparison between the literary talents and tastes of Tiberius and Germanicus serves to render Ovid's given reason for his choice of Germanicus as patron unconvincing. Calendrical considerations also obtrude. Germanicus was honoured in some calendars with two anniversaries, his birthday on 24 May and his triumph of 26 May AD 17, but there is no evidence that Ovid knew of them.[7] Indeed, the dedicatory prooemium to Germanicus indicates that Ovid did not expect to find calendrical honours to the young Caesar at this stage in his career (1. 9–12, 15–16). All entries with which he honours Tiberius' heir - 1 January, 13 January, and a single sporadic allusion in the introduction to book 4 (lines 81–4) are days and months which have no known association with Germanicus. It appears that Ovid is artificially incorporating his new patron into the Roman calendrical year because he knows of no specific personal connection the young Caesar had with it at

---

[6] Although if Horace was excluded from that list by Tiberius himself, perhaps it was not Tiberius' literary taste that influenced that exclusion so much as the fact that the poet had immortalized the name of Marcus Lollius (*Od*. 4. 9). Tiberius had suffered appalling indignity at the hands of Lollius and he savagely attacked his memory as late as twenty years after Lollius' death (Tac. *Ann* 3. 48).

[7] His birthday was recorded in the *Feriale Cumanum* and later in the *Acta Arvalium* of AD 38 (*CIL* vi. 2028), and later again in the 3rd-cent. *Feriale Duranum* (Degrassi (1963) 461). His triumph was recorded by the *Fasti Amiternini* and the *Fasti Ostiensis* (Degrassi (1963) 462).

the time he was rewriting the *Fasti*. Our study of the passages honouring Germanicus will subsequently support this notion.

Yet the poet would have been spared the efforts of such contrivance had he selected Tiberius as patron. As the new Pontifex Maximus, Tiberius was head of the priestly college in charge of the Roman calendar and as such a natural dedicatee for a poem setting it to verse. As the new Princeps and heir of Augustus, certain days of the calendar would now be celebrated to honour his anniversaries. Above all it was Tiberius alone who had the authority to recall Ovid. Germanicus could only intercede on the exile's behalf. Not only is Ovid's reason for choosing Germanicus instead of Tiberius as patron a literary fiction; he also made his task of revising the *Fasti* far more difficult in bypassing the Princeps in favour of his heir. Ovid's choice of Germanicus therefore suggests that strained relations existed between himself and Tiberius. An attempt at seeking the real reason for his choice of new patron must be made. The exile poems help to shed some light on the matter.

Ovid's first published tribute to Germanicus appears in *Ex P.* 2. 1, dated to AD 13.[8] In an earlier poem he had already referred to Germanicus as one of the youths growing up under Caesar's name to give that 'domus' eternal sway over the world (*T* 4. 2. 9–10), but the individual himself is neither named nor singled out for special mention in the poem honouring Tiberius' anticipated Pannonian triumph in AD 12. Only in *Ex P.* 2. 1 celebrating the same triumph after its actual occurrence is Germanicus hailed by name and accorded individual tribute by Ovid. The first forty-eight lines celebrate the splendour which 'fama' had reported to Ovid of the joyous occasion of Tiberius' triumph. It comes as something of a surprise to find the entire second half of the poem turning to an invocation of Germanicus, who Ovid had heard had participated in the triumph of his father (*Ex P.* 2. 1. 49–68). The exile prophesies for him a glorious destiny as conqueror and triumphator, and promises to celebrate that destiny in verse should his miserable circumstances in exile permit.

Amidst all the honours he is predicting for Germanicus, Ovid is careful to stress the young Caesar's junior status in contrast with that of Tiberius, who in turn has paid respect to the *iustitia*

---

[8] Frazer (1929) ii. 130; Syme (1978) 88.

of his own father (i.e. Augustus (*Ex P.* 2. 1. 33)). Germanicus is the son of the present triumphator who will rejoice in the future achievements of his son with the same delight he now feels at his own. Germanicus' honours are still clearly in the future; at present he is the greatest of youth in war and peace ('iuvenum belloque togaque maxime' (*Ex P.* 2. 1. 61–2)). Thus we find that Ovid has selected the young Caesar as potential patron even before he had achieved a military triumph in his own right, even before Tiberius had assumed sole power, and while Augustus still ruled the empire. What, then, was so significant about Germanicus' participation in Tiberius' triumph on 23 October AD 12[9] that decided Ovid to elevate him to the status of patron who had it within his power to achieve his recall from exile?

The year AD 12 was of no small significance to Germanicus. His political career had begun in AD 7, the same year Agrippa was banished by Augustus (Dio, 55. 31–32. 2). Dio reports that although he was holding the office of quaestor at the time, Germanicus was dispatched with reinforcements to Tiberius in Dalmatia in place of Agrippa who was banished to an island by Augustus.[10] His rapid advancement thus seems to have been a result of the misfortune of the third and last son of Julia and brother of his wife, Agrippina. The following four years were spent on campaign. In the meantime another child of Julia I, Julia II, was banished in AD 8, as was Ovid himself. Ovid's early letters from exile, datable to AD 9, make clear (in conspicuous contrast to the *Fasti* thus far written), that Tiberius was now unquestionably Augustus' political heir (*T.* 2. 165). Germanicus finally returned to Rome in time for the beginning of AD 12, when he assumed the consulship for the first time and held it throughout the year. It was in this year that the Roman public became properly acquainted with the young Caesar whose only previous public appearance in the city seems to have been at the gladiatorial games he held with his brother in honour of Drusus in AD 7.[11]

Germanicus had been absent from the city for virtually the

[9] The day is recorded by the *Fasti Praenestini* (Degrassi 1963) 135; for the year, see Sumner (1968) 274 n. 107.

[10] There is nothing strange in men of quaestorian rank commanding legionaries, even whole legions, especially if those men were members of the imperial house. See Levick (1976*b*) 317. Also Tac. *Ann.* 2. 36.

[11] Levick (1976*b*) 330–1; Dio, 55. 27. 1.

whole of his career thus far. In AD 12 he had the chance to compensate. He kept a very high profile by being extremely active in
the courts, impressing many with his great eloquence and attain-
ing immense popularity for himself with the people (Tac. *Ann.* 1.
7. 9; Suet. *Cal.* 3. 2; Dio, 56. 26. 1). Then in October he took part
in his adoptive father's triumph, he himself receiving the triumphal insignia for his contributions to the northern campaigns.
Tiberius' triumph, indeed, was the first public testimony after
the alleged dynastic coup of AD 8 to the people of Rome of
Germanicus' place in the dynastic pecking order. It was also a
public manifestation of the approval he received from both
Tiberius and Augustus. (Augustus had written a letter commending Germanicus to the Senate in the same year: Dio, 56. 26. 2.) It
is this pecking order which is reflected in Ovid's first poem paying tribute to Germanicus discussed above, in which the details
of that triumph were reported to him (*Ex P.* 2. 1. 49). It appears
that it was the triumph of AD 12 which first brought Germanicus
to the notice of Ovid as a promising patron.

Germanicus' high profile as heir to Augustus and Tiberius is
not the whole story, however. He had another advantage no less
significant to Ovid, and that not only his 'benevolentia singularis'
(Suet. *Cal.* 3.) and his 'clementia' (Tac. *Ann.* 2. 73).[12] Augustus,
in AD 12, was 74 years old. The aged ruler could die at any time.
Ovid had to have a secure back-up, someone with the appropriate
influence to whom he could appeal not only for as long as
Augustus survived, but also at the accession of his heir. On the
evidence of the fact that the poet did not rededicate the *Fasti* to
Tiberius, and the fact that he never appeals to him directly as an
individual in his exile poetry (only when his name is subsumed
into the imperial *domus*), it is clear that Ovid entertained no hope
that Tiberius would respond to his pleas. But it can be shown
that Ovid possibly had reason to believe that both Augustus and
Tiberius would listen to Germanicus.

First, there were family connections: blood and marital ties
placed Germanicus in a unique position to influence all branches
of the family of Augustus, even opposing dynastic factions. On
the one side he was the grandson of Livia and the son of Nero

---

[12] Frazer (1929) ii. 3 believes Ovid's choice of patron in Germanicus was that
his 'well-known clemency and humanity gave Ovid some ground for hope'. I
would not dispute this, but it is not the whole story.

Drusus, deceased brother of Tiberius who was devoted to his memory. The dedication of the temple of Concord in January AD 10 in their joint names was the most recent manifestation of this. Germanicus' sister Livia Julia was married to Tiberius' son and his own brother by adoption, Drusus Caesar, with whom he was on excellent terms (Tac. *Ann.* 2. 43. 6, 53. 1; Dio, 57. 18. 7). On the other side he was the grandson of Octavia and great-nephew of Augustus, and was therefore the only adult male descendant of the Princeps' own blood still in favour (Claudius was deemed unfit for public office). The advantage of blood relationship with Augustus was augmented by the fact that he was married to the only female descendant and now closest blood relative of the Princeps still in favour: Agrippina, daughter of Julia I and grand-daughter of Scribonia. Germanicus was the father of the direct descendants of the two wives of Augustus, Scribonia and Livia, and of Augustus himself. Germanicus was the crucial lynch-pin which held together the imperial *domus*.

Second, Germanicus enjoyed the political patronage of both Augustus and Tiberius. Augustus' favour for his grand-nephew was amply demonstrated by the fact that he requested Tiberius to adopt him as his son prior to his adopting Tiberius himself in AD 4, even though Tiberius had a son only a little younger than Germanicus (Tac. *Ann.* 1. 3. 5). That favour was publicly re-endorsed at Germanicus' election to the consulship without the prerequisite of the praetorship (a privilege not enjoyed by Tiberius and Nero Drusus), and his being awarded with the *ornamenta triumphalia* at Tiberius' triumph of AD 12 along with the generals of consular rank.[13]

A bond of affection, at least on the surface, augmented Germanicus' blood relationship with Tiberius. It seems clear that, if any mistrust or rivalry existed between the two at this time, or hatred between Livia and Agrippina and Tiberius and Livia which could equally jeopardize Germanicus' powers of influence, Ovid did not have cognizance of the fact.[14] He can only

---

[13] Dio, 57. 17. 2. Ovid alludes to honours and decorations for the generals (*Ex P.* 2. 1. 30; 2. 89–90) and participation in the triumph of 12.

[14] Suetonius (*Cal.* 4) claims that Augustus wanted Germanicus in preference to Tiberius as his successor; Tacitus (*Ann.* 1. 3. 5) and Suetonius (*Tib.* 15. 2) claim that Tiberius was compelled to adopt Germanicus; Dio (57. 13. 6) thinks that Tiberius had, from the beginning, suspected Germanicus as lying in wait for the

have heard rumour of the popularity of the young man with his family, and that it was in consideration of the love and respect felt for him by Augustus and his relatives that Augustus had him adopted by Tiberius in AD 4.[15] Ovid's ignorance of any ill-feeling of Tiberius towards Germanicus suggests one of two things: that Tiberius' practice of not making known his private feelings (Tac. *Ann* 1. 52; cf. *Ann* 1. 7. 11, 69. 7) misled the general public, perhaps even those closest to him, into believing that he held Germanicus in affection; or that at this point, before the death of Augustus, relations between Germanicus and Tiberius were genuinely affectionate and cordial.

Events after the triumph of AD 12 indicated that Germanicus continued to enjoy full political endorsement from both Augustus and Tiberius, and continued to enjoy the favour of Tiberius even after the death of Augustus. At the beginning of AD 13, Augustus had accepted a fifth decennium as leader of the state. Tiberius was granted tribunician power for the second time (Dio, 56. 28. 1; Tac. *Ann.* 1. 10. 7;) and *imperium* over provinces and armies equal and equivalent to that of Augustus (Vell. 2. 121. 1; Suet. *Tib.* 21. 1). He was *collega imperii*. Germanicus was dispatched to the Rhine that year, invested with *imperium proconsulare* and won his first imperatorial salutation.[16] After the death of Augustus some of the legions in Germany mutinied and attempted to force Germanicus to assume control of the Principate, but he demonstrated unshakable loyalty to his adoptive father (Suet. *Tib.* 25. 2–3; *Cal.* 1; Tac. *Ann.* 1. 34, 35, 37) and they accepted from him the oath of allegiance. Tiberius publicly acknowledged his gratitude. He brought Germanicus' achievements to the notice of the Senate with generous praise of his *virtus* (Tac. *Ann.* 1. 52). The first action of the Senate in the year AD 15 was to award Germanicus a triumph (*Ann.* 1. 55. 1.). Further campaigns inter-

sovereignty. Tacitus (*Ann* 1. 33. 5) claims that Germanicus was troubled by the secret hatred of his uncle and grandmother, and that Livia felt a stepmother's hatred towards Agrippina. Dio (57. 3. 3) and Suetonius (*Tib.* 50. 2–51) say that Tiberius hated Livia.

[15] Suet. *Cal.* 4. The affection both Livia and Augustus held for the children of Germanicus is also evinced by Suet. *Cal.* 7. Augustus' affection for Germanicus and Agrippina is suggested by Suet. *Cal.* 8: 'Valebis, mea Agrippina, et dabis operam ut valens pervenias ad Germanicum tuum.'

[16] Not in the year 11, as erroneously stated by Dio (56. 25. 2), nor in 14, as stated by Tacitus (*Ann.* 1. 14. 3). See Syme (1978) 57–8.

vened before the event could materialize, campaigns that earned
him his second imperatorial salutation: 'nomenque imperatoris
auctore Tiberio accepit' (*Ann* 1. 58. 5). At the end of AD 16
Tacitus records the dedication of a triumphal arch at Rome 'ob
recepta signa cum Varo amissa ductu Germanici, auspiciis
Tiberii' (*Ann.* 2. 41. 1).

Public actions of both Germanicus and Tiberius thus demonstrated that they were on the best of terms. And Ovid's continued
confidence in Germanicus' favour and influence with Tiberus is
manifested by the fact that his first public tribute to him in AD 12
is followed up over the years 13–16 by poetic epistles to the young
Caesar's acquaintances or associates (Cassius Salanus, *Ex P.* 2. 5),
Sextus Pompey (*Ex P.* 4. 5), Carus (*Ex P.* 4. 13), P. Suillius
Rufus, (*Ex P.* 4. 8), containing both tributes to the prince and
pleas to the addressees to intercede with him on his behalf.[17]
That to Suillius, written after the death of Augustus, is most significant for divining the suppliant–saviour relationship that Ovid
establishes between himself and Germanicus. Ovid exhorts
Suillius to supplicate on his behalf the gods he worships (*Ex P.* 4.
8. 21–4):

> tu modo si quid agi sperabis posse precando,
>   quos colis, exora supplice voce deos.
> di tibi sunt Caesar iuvenis. tua numina placa.
>   hac certe nulla est notior ara tibi.

Only do, if you hope that anything can be done by prayer, prevail upon
the gods whom you worship with a suppliant's voice. Your gods are the
young Caesar. Propitiate your divinity. Certainly no altar is better
known to you than this.

The similarities in language between this poem and the proem of
the *Fasti* dedicated to Germanicus are striking.[18]

To sum up: there can be little doubt that Ovid rededicated the
Fasti to Germanicus because he was confident that the young
heir's favour with Tiberius, first noticed in the triumph of AD 12,
had in no manner diminished after the death of Augustus. It was
a belief in that good relationship which was the inspiration to
dedicate his poem to Germanicus, and a belief that it was within

---

[17] For the connection of these individuals with Germanicus and the dates of
the poems, see Syme (1978) 87 ff.

[18] See n. 1.

his power to induce Tiberius to mitigate his exile. Poetic skill was
only the convenient pretext. Yet it was not long before he again
put down the *Fasti*. Why he did so will be examined at the end of
this chapter.

Germanicus and Janus

The first calendrical entry Ovid contrives for Germanicus is
1 January in association with Janus, whose day it is. The disquisition on Janus is lengthy (1. 63–284), covers a variety of themes
ranging from the inauguration of the consuls to the *aition* of the
New Year, but is punctuated only twice with an invocation to the
new patron of the *Fasti*. Those invocations are made at the beginning and the end of the long passage, both in connection with the
theme of 'pax' and the closure of the doors of Janus. These passages warrant investigation for several reasons. One is that
Germanicus is unknown from any other source to have any connection with Janus; another is that Ovid openly contradicts himself within the passage as to the significance of the opening and
closing of the doors, indicating that he is uncertain about the
ostensibly age-old tradition referred to by Augustus in his *Res
Gestae* (13); another is that Syme accuses Ovid of negligence in
omitting mention of Augustus' proud boast that Janus had been
closed three times 'me principe'.[19]

Ovid invokes the name of Germanicus in the first line celebrating the first day of the year (1. 63–70):

> Ecce tibi faustum, Germanice, nuntiat annum
>   inque meo primum carmine Ianus adest.
> Iane biceps, anni tacite labentis origo,
>   solus de superis qui tua terga vides,
> dexter ades ducibus, quorum secura labore
>   otia terra ferax, otia pontus habet:
> dexter ades patribusque tuis populoque Quirini.
>   et resera nutu candida templa tuo.

Look, Germanicus, Janus is announcing a well-omened year for you and
is first to lend his presence to my verse. Two-faced Janus, source of the
silently gliding year, who alone of the higher beings see your own back,
be auspicious to the commanders through whose labours both the fertile
earth and the sea enjoy peace and freedom from care. And be auspicious

---

[19] Syme (1978) 24; see also (1979) 193–4.

to your senators and to the people of Quirinus, and with your nod unbolt the white temples.

It is apparent from these lines that Ovid is, in retrospect, alluding to the first item on the Senate's agenda for the first day of the year 15: a decree awarding a triumph for Germanicus (Tac. *Ann.* 1. 55. 1).[20] Ovid's association of Germanicus with Janus, both god of the New Year and proclaimer of peace, is thus comprehensible. It was the first (and only) triumph decreed for Germanicus, and Ovid was no doubt delighted that his prediction made somewhat precipitately two years before (*Ex P.* 2. 1. 49–68) was at last to be realized.

The theme of association between Germanicus and Janus as harbinger of peace is reiterated only once more at the end of the passage. The context is Janus' explanation of when and why the Gates of War are open and closed (1. 279–81):

> 'ut populo reditus pateant ad bella profecto,
>   tota patet dempta ianua nostra sera.
>   pace fores obdo, ne qua discedere possit;'

'So that the means of return may be available to the people after they have marched out to war, the bolt is removed and my entire gate stands open. I bar the doors in times of peace so she cannot get away.'

He then prophesies (1. 282):

> 'Caesareoque diu numine clusus ero.'

'And under the divine sway of Caesar I will be closed for a long time'.

The poet then concludes the passage with a prayer for eternal peace and the eternal keeping of the ministers of peace (the Caesars).[21]

While Ovid's connection between Germanicus and Janus is

---

[20] It has been thought that Tacitus was mistaken and that the decree should belong not to the beginning but the end of the year. Syme (1978) 61 shows why Tacitus cannot be confuted. It is also clear that Ovid has understood the decree to belong to 1 Jan., which gave him the opportunity to honour Germanicus on Janus' day.

[21] Syme (1979) 194 believes this couplet alludes to the triumph which Germanicus held in May AD 17. In so doing he implies that Ovid was actually still writing up to AD 17, the year of his death (cf. Syme (1978) 63). The couplet, however, could well have been inserted by Ovid immediately upon his hearing of the decree awarding the triumph in 15. The theory that Ovid had ceased writing by the end of 16 will be presented later in this chapter.

comprehensible in the light of the decree for his triumph on
I January AD 15, there is no evidence at all that the gates of Janus
were closed at this time. Not surprising, in view of Tacitus'
'decernitur Germanico triumphus manente bello' (*Ann.* 1. 55. 1).
This is not the first time that Ovid had been over-hasty with a
prediction.[22] Yet since the imposition of peace could be assumed
to be the prerequisite of a triumph, Ovid's precipitance here is
perhaps more comprehensible than on previous occasions, even if
no less tactless. Which now brings us to the question of Ovid's
confusion over the Gates of Janus, and Syme's accusation of negligence with regard to the three closures during the Principate of
Augustus.

In the middle of his verse devoted to the celebration of Janus,
Ovid puts the following words in the mouth of the god (1. 121–4):

> 'cum libuit Pacem placidis emittere tectis,
>   libera perpetuas ambulat illa vias:
> sanguine letifero totus miscebitur orbis,
>   ni teneant rigidae condita bella serae.'

'When it pleases me to discharge Peace from her tranquil dwelling, she is
free to be continually on her way. The whole world will be embroiled in
fatal bloodshed, should my rigid bars not keep warfare impounded.'

Janus closed his doors to contain war in order to let peace wander
freely and unhindered. A direct contradiction to his later statement, already cited, that the Gates of Janus closed to contain
peace, lest it escape (1. 281–2). How to account for this? A brief
excursus on sources must now intervene in order to arrive at an
understanding as to why Ovid failed to notice all or any one of the
three closures of the doors of the divine janitor under Augustus.[23]

The most crucial evidence for the closures under Augustus
comes from *Res Gestae* 13:

Ianum Quirinum, quem claussum esse maiores nostri voluerunt, cum per
totum imperium populi Romani terra marique esset parta victoriis pax,
cum prius, quam nascerer, a condita urbe bis omnino clausum fuisse pro-
datur memoriae, ter me principe senatus claudendum esse censuit.

---

[22] His prediction of a triumph for Germanicus in a poem ostensibly written to
celebrate the triumph of Tiberius in AD 12 could hardly have been regarded as
tactful (*Ex P.* 2. 49 ff.).

[23] The sources for Janus are also treated by Syme (1979) but with a completely
different slant.

Janus Quirinus, which our ancestors decreed should be closed when
peace had been acquired by victories throughout the whole empire of the
Roman people on land and on sea, though prior to my birth from the
foundation of the city it has been recorded to have been closed only
twice, the Senate voted should be closed three times while I was
Princeps.

In the context of the *Res Gestae* as an inscription this passage is
noticeable as an instance of untoward verbosity. The only other
instances in any way similar are at 17. 2 and 34. 2, both of which
understandably require more elaborate explanation because they
were innovations. By contrast Augustus felt no need to explain
the Ludi Saeculares (22. 2), the significance of placing the laurel
from the fasces in the Capitol (4. 2), or of performing the lustrum
for the first time in forty-one years (8. 2). His audience already
knew. So at *RG* 13 why does he not simply say 'Ianum Quirinum
ter clausi' with the names of the consuls of the relevant year(s) to
indicate the date? He had been meticulous in specifying the year
of his other achievements (e.g. 2. 2, 4; 5. 1; 6. 1; 11; 12. 2; 15. 2, 3, 4;
16. 1, 2). The passage is also remarkable in the fact that Augustus
constructs an epoch which ends with his birth instead of with his
entry into public life when the *Res Gestae* begins. He describes
the period since his birth, that is when the three latest closures
took place, as 'me principe'. This latter phrase is used elsewhere
(cf. 30. 1, 'ante me principem'; 32. 3, 'me principe') to denote a
period of time. Yet Augustus dates the beginning of his authority
as Princeps at 7. 2 from 28 BC when he received the title 'princeps
senatus' (Horace (*Od.* 1. 2. 50) shows 'princeps' already in use as a
title (informally) during his consular period, i.e. from 31 BC). In
this the Janus passage, he is now backdating it to his birth! Why
the inconsistency between the Janus paragraph and *RG* 7. 2 in the
distinction between epochs?[24]

W. Ensslin made the suggestion that Augustus, with the
expression 'prius quam nascerer', wanted to make a distinction
between the former age and the present, the Golden Age of
peace, and so present himself as 'Friedensfürst' who 'mit dieser
auffallenden Formulierung der Zeitbestimmung an alle diese
Vorstellungen von der Bedeutung seiner Geburt erinnern wollte'.
He also notes that all the portents surrounding Augustus' birth

---

[24] The anomalies evident in *RG* 13 concerning the tradition of Janus are noted
by Judge (1979) 21.

reported by Suetonius (*Aug.* 94) give rise to the same impression
of the birth of a new age.[25]

Ensslin's interpretation is indeed plausible. And the inconsistency in epoch definitions between *RG* 13 and other passages, the
unnecessary details supplied for an allegedly ancient, well-known
tradition, and the absence of specific dates, do encourage a suspicion that Augustus was somehow meddling with (inventing?) tradition here.[26] One thing is clear. The principal source for the
three closures of Janus under Augustus raises more questions
that it resolves. Remarkably, it is the one source for the gates of
war which was not put under scrutiny by Syme.[27] Are the other
sources any more enlightening?

Livy (1. 19. 3) tells us that since the reign of Numa the temple
of Janus had been closed twice: once in the consulship of Manlius
at the end of the first war with Carthage, and again after the battle
of Actium. Livy may well have acquired his information concerning the closures under Numa and Manlius from the annalist
L. Calpurnius Piso (in Varro *LL* 5. 165), incidentally our oldest
source on the subject. Livy himself is proud to tell us that he was
fortunate enough to witness the third closure after the battle of
Actium. Yet how odd that, having been so specific as to the year
of the second closing, Livy is so vague as to the date of the third.
The battle of Actium took place on 2 September 31 BC. Later evidence indicates that the closure of Janus did not take place until
11 January 29 BC,[28] fourteen months later. 'After the battle of
Actium' suggests that the event took place either the same year,
or at the latest the year after. Is Livy being deliberately misleading? It is thought that he had written this section of the history at
latest by 25 BC,[29] which explains why he mentions only one closure of Janus. But how curious that an historian who claims to
have witnessed an event fails to record the date. He set a pattern,
it seems.

Horace mentions the closure of Janus in two poems addressed
to Augustus and composed *c.*13 BC, in an Epistle (2. 1. 255–6) and

---

[25] Ensslin (1932) 363–4.

[26] A genuine precedent for the Augustan ceremony of opening the doors is very
questionable—Latte (1960) 132; also Wissowa (1912) 105.

[27] Syme (1979).   [28] Syme (1978) 25.

[29] Ogilvie (1965) 94. Luce (1965) 238 suggests the years before 27 BC; Syme
(1978) 170 believes that Livy embarked on his vast enterprise as early as 30 or 29.

in the last Ode (4. 15. 6 ff.).[30] He mentions no date (excusable in a poet not versifying a calendar!) and does not say to which of the three closures he is referring. Syme believes the reference in both cases is to the third closure. And both references, says Syme, are linked (illicitly) to the humbling of the Parthians:[31]

> claustraque custodem pacis cohibentia Ianum,
> et formidatam Parthis te principe Romam.

and bars confining Janus, custodian of peace, and Rome with you as leader, a terror to the Parthians . . . *Ep.* 2. 1. 255–6)

> tua, Caesar, aetas
> fruges et agris rettulit uberes
> et signa nostro restituit Iovi
> derepta Parthorum superbis
> postibus et vacuum duellis
> Ianum Quirini clausit et . . .

Your age, Caesar, has restored abundant produce to the fields and returned to our Jove the standards torn down from the proud portals of the Parthians, and has closed the shrine of Janus Quirinus in the absence of war, and . . . (*Od.* 4. 15. 4–9).

I see no need to interpret Horace's closure of Janus as being historically linked with the conquest of the Parthians. Horace is merely listing, in both poems, a number of unrelated events. There is no way that 'et' can be used to link phrases causally. Even the tenses used cannot be made to imply causal connection. The achievements of the age are being cited with no attempt at chronology or causal connection. Virgil, too, set the Parthians and Janus side by side (*Aen.* 7. 606–7). Contrast between peace and war would no doubt appeal as a poetic device. Perhaps Horace had his fellow bard in mind.

Horace is saying that the closure of Janus was merely one of the many achievements of Augustus. There is no attempt to imply that there was more than one closure. The poet was not concerned with the number of times. Augustus brought peace to the whole world and closed Janus. It is far more aesthetically pleasing (and indeed more flattering to Augustus) simply to state the fact.

---

[30] Both poems are addressed to Augustus and composed *c.* 13 BC: Syme (1978) 172.

[31] 'Horace had neglected in *Odes* 1–3 to register the first and second closures' (Syme (1978) 27 n. 3).

A number of closures inevitably implies a number of openings. A number of openings implies wars and more details and problems than a poet needed. The gates of Janus are reported to have remained closed during the entire forty-three years of the reign of Numa, after all (Plut. *Num.* 20. 2; *de fortuna Romanorum* 9), so perhaps Horace is attempting to graft an ideal of prevailing peace (was Augustus imitating this technique in the *Res Gestae*?) onto the entire Principate of Augustus.

Velleius, writing in about AD 30, emulates Horace in mentioning only one closure of Janus. With an important difference, however. The historian is explicit in stating that, under Augustus, the doors of Janus were closed once only (2. 38. 3):

Immane bellicae civitatis argumentum, quod semel sub regibus, iterum hoc T. Manlio consule, tertio Augusto principe certae pacis argumentum Ianus geminus clausus dedit.

It is dire evidence of a warlike state that evidence of certain peace was provided by the closure of twin-faced Janus only once under the kings, a second time in the consulship of the aforementioned Titus Manlius, and the third time in the principate of Augustus.

Velleius is as annoyingly evasive about the date of the third closure as is Livy. Again, why give the year for the second closing in the Republic but not the third under Augustus? And why only one, and not three, closures under Augustus? There is no excuse for poetic aesthetics here.[32] Perhaps he has just regurgitated Livy's record without updating his facts. Yet even if he had not bothered to go and read the *Res Gestae* on the Mausoleum in the Campus Martius, would not the three closures have been common knowledge anyway?

Verrius Flaccus' *Fasti Praenestini* take us back to Augustus' own lifetime and to the very years when Ovid was composing the *Fasti*. Yet mutilations to the text conceal vital information forever. What we can glean from the little we have only demonstrates what we are missing. Mommsen's reconstructed entry is

---

[32] Syme (1979) 194: 'The design of this crafty composer is patent. Exalting Tiberius Caesar, he did not care to obtrude a uniquely Augustan theme. To mention a second and a third repetition would have disturbed an exposition all too selective.' But why did Velleius mention the Gates of Janus at all if he did not care to obtrude a uniquely 'Augustan theme'?

as follows, the words within the brackets showing the extent of the reconstruction:[33]

D[ebellavit hostes Imp. Caesar Augustus tertium] / ab Romulo et Ianum c[lausit se V et L. appuleio cos].

Imperator Caesar Augustus totally vanquished the enemy for the third time since Romulus and closed Janus in his fifth and in L. Appuleius' consulship.

A date at last! The inscription provides the letters denoting the day and month: three days before the Ides, or 11 January. Mommsen was able to reconstruct the year only with the help of Cassius Dio (51. 20. 1, 4) and Orosius (6. 20. 1), who were considerate enough to supply the consuls' names. But how probable is it that Verrius provided the dates for the other closures as well? Did he, like Horace, choose to conflate the three closures or did he in fact provide three separate entries on the appropriate dates? We have no way of knowing as the text is so fragmented. No other inscribed calendar records any closure of Janus at all, not even the *Fasti Maffeiani* dated 8 BC by Degrassi and the most complete which has survived. The *Fasti Praenestini* (AD 6–9) were the first extant evidence for the date of the first closure of Janus under Augustus, then, and they were cut about thirty-five years after the event.

Of all the authors cited so far, that of the *Fasti Praenestini* was the most intimately connected with Augustus. Verrius had been entrusted with the onerous task of educating the Princeps' grandsons, and one might justifiably assume that Augustus played his part in instructing Verrius in what was, or was not, to be handed on to the younger generation. Such instruction might be suspected of having made itself manifest in his own calendar. But why 11 January, the festival of the Carmentalia? Why not 1 January, the day reserved for the honour of Janus (Ovid, *F* 1. 63 ff., 89 ff.), or even 9 January, when Ovid says that Janus was 'agonali luce piandus' (1. 318)?

Lucius Annaeus Florus[34] wrote an epitome of the history of Livy. He is no more helpful than anyone else. He states that Augustus closed Janus once, and the date he supplies (4 BC) is

---

[33] Degrassi (1963) 113 agrees with Mommsen's reconstruction.

[34] Writing in the late 1 to mid-2nd cent. AD. Forster in the introduction to Florus, Loeb pp. vii–viii.

twenty-five years out from that supplied by Verrius as reconstructed by Mommsen (2. 34. 64). He unambiguously links
Augustus' one closure with the return of the standards by the
Parthians (perhaps another misinterpretation of Horace's poems?
He can't have got it from Livy!), and there is no hint that there
was any other closure. Understandable, as it would have spoiled
the climax of Florus' work which culminates with world peace
and Augustus' deserved deification. Chronology is sacrificed for
the sake of literary structure and the moral lesson.

This survey of the sources so far might encourage one to suspect that Augustus meant 'tertium' instead of 'ter' at *RG* 13, and
that there was indeed only one closure during his reign. Yet
Suetonius puts paid to that idea. The biographer is the first
extant author after Augustus himself to record three closures of
Janus in the Augustan period (*Aug.* 22). Perhaps it is because he
had access to senatorial decrees for the period that he was able to
provide such information. He does not mention the senatorial
decrees, but Augustus does. Yet no dates are given by Suetonius,
nor elaborations. Clearly a minor interest to readers of imperial
biography. Or by now such a commonplace of history as to
require no further mention?

Cassius Dio at last comes to the rescue. He states that, in
Augustus' fifth consulship, with Sextus Apuleius as colleague,
the Senate decreed that the gates of Janus be closed (51. 20. 4).
Dio also provides the year of the second closing—in 25 BC (53. 26.
5). Syme has calculated that January of 24 BC would be 'better,
perhaps'.[35] The third closing poses a problem. It is not registered
by Dio, although he does record that the Senate decreed its closing in 10 BC; the ceremony had to be postponed because of
troublesome Dacians on the Danube (54. 36. 2). Nothing more is
heard on the subject. The only author to record the third closure
of Janus is the Christian writer Orosius (6. 22. 1), but his evidence, compounded of 'error and fraud', would only perplex 'the
unwary or the retarded'.[36] Syme devoted much scholarship
towards calculating when the third closure of Janus under
Augustus took place.[37] Material provided by the ancient sources
did not made his task easy.

It is expedient to recapitulate here, even at the cost of

---

[35] Syme (1978) 25.   [36] Ibid. 26.   [37] Ibid. 24–7.

repetition. The testimony of Augustus himself, inscribed on columns in front of his mausoleum after his death, is evasive in its absence of dates, baffling in its elaboration of an ostensibly well-known Roman tradition, inconsistent and perplexing in its definitions of epochs. Livy, Horace, Flaccus (?), and Velleius mention only one closure of Janus, and none gives a date except Flaccus. Janus is ignored altogether by other *fasti*, if the Maffeiani is at all representative. Numismatic silence enhances the almost conspiratorial elusiveness of contemporary sources.[38] Suetonius is the first to imitate Augustus in mentioning three closures without dates. Dio provides two dates, but one does not go unchallenged. Orosius' contribution is dismissed as fraud.

To revert to Ovid: should we be surprised that he is no more enlightening with dates and the number of closures than any other contemporary or ancient source? What, then, about his confusion with the subject? It will be remembered that in his earliest reference to the doors of Janus, he seems to think that it was War that was contained behind the closed doors (1. 121–4). Later, in reference to Germanicus, he states that it was peace (1. 281 ff.). Now the notion that it is War, not Peace, shut up in the closed temple had already appeared in Virgil (*Aen.* 7. 607–15). Janus is then the guardian of war rather than peace (607–10):

> sunt geminae Belli portae (sic nomine dicunt)
> religione sacrae et saevi formidine Martis;
> centum aerei claudunt vectes aeternaque ferri
> robora, nec custos absistit limine Ianus.

There are the twin gates of war (as they call them by name), sacred by religious law and the dread of savage Mars; a hundred bolts of bronze and the eternal strength of iron secure them, nor does Janus ever desert his guardianship of the threshold.

Frazer observed that the interpretation of the Doors of Janus as the Gates of War more aptly applies to the title of Quirinus bestowed on the god.[39] Quirinus was especially a god of war,

---

[38] Sutherland (1987) 15 suggests that the unavailability of mints is responsible for the numismatic silence on major events, including the two closures of Janus in 29 and 25 BC. It is true that coins celebrated the closure of Janus under Nero ('pace p.R. terra marique parta Janum clusit s.c.', see Sutherland (1984) 153, 166 ff.; 169 ff.), yet not under Vespasian for all his lavish advertisement of Pax (Syme (1979) 212).

[39] Frazer (1929) ii. 104.

noted Frazer, and the epithet Quirinus applied to Janus was understood to signify that he was the Lord of War (Macr. *Sat.* 1. 9. 16: 'Quirinum, quasi bellorum potentem, ab hasta quam Sabini curin vocant').

With Virgil's passage in front of us then, Ovid's original statement that the Doors of Janus contained War, not Peace, becomes more comprehensible. But suddenly at 1. 253 he has Janus say he was guardian of peace: 'nil mihi cum bello: pacem postesque tuebar' which is consistent with the still later passage that it was Peace contained within the closed doors (1. 281). Ovid is now harking back to Horace's Epistle already cited (2. 1. 255). The paradox in the evocation of Janus (a natural expectation?) suddenly becomes evident in Horace too: in his Ode, Janus is simply referred to as Quirinus (4. 15. 9), which Frazer showed is more appropriate to the guardian of war. Virgil does not escape scrutiny now either. In contrast with his previous allusion to Janus as guardian of War, he later has Aeneas and Latinus invoking Janus in a prayer that peace shall remain unbroken over Italy (*Aen.* 12. 198 ff.). Is he not implying, then, that Janus is now guardian of peace?

Ovid's confusion is precedented. His treatment of the Doors of Janus, taken in the context of the other ancient sources on the subject, is not peculiar at all (*pace* Syme). If anything, it can be perceived as informative. Ovid's treatment reflects the uncertainty amongst contemporaries as to the meaning of the ancient custom of closing the gates of Janus in peace and opening them in war. It imitates the paradoxes in the evocation of Janus as guardian of war and peace in Virgil and Horace. It reflects the uncertainty as to when, exactly, Augustus closed the gates of Janus, and how many times, which in turn poses the question as to the extent of the general awareness of the significance of the event when it (they) occurred. Ovid neatly sidesteps the latter uncertainty by logically discussing the question of closing the doors in general terms under the opening day of the year, dedicated to Janus.

In the light of Ovid's treatment of Janus set against the background of the other ancient sources, Augustus' laborious explanations of the tradition of Janus Quirinus perhaps become more comprehensible. So few Romans understood it that he had to spell it out. One might suspect that he instructed Verrius Flaccus to annotate it in his calendar for the same purpose. Ovid never saw it, nor any calendar recording the closure of the Gates of Janus. His own version is ample proof, but if further were needed, he virtually says as much. Having finished with Janus he says (1. 289): 'quod tamen ex ipsis licuit mihi discere fastis . . .'. Neither, of course, could he have seen the *Res Gestae* version, inscribed years after he went into exile.

This cursory examination of the sources for the tradition of the Gates of War has highlighted rather than solved any problems. The value of Ovid's record, however, is considerable. It points to the fact that, as late as the last decade of Augustus' life, the ostensibly ancient tradition connected with the gates of Janus was still in the process of being formulated. Paradoxes and misunderstandings still abounded, until Augustus felt obliged to interpret it, in writing, for all.

Thus, in the case of Ovid's association of Germanicus with Janus, it would appear that the two invocations at the beginning and end of the disquisition on Janus are tacked on to what had already been written before his exile. Over-anxious to praise the younger Caesar for having been awarded a triumph on the first day of the year in AD 15, and having no genuine means of incorporating his new patron into the calendar where he did not yet belong, Ovid improvised with what he already knew. With that information he then constructed what he expected to happen. That his expectation did not materialize does nothing to diminish the importance of his evidence. That he expected the Gates of Janus to be closed after the decree of a triumph for Germanicus indicates (*a*) that he was aware that they were open at the death of Augustus;[40] (*b*) that although the evidence for Janus is so confused in the ancient sources, his expectation that Janus would be somehow involved, suggests how successful Augustus had been in establishing this as a symbol of state and heightening an awareness of this new concept which he (probably) introduced. That opening and closing the Gates of War was to elicit no interest from Tiberius, Ovid was not to know.

Germanicus and the Name 'Augustus'

Germanicus is invoked for the second time in Ovid's calendar on 13 January (1. 587–616 (too long to cite here)). For the second

---

[40] They were opened for the third and last time in 1 BC (Syme (1979)).

time the poet is confronted with the problem of associating Tiberius' heir with a day and a festival with which he has no known connection. It is the ides of January, and an NP day on that account. Ovid swiftly acknowledges the day dedicated to Jupiter by relating the sacrificial activities of the god's priest, the *flamen Dialis*, in the first couplet. He then states that it is also the anniversary of the day when every province was restored to the Roman people,[41] the day when Germanicus' grandfather was endowed with the name 'Augustus'. The rest of the passage builds up to a eulogy of the great name with its divine and augural connotations, and culminates in a prayer for good auspices for the present-day heir to the title of the ruler of the world.

Praise of the name Augustus, which Ovid logically believes Tiberius' heir will one day inherit, appears to be the only means by which Ovid can here insert Germanicus into the *Fasti*. This means is however consistent with the new proem of his revised book 1, where praise of the young Caesar's 'pater' and 'avus' is promised in the forthcoming pages (1. 10). Possible evidence against the idea that the whole passage eulogizing the name Augustus was composed in order to honour Germanicus from exile is contained within the lines where it is difficult to determine whether they were written before or after Ovid's banishment. For example the line 'hic socium summo cum Iove nomen habet' (1. 608) might imply that Augustus is still alive, and the plural pronoun in 'protegat et vestras querna corona fores' (1. 614) would then refer jointly to Augustus and Tiberius. It follows then that the 'heres' to the cognomen Augustus in line 615 would be Tiberius, and Germanicus thus receives no further mention. On this interpretation the invocation to Germanicus at 1. 590 is merely a quick and solitary insertion into the passage by Ovid at a later period.

Yet lines 1. 608 ff. are tantalizingly ambiguous, the equivocation undoubtedly arising from the fact that the same names were shared by the first and second emperors. Ovid could address Tiberius only as 'Caesar' or 'Augustus' (he would never dare use his *praenomen* 'Tiberius' even though it does scan in the vocative!), and the passsage might therefore still reflect later composition.

---

[41] See Dio, 53. 9. 6. For a discussion of Mommsen's reconstruction of the *Fasti Praenestini*, and the mistaken idea that Augustus claimed to have 'restored the Republic' on the day, see Millar (1973) 50 ff. and Judge (1974) 279–311.

Tiberius inherited the name 'Augustus' in his father's will, and although he did not utilize it in the West, he did so in his correspondence to the East (Suet. *Tib.* 26. 2) where Ovid was now located. Alternatively, as with the case of the doors of Janus, Ovid might be working on his expectation of what would happen (i.e. that Tiberius would assume the title in Rome) rather than on knowledge of what did happen. He actually refers to Tiberius as 'Augustus' at *Ex P.* 4. 9. 70. The holder of the name that ranks with supreme Jove in 1. 608 might then be an allusion to Tiberius,[42] 'vestras' in 1. 614 a joint address to Tiberius and Germanicus, and the heir to the great surname of Augustus at the end of the passage would then be Germanicus.

This second possibility which Ovid's ambiguity permits is more feasible, for although there is no certain criterion upon which to form a judgement, there are a number of reasons why it is most likely that the entire passage was composed from exile. The passage begins with an invocation to the grandson of Augustus and is celebrating (erroneously, see below) the anniversary of the day upon which the grandfather received the title: 'et tuus Augusto nomine dictus avus' (1. 590). That *cognomen* then becomes the central theme of the entire passage. This comprises an exhortation to Germanicus to peruse a long roll-call of 'cognomina ex virtute', many significantly hereditary, won by famous Roman generals of the past for conquest of various lands (Africanus, Numidicus, Magnus, Maximus, and the addressee's natural father, Germanicus at 1. 597) which the poet utilizes in the build-up to the climax of his eulogy of the name 'Augustus'. The climax comes at 1. 608 ff. in praise of the name which is distinguished from the aforementioned by its associations not with military achievement but with 'summo Iove', and with the epithet 'august' which is derived from things divine. The emphasis here is clearly on the nature of the name itself rather than on the identity of the bearer of the name. The denouement comprises a prayer to Jupiter to augment the imperium and the years of the 'dux', and an invocation to the gods that the same omens which attended the father when assuming power (obviously the same

[42] Cf. the religious connotations attached to 'dux venerande' at 1. 646; also 610 'templa sacerdotum rite dicata manu' with 640 'nunc te (Concordia) sacratae constituere manus', all of which refer to Tiberius and which would be appropriate to one bearing the name 'Augustus'.

person as the 'dux') should also wait upon the heir to the great *cognomen* when he should eventually take upon himself the 'orbis onus' (616).[43]

If Ovid wished to achieve artistic symmetry in the passage eulogizing the hereditary title 'Augustus' which begins with an invocation to the grandson of the original holder and invokes the *cognomen* of his natural father (which he had already inherited) in the middle he would have to acquire a balance in design either by invoking his addressee once more at the end, or at least by alluding to his presence in relation to the central theme. On artistic grounds, the 'pater' here must be his adoptive father Tiberius (recalling his relationship to Germanicus at 1. 10), the heir to the name 'Augustus' none other than Germanicus. The final invocation to Germanicus as 'tanti cognominis heres' (1. 615) is a fitting conclusion to a passage that began with an invocation to the grandson of the one who had first received the title 'Augustus'.

Further inference lends support to the theory that the passage in its entirety was composed from exile. The study of the early passages devoted to Livia in the *Fasti* (Ch. 4) has shown that Ovid went to great lengths to avoid even the most oblique allusion to Tiberius in the first edition of his poem. It is not credible therefore that Tiberius should be honoured here as the heir to the name 'Augustus' before the death of the original holder of the title and before the poet went into exile. Similarly the plural pronoun in reference to the oak crown over the doors, which must include Tiberius if Augustus is still alive, would be thoroughly inconsistent with Ovid's assumed posture towards Tiberius before his exile. The allusions to Tiberius, therefore, are made after he had become Princeps. Ovid has it then that it is Tiberius who is now the holder of the name that ranks with that of Jove, he is the 'dux' of 1. 613, and the 'pater' of 1. 616. This being the case Tiberius cannot also be the heir referred to in the final couplet. Having praised the present holder of the title (1. 613) Ovid then looks beyond Tiberian time to the day when Germanicus inherits the great name that was originally bestowed upon his grandfather on this day in 27 BC. The theme of the name Augustus, beginning with an invocation to Germanicus, is thus neatly terminated by a

[43] On the burden, see Tac. *Ann.* 1. 11. 2, 'regendi cuncta onus'.

return to the original addressee and new patron of the poem itself.[44]

Ovid's choice of 13 January as the anniversary of Octavian's assumption of the *cognomen* 'Augustus' is, however, at variance with other calendars. According to the *Feriale Cumanum* and the *Fasti Praenestini*, Octavian received the title on 16 January.[45] Yet Ovid has reserved that day for praise of Tiberius' dedication of the temple of Concord, culminating in a eulogy of Livia as the consort of mighty Jove. An excellent opportunity missed, one might think, to eulogize Tiberius as the new Augustus on the anniversary of the conferment of the title of his adoptive father in 27 BC. Why then does Ovid choose the 13th?

Unlike 16 January, the 13th had no known connection with Tiberius; in choosing it the poet spared himself the obligation to celebrate the day by praising Tiberius in direct connection with the name 'Augustus' and so making more blatant (and tactless) the contrived incorporation of Germanicus in association with the name. Furthermore, the edict that was issued in rendering thanks to Octavian by conferring upon him the name 'Augustus' and the honour of the 'querna corona' over his door, came about as a result of his having resigned all powers and provinces to the Senate and people of Rome just three days before—on 13 January.[46] Ovid is therefore simply conflating events and celebrating them on the earlier day.

Conflating events was not unforgivable, it seems. Verrius Flaccus' entry for 13 January incorrectly celebrates the placement

---

[44] Frazer (1929) ii. 229 believes the end of the passage to have been penned after the accession of Tiberius because he finds there an allusion to Tiberius' feigned reluctance to accept sole rule and his refusal to allow the civic crown to be hung over his door. But he also understands the heir to be Tiberius, which is, in my view, not logically connected with either Ovid's studied omission of Tiberius before his accession, or with the period after Tiberius had assumed sole power. Bömer (1957–8) ii. 70 also believes there is difficulty in discerning whether 1. 613 ff. belong to the first or second edition and presents a good case for the choice of either. Yet he settles for the likelihood of their belonging to the first edition. Neither Frazer nor Bömer considers that the passage in its entirety might be more satisfactory artistically as a post-exilic composition. Even Syme (1978) 29 believes the 'heres cognominis' is meant to signify Tiberius.

[45] 'Imp. Caesar Augustus est appellatus ipso VII e Agrippa III consulibus' (*Praen.*); 'XVII i. Februarias. Eo die Caesar Augustus appellatus est. Supplicatio Augusto' (*Fer. Cum.*), Degrassi (1963) 400.

[46] Dio, 53. 12 ff., 16; Suet. *Aug.* 7. 2; Syme (1939) 313.

of the oak crown when it should belong to the 16th, and in recording the name 'Augustus' he antedates by three days the conferral
of the title, even though he correctly records this event on 16
January.[47] Augustus himself was apparently not bothered by specific dates either, judging by his own non-chronological order of
his honours in 27 BC (*RG* 34. 2). Moreover, neither date was celebrated in the calendar as a public holiday to honour these
events.[48] It is possible that more was made of them a generation
later than when they actually occurred. Perhaps the growing
emphasis on the 'domus Augusta', evident both in the *Tabula
Siarensis* and in Ovid's exile poetry (*Ex P.* 4. 9. 105–10 of AD 15),
as well as in the present passage, was responsible for this.[49] No
extant calendar of earlier dating than Verrius or Ovid (e.g. the
Caeretani, Maffeiani, Feriale Cumanum) records them.

Finally, the Ides of January, as of every month, was a day
sacred to Jupiter (*F* 1. 56).[50] Ovid invokes Jupiter at three strategic points in this passage, thus making the connection between
the god and the bearer of the name 'Augustus' an important
theme. The first is at the introductory couplet (1. 587), the second
at the first and last line of the climax glorifying the nature of the
name that ranks with supreme Jove (1. 608, 612), the third in his
exhortation to the god which begins the denoument (1. 613).

Before his exile Ovid had more than once compared Augustus
with Jupiter. In the *Metamophoses* Jupiter is the ruler and father
of heaven, Augustus his counterpart on earth (*Met.* 15. 353–60).
The theme is reiterated in the pre-exilic *Fasti*: 'hoc tu per terras,
quod in aethere Iuppiter alto, / nomen habes : hominum tu pater,
ille deum' (2. 131–2). After exile, however, Ovid goes further by
actually identifying Augustus with Jupiter and his poems from
Tomis abound with such references.[51] The only post-exilic reference to Augustus in the *Fasti* is incorporated after the ruler's

---

[47] corona querc. . . . . .Augusti poner. . . .p.R rest. .u. . . are the only remains of
Verrius' entry. For Degrassi's reconstruction see (1963) 396. Also Judge (1974) 298.

[48] Both were, however, NP days; 13 Jan. because the Ides of all months were
NP, and 10 Jan. became NP to commemorate Tiberius' temple of Concord
(Degrassi 1963) 398).

[49] For the *Tabula Siarensis* see González (1984) 55–100; *AE* (1984) 137–45. For
the emphasis on the 'domus Augusta', see Millar (1988) 12.

[50] See also Wissowa (1912) 114.

[51] The numerous examples are cited in Scott (1930) 52 ff.

death and it is entirely consistent with the ruler's new elevated status in the eyes of the now degraded and suppliant poet: Livia is the only woman found worthy of the couch of great Jupiter (1. 650).

Jupiter's day would then seem a logical choice to celebrate the great name of 'Augustus' so commonly associated by Ovid with Jupiter and which he is now claiming Germanicus will one day inherit. Yet in the passage under scrutiny, a distinction may be detected between Ovid's former identification of Augustus with Jupiter and his present treatment. Here Jupiter and the holder of the name 'Augustus' are not identical but separate, the latter explicitly subject to the great god's power and goodwill (1. 612–14). And in this context the poet's treatment here of 'querna corona' is noteworthy. At 4. 953–4, written before exile, Ovid had prayed for a long life for the house decorated with the oaken wreath. After exile but before the death of Augustus, it was the oaken crown that had marked the residence of Augustus as the home of Jupiter (*T* 3. 1. 35–8):

> 'et Iovis haec' dixi 'domus est?' quod ut esse putarem,
>   augurium menti querna corona dabat.
> cuius ut accepi dominum, 'non fallimur,' inquam,
>   'et magni verum est hanc Iovis esse domum,'

'Is this the home of Jove?' I said, for a wreath of oak-leaves prompted my mind to suppose it to be so. When I heard who its master was, I said 'I am not mistaken, and it is true that this is the house of mighty Jove.'

the poet employing the conceit (while Augustus still lived) that the house of Augustus and the house of Jupiter were one and the same (cf. *Met.* 1. 175: the house on the Palatine is a counterpart of Olympus).

Later on in the same poem Ovid refers to the inscription explaining why the crown was bestowed (*T* 3. 1. 47–8):

> 'causa superpositae scripto est testata coronae:
>   servatos civis indicat huius ope.'

'The reason for the wreath placed above it is testified by an inscription: it proclaims that with his help citizens have been saved.'

The poet is thus providing the oak crown with its formal identity and ideological point given it by Augustus who had been awarded it for having saved citizens (Dio, 53. 16. 4), and who had had it advertised on coins exhibiting the door of the house with the

oaken crown over it and the inscription 'ob cives servatos'.[52] Ovid
uses this ideology to best advantage, as the oak crown has a special relevance to the exile who is able to invoke it as justification
for his recall (*T* 3. 1. 49–52):

> adice servatis unum, pater optime, civem,
> qui procul extremo pulsus in orbe latet,
> in quo poenarum, quas se meruisse fatetur,
> non facinus causam, sed suus error habet.

Add, best of fathers, one citizen to those who have been saved; one who,
banished far off, escapes notice on the edge of the world. The cause of
his punishment, which he admits himself to have deserved, was not a
crime but his own mistake.

By contrast, in this post-exilic, post-Augustan exhortation in 1.
614 of the *Fasti*, the Augustan attribute of the oak crown seems to
have been shifted from the ruler who had won it to the ruler who
was yet to win it. Juxtaposed with the exhortation to Jupiter to
augment the ruler's imperium and years, Ovid's petition to the
oak crown to adorn the doors of the residence on the Palatine
suggests that it was not yet there, that the palace was not yet
identified as the house of Jupiter, and that the residents (Tiberius
and Germanicus) had not yet been awarded the honour of saving
citizens (Tiberius refused to allow the civic crown of oak to be
hung up at his door (Suet. *Tib.* 26). The line 'protegat et vestras
querna corona fores' is an expression of hope that Tiberius and
Germanicus will save citizens, namely, the poet himself.[53]

As a day sacred to Jupiter 13 January was thus as advantageous
a day to incorporate Germanicus in the calendar as was the fact
that the day had associations with the *cognomen* Augustus and
none with the new ruler, Tiberius. 13 January is the last entry of
Germanicus in the *Fasti*. There are two allusions to the *domus
Augusta*, one at 1. 701 ('gratia dis domuique tuae') and one at 1.
721 ('ut . . . domus quae praestat eam cum pace perennet'), both
in connection with the theme of peace which permeates the
reworking of book 1.[54] Germanicus as heir and peacemaker is naturally subsumed in these references, even if not explicitly

---

[52] Sutherland (1987) 8. See also *RG* 34. 2.

[53] Frazer's interpretation is that 'the courtly Ovid hints at the feigned reluctance of the new emperor to accept the crown, and expresses a polite hope that his
modest hesitation may yield to the wishes of his loyal subjects' ((1929) i. 230).

[54] Fantham (1985) 258 ff.

invoked. Apart from a sharp outburst at 4. 81 when memories of his home-town overwhelm the exile, Germanicus is mentioned by Ovid no more.

Why Ovid Abandoned the Fasti

Earlier in this chapter I tried to show that it was Germanicus' pivotal position and political standing within the family of Augustus that must have inspired Ovid to rededicate the *Fasti* to him. Now I hope to demonstrate that the young Caesar's subsequent loss of favour with Tiberius and the political crisis of AD 16 would give Ovid reason to lose confidence in Germanicus' powers as patron and abandon the *Fasti*, and cease all his pleas from exile, for good.

The last datable epistle from exile belongs to Pomponius Graecinus as suffect consul (*Ex P.* 4. 9. 5) in AD 16. The poem's reference to Ovid's celebrating the birthday of the god Augustus at lines 115–16 might place it after 23 September,[55] and the allusion to Pomponius' brother Flaccus, who will assume the fasces and inaugurate the following year, at lines 59 ff., dates it before the year 17. Germanicus is not personally invoked, yet the 'domus regnatrix' is at *Ex P.* 4. 9. 105–9, implying a sustained belief in imperial solidarity. No hint then, in the autumn of 16, that Ovid was aware of anything to the contrary between Germanicus and Tiberius. Nor indeed is there in his final letter to Sextus Pompeius (*Ex P.* 4. 15. 23–4) (AD 16?) which still invokes the 'numina' comprising the 'domus Augusta'. Hope still lived.

When did Ovid revise the *Fasti* for Germanicus? The one poem to invoke the aid of Germanicus directly is that addressed to Suillius Rufus (*Ex P.* 4. 8). It is datable to after the apotheosis of Augustus on 17 September AD 14 ('et modo, Caesar, avum, quem virtus addidit astris' line 63),[56] and is that which contains Ovid's promise to Germanicus to devote to him his poetic talents in return for a mitigation of his sentence. The death of Augustus had evidently provided fresh hope and opportunity to the exile to

---

[55] The arrangement of *Ex Ponto* bk. 4 is not dictated by chronology, see Syme (1978) 43–4.

[56] '. . . Divo Augusto honores caelestes a senatu decreti', in *Fast. Amit.* (Degrassi (1963) 510). Vell. 2. 124. 3; Tac. *Ann.* 12. 69. 4.

direct his energies towards pleasing the new patron he had discovered in the triumph of October, AD 12 (*Ex P.* 2. 1. 49 ff.).

Having found the earliest possible date of the poem, it is difficult to be more precise with a terminal date. Bömer places it
immediately after the death of Augustus, while Syme, conjectur-
ing that Suillius was quaestor serving on the Rhine under
Germanicus in 15, assigns the poem to 15 or 16.[57] Yet there is no
hint of the triumph voted in 15. The poet had already exuberantly
prophesied a glorious triumph for Germanicus back in 13 (*Ex P.*
2. 1.), and if he had heard nothing of its realization in the subsequent two years, he would naturally be more restrained now in
eulogizing Germanicus' military achievements.[58] Perhaps this
accounts for emphasis upon the poetic nature of the patron. The
poem may well belong to 15, but before news of the triumph
decreed in January of that year had reached him.

The edition of the *Fasti* which introduces Germanicus is
assumed to be an attempt at fulfilling the promise of poetic tribute in the letter to Suillius of, let us say, the first months of AD 15.
It is therefore subsequent to that epistle. The latest event entered
in Ovid's calendar is the German triumph of Germanicus voted
by the Senate on 1 January AD 15 (1. 285–6). The time required for
the exile to have received news of this and to have adjusted his
poem accordingly cannot be certain. He claims on several occasions that return mail between Rome and Tomis could take as
long as a year (*Ex P.* 3. 4. 59–60; 4. 11. 15–16). Elsewhere he claims
that a one-way trip from Tomis to Rome, even via the winter
snows of Thrace, could take less than ten days (*Ex P.* 4. 5. 5–8).
The latter figure strains credulity somewhat, as a courier travel-
ling at very high speed, that is, at a rate of over 150 miles per day,
took nine days to carry news of the revolt of the Rhine army to

---

[57] Bömer (1957–8) i. 18: 'Auch enthält das noch ins Jahr 14 datierte Gedicht
Pont. IV 8 eine so eindeutige Ergebenheitsadresse an Germanicus, dass kein
Zweifel daran besteht, dass Ovids Annäherungsversuche auf die Zeit unmittelbar
nach dem Tode des Augustus zurückgehen.' Syme (1978) 89, 93: Suillius' interest
to Ovid is not his marriage to Ovid's stepdaughter but his devotion to (and presumably influence with) Germanicus. Suillius' devotion to Germanicus 'di tibi
sunt Caesar iuvenis' (8. 23) recalls that of Sextus Pompeius: 'tempus ab his va-
cuum Caesar Germanicus omne / auferet: a magnis hunc colit ille deis' (5. 25–6).

[58] See the poem to Carus, tutor to the sons of Germanicus, written in the winter of 14–15 (*Ex P.* 4. 13. 40). Ovid's exhortation at 45–6 implies that he is now less
certain about the prospect of a triumph.

Galba in Rome in January AD 69. On average, an imperial courier
travelled about 50 miles a day.[59] And Ovid is unlikely to have
been permitted to use the *cursus publicus* usually reserved for official business dispatches and personages and which, in Pliny's day
and possibly before, required a permit (*Ep.* 10. 45–6). And even
that was not always reliable, judging from Claudius' complaint
about the problem of coping with corruption among Roman officials in charge of transport provision in the provinces (*ILS* 214).
Any private service at Ovid's disposal is very likely to have been
erratic and unreliable, especially in an outpost such as Tomis.

Anytime from mid-15 onwards is perhaps a reasonable estimate
of the time required for Ovid to have received news of the triumph voted for Germanicus which is evinced in the *Fasti*. The
date of the revision can be narrowed down to the period mid-15 to
late 16, when, I will argue, he ceased writing altogether.[60] Jerome
registers Ovid's death under the year AD 17 (*Chron.* p. 171 H), but
does not say when. Months, perhaps as much as a year after Ovid
had laid down his pen. Was it simply weariness of sending so
many vain entreaties to Rome that caused the poet to discard the
Fasti once more? Or did tensions in the political arena make him
realize that the new patron of the *Fasti* was powerless to help
him? The first alternative cannot be answered; an attempt can be
made at the second.

It has been shown that, publicly, solidarity existed between
Germanicus and Tiberius. Following his triumph on 26 May AD
17, Germanicus was given *maius imperium* over all the eastern
provinces, and granted a consulship with Tiberius in 18. Yet an
undercurrent of tension between the two may have been evident
to avid 'Caesar watchers' from as early as 15. In Tacitus' view,
Germanicus' continued campaigning in Germany after he had
been decreed his triumph in January 15 contributed to a growing
mistrust by Tiberius, even though Tiberius was anxious to avoid
open offence to his heir.[61] He was already worried by the rela-

[59] See *OCD*[2] Postal Service (Roman). An inscription from Pisidia of early
Tiberian date makes reference to rights regarding transport services. For text and
commentary, see Mitchell (1976) 106–31.

[60] Syme's view (n. 20) that Ovid was still writing in AD 17 is not tenable. The
last datable epistles were written before the beginning of that year.

[61] In the course of the year 15 he proposed a salutation to Germanicus for
achievements far from spectacular. Tiberius did not choose to add that salutation
to his own total. Tac. *Ann.* 1. 58. 5; Syme (1978) 61.

tionship between Germanicus and his eight legions since the mutiny in AD 14 (*Ann.* 1. 7, the first suggestion of unease in Tiberius). Germanicus, for his part, tried to avoid exacerbating the suspicions that he felt Tiberius harboured; it was for this reason that he excluded his own name on the monument set up after his victory in 16 (*Ann.* 2. 22. 2). The mistrust is most evident in the exchanges between the two regarding the conclusion of the German campaigns. Germanicus was advised by frequent letters from Tiberius to return home for the triumph already decreed for him, citing his own considerable experience to show that little more was likely to be achieved (*Ann.* 2. 26. 3) Germanicus pleaded for another year to complete his enterprise properly but Tiberius insisted, invoking Germanicus' sense of duty and offering him the inducement of a second consulship. Had Tiberius let the matter rest there, his arguments might have been regarded as reasonable, but Tacitus then has him commit a diplomatic blunder: having said that the campaign should not continue, Tiberius adds that, if it must go on, Germanicus should give Drusus a chance to win his triumphal honours (*Ann.* 2. 26. 3). Tacitus implies that it was the latter argument that caused Germanicus to yield, the idea now firmly implanted in his mind that jealousy was the motive for his premature recall.

If Tacitus' re-creation of the tensions between Tiberius and Germanicus at this time is authentic, then Germanicus would clearly not want to exacerbate a precarious situation by risking any further annoyance to Tiberius: for example, by petitioning on behalf of a disgraced poet who did not in any case enjoy the goodwill of the Princeps. Tacitus further reports that Tiberius did not succeed, despite his efforts to the contrary, in convincing people of the sincerity of his affection for Germanicus (*Ann.* 2. 42. 1). That Ovid eventually became aware of these tensions—and the concomitant limitation of Germanicus' influence over Tiberius—is utterly conceivable, and would have no doubt reduced his faith in his imperial patron. The reduction of such faith would have made him pause in his revision of the *Fasti*. It is naturally difficult to say when he might have become aware of such tensions: perhaps mid-16 is a reasonable estimate for when that pause took place (see below). The question is, approximately when was faith in his patron destroyed completely?

Strained relations between Germanicus and Tiberius were sig-

nificantly increased by immediately subsequent events which
Ovid must have seen as affecting his situation. Tacitus says that
'sub idem tempus' that Germanicus felt obliged to return to
Rome on account of his father's jealousy, a certain Libo Drusus,
of the family of Scribonii, was accused of revolutionary schemes
(*Ann.* 2. 27). The nature of the crime as preserved by Tacitus
does not properly justify the penalties imposed, yet the extent of
the gravity of the case in the mind of the accused was brought
home when he could find no advocate. He committed suicide
forthwith. The trial nevertheless went ahead and he was posthumously convicted (Tac. *Ann.* 2. 27–31).

The gravity of the case in the view of Tiberius is demonstrated
by the extravagance of the rewards to Libo's accusers, and of the
thanksgivings and offerings to Jupiter, Mars and Concord subsequent to the trial (Tac. *Ann.* 2. 32; Dio, 57. 15. 5). The day of
Libo's suicide, 13 September in the year AD 16 was even observed
as an NP day in the calendar. The entry made for this day in the
Fasti Amiternini reads thus:[62]

Feriae ex senatus consulto, quod eo die nefaria consilia, quae de salute
Ti. Caesaris liberorumque eius et aliorum principum civitatis deque re
publica inita ab M. Libone erant, in senatu convicta sunt.

Holiday by decree of the Senate because on that day the abominable conspiracy plotted by M. Libo against the safety of Tiberius Caesar and his
children and other leaders of the state and concerning the Republic was
exposed in the Senate.

This entry is significant for more than one reason: not only is this
the first time that the death of a conspirator is entered and celebrated as a public holiday in the Roman calendar; it also specifies
that not just Tiberius but also his heirs had been threatened. The
implication is that Germanicus too was put at risk by the conspiracy of Libo.

This point must be investigated. The exact nature of the conspiracy is not easy to determine, but it is clear that the charges
laid against Libo were far more serious than at first appears.
Suetonius (*Tib.* 25) has it that Tiberius genuinely believed that
there was a plot to overthrow him, and even implies, in conflating
several events including that of Libo, that Tiberius thought
Germanicus was interested in unseating him: 'simulavit et vali-

[62] Degrassi (1963) 509.

tudinem, quo aequiore animo Germanicus celerem successionem vel certe societatem principatus opperiretur.' The truth of Germanicus' involvement is less important than what Tiberius believed.

Seneca (*Ep.* 70. 10) on the other hand has it that it was Libo who was aiming higher than anyone could reach in that period. What that means is unclear. Tacitus however considered it important enough to note that Libo's great-grandfather was Pompey and his aunt Scribonia, former wife of Augustus (*Ann.* 2. 27. 2). In connection with that we note that Seneca supplies the significant anecdote that Scribonia, a 'gravis femina', was in fact involved in the affair. She staunchly supported Libo, giving him courageous advice not to commit suicide and so make life easier for Tiberius (Sen. *Ep.* 70. 2).

The fact that the discarded wife of Octavian should now be found, at the great age of 85 (she was in fact Libo's great-aunt[63]), indefatigably lending her name and support to an allegedly harmless individual whom Tiberius took very seriously indeed, points to the true nature of the crime. Scribonia had seen Julia, her only child by Octavian, destroyed, and in turn all Julia's children, with the exception of Agrippina. Scribonia's participation in the present intrigue most strongly suggests that the case of Libo was a cover for a dynastic conspiracy designed to oust the descendants of Livia, Scribonia's replacement in Octavian's affections, for the purpose of ensuring the survival of her own.[64] The gravity with which Tiberius treated Libo gives full support to such an idea. Yet for him to admit that it was a dynastic coup was not a politic move. Hence the difficulty in reconciling the seriousness of the charge with the apparently ludicrous actions of Libo which initiated proceedings against him (Tac. *Ann.* 2. 27, 30).

But was Germanicus really under threat from such a conspiracy? Germanicus himself was not related to Scribonia, but he was a very powerful consort to her only surviving granddaughter and

[63] Syme (1986) 256.

[64] As Levick (1976a) 41–2, 150 has very convincingly shown. Proposographical speculation is not in all cases profitable, but as the fate of Scribonia's descendants through Augustus was so consistently dire after the marriage of Julia and Tiberius broke down it would seem inconceivable to think that she would passively sit and watch her children and descendants disgraced and destroyed. The sources are suggesting that she did not. And the mere survival of her descendants necessitated the destruction of the son of Livia.

was father of her direct descendants. In AD 16 those six descendants were still young and in need of powerful protection. He also bore the doubly charismatic name of Germanicus Caesar, a name no possible 'Scribonian' replacement stepfather could compete with, especially with regard to the army, no matter how distinguished a pedigree he may have had. To wipe Germanicus out would also have risked incurring the rage of the Roman populace—and perhaps of the Rhine legions which, only two years before had offered him the empire—against the conspirators. The extravagant grief and recriminations at the mystery surrounding his death three years later supports this idea (Tac. *Ann.* 2. 82). Surely Germanicus must have been destined to be spared, even though he was the grandson of Livia.[65] To plot the assassination of all three adult Caesars would not be at all a viable plan for a successful overthrow of Tiberius and his natural son, Drusus. The preservation of Germanicus was the best guarantee that his children, Scribonia's descendants, would survive.

Yet if Germanicus was intended to be spared, how to account for the *Fasti Amiternini* declaring that both Tiberius and his sons were at risk? To do so we must first consider two other inscriptions which similarly lure the observer into forming the wrong impression. Linderski[66] has shown how it is in the context of embellishing and expurgating history that we have to place an inscription of AD 42 incorporating the discarded and disinherited Julia I as a happy part of the monolithic 'domus Augusta'. If all literary sources pertaining to her catastrophe had perished, he says, this inscription would have stood for all times as a document of co-operation between the happy family of Iulia, 'divi Augusti filia', 'divus Augustus', and 'diva Augusta'.[67]

The same might be said of the *Tabula Siarensis*, recording honours decreed for the dead Germanicus in AD 19.[68] The inscription places great emphasis upon the monolithic 'domus Augusta' comprising Tiberius Caesar Augustus, his mother the Augusta, Drusus Caesar, Antonia the mother of Germanicus Caesar, Agrippina his wife and Livia his sister, the deceased Germanicus himself, his deceased father Nero Drusus, etc. This document too might have stood as a monument to a happy unity of Caesars

[65] *Contra* Levick (1976a) 151.   [66] Linderski (1988) 181–90.
[67] Ibid. 200.   [68] See n. 47.

if we were not well equipped with the literary sources which tell a very different story.

It is in the same context, I believe, that we should look at the *Fasti Amiternini*, dated AD 20, the year after the death of Germanicus. The words 'de salute Ti. Caesaris liberorumque eius' promote an ideal of unity within the 'domus Augusta', a unity which Tacitus' words indicate had begun to erode, in the case of Tiberius and Germanicus, by the year 15. The very fact that the inscription declares that the whole family was threatened tempts one to suspect that it was not the whole family which was threatened, that the alleged conspiracy of Libo was aimed at a selected member or members only, a selection which did not, for practical reasons, include Germanicus. The idea that the whole family was threatened is promoted in the inscription to maintain the view of the emperor and imperial family as a united front.

If this theory is correct, then it was the 'conspiracy' of Libo, occurring, as Tacitus says, at the same time as Germanicus felt impelled to return to Rome on account of his father's ill-feeling, which served to worsen already deteriorating relations between himself and his father, even if Germanicus was unaware of the conspiracy. Germanicus' intimate connection with the Scribonian side of the family would in itself make the besieged Princeps highly suspicious of his immediate heir, and seriously doubt that Germanicus too was meant to be destroyed. It is news of the same conspiracy, understood as a dynastic coup, which I propose finally brought home to Ovid the complete fallacy of the monolithic institution of the 'domus Augusta', and the accompanying idea of any bond between Germanicus and Tiberius which gave him faith in the possibility of recall.

This being so, then the fact that the last datable epistle of Ovid's from exile is late AD 16 need not surprise. Bad news travels fast. Germanicus' powers as patron, which had looked so very promising within the 'domus Augusta' between AD 12 and 15, had, from Ovid's point of view, now been rendered obsolete. And once he had made the blunder of backing the wrong horse publicly, in his poetry, what patron could help him now? His final epistle reveals a realization of the fact by speaking of his Muse in the past tense,[69]

---

[69] In the penultimate, in which the 'domus' still exists, he had spoken of his Muse as having a future: *Ex P.* 4. 15. 39–42.

knowing full well now that his poetry had lost its power to help him (*Ex P.* 4. 16. 45–52):

> dicere si fas est, claro mea nomine Musa
>> atque, inter tantos quae legeretur erat.
> ergo summotum patria proscindere, Livor,
>> desine, neu cineres sparge, cruente, meos.
> omnia perdidimus: tantummodo vita relicta est,
>> praebeat ut sensum materiamque mali.
> quid iuvat extinctos ferrum demittere in artus?
>> non habet in nobis iam nova plaga locum.

If it is permissible to say so, my Muse was renowned, and she was recited amongst the great. Therefore, Envy, refrain from tearing at one who has been displaced from his native land. Nor scatter my ashes, cruel one. We have lost everything. Life alone is left, so that it may provide the consciousness of torment and its source. What point is there in thrusting steel into dead limbs? There is no place left in me now for a new wound.

These words are telling us that the poet knew that all his poetic efforts would henceforth be in vain. He does not say why. Yet he is saying that he has no further reason for writing poetry, indeed, for living. It was not death then, that caused Ovid to lay down his pen. It was the deprivation of a reason to write that precipitated his death.

EPILOGUE

A STUDY of the cultural and political background to the *Fasti* has illustrated how the Roman calendar as a subject for 'epic' was a viable option for an elegist trying to adapt his talents to the service of the late Augustan regime. Ovid turned the technical difficulties inherent in the task to advantage by creating a new genre, a new elegiac medium which could accommodate both a Callimachaean spirit and a celebration in a lighter vein of 'magna', hitherto the preserve of heroic hexameters. The calendar also gave him the opportunity to imitate in poetry the episodic and decorative techniques of Augustan architectural sculptors. Their example demonstrated how it was possible to avoid the dangers implicit in narrating the career of Augustus and still find a balance between catering to the ambitions of the ruler and to the artist's own individual style.

The study of the *Fasti* itself has elicited much information about its author. The portraits which adorn Ovid's calendar indicate that, before his exile, he was finely attuned to the political and cultural currents of his times. His protagonists are portrayed in roles which were complementary to their individual functions within Augustus' political and religious programme. After his exile and the death of Augustus, his treatment of Tiberius and Livia shows the poet's understanding of the political realignments effected by the terms of Augustus' will in so far as it mirrors that of the Roman senate—and of Livia herself. At the same time, that treatment is the work of an author ill-informed about the temperament and style of government of the new ruler, an author led by his situation as suppliant into making tactless errors about the relative status of Tiberius and the Augusta. Ovid's decision to rededicate the *Fasti* to Germanicus exposes the exile who somehow knew that Tiberius would ignore his pleas, yet an outcast who had enough faith in the power of imperial patronage to entertain a hope of returning to Rome. It has been posited that

Ovid finally became aware of a crisis within the imperial *domus* in late AD 16, that it was then that he lost confidence in his patron's powers, abandoned all hope of salvation and laid down his pen for ever.

An historical study of the *Fasti* discloses aspects of members of the ruling family which add depth and insight into the processes by which Augustus imposed himself upon the age. The numerous references to Julius Caesar demonstrate the way in which memory of the first Caesar could be reshaped to augment Augustus in both a political and a religious role. Ovid's pre-exilic portrayals of Livia project her in the guise of Roman *matrona* which enhances the ruler as religious and moral revivalist. They point to a desire of Augustus to associate his consort with, and to exercise control through her patronage of, the ancient female cults of Rome. The variety of roles assigned Augustus himself illuminates the way in which the carnage perpetrated by him at the beginning of his career was legitimized in religious terms on a national level; the way in which his identity, and that of all subsequent Caesars, was infused into the heart of Roman religion; the way in which that religion, which focused on the past, could be adapted to accommodate a living individual as designated, hereditary ruler of the Roman world.

An historical study of the *Fasti* has revealed how a mythology could be created to transform Republican titles into roles of monarchical stamp. It is the *Fasti* which contains the essential features, hitherto obscured, that were at the heart of the transformation, in religious terms, from Republic to Monarchy. The way in which that transformation was affected is witnessed by no other contemporary source.

APPENDIX

Omissions in the *Fasti*

THE need for this appendix has been occasioned by Syme's treatment of the *Fasti* in chapter 2 of his *History in Ovid* (1978). There he provides a summary catalogue of the Augustan anniversaries registered in the six books of the poem, concludes that the total sum is not large, and makes note of the omissions. It is the omissions, which 'may (or may not) prove instructive for some purpose or other', which most attracted Syme's attention. Two of them consume the major part of his study of Ovid's calendrical verse.

It is those same omissions which will be the subject of the present study. Syme lists five in all, in ascending order of seriousness. They are:

1. Octavian's assumption of imperium on 7 January 43 BC.
2. Dea Dia, 'the goddess to whom sacrifice was made by the Arvales, a confraternity revived by Augustus from ancient desuetude and intended to convey high prestige'.
3. The Ludi Saeculares.
4. The three closures of Janus.
5. The adoption of Tiberius on 26 June AD 4.

Of these omissions, it is (4) and (5) which received in-depth treatment by Syme. I propose to provide a similar treatment to all of them now with the exception of (4) 'The Three Closures of Janus', which has been treated at length elsewhere in the present work (see Ch. 5, 'Germanicus and Janus'). The other omissions to receive scrutiny here will reveal that Syme was not only unjustified in scolding Ovid for his negligence; they will also suggest that his dating of the *Fasti* to the years AD 1–4 is erroneous, and support the theory, postulated throughout this book, that Ovid was stating the truth when he said that the composition of the *Fasti* was interrupted by his banishment (*T* 2. 551–2). That the poem was written, in other words, in the years immediately prior to AD 8. This is the purpose for which I believe the omissions noted by Syme indeed 'prove instructive'.

1. *Caesar's Assumption of Imperium, 7 January 43 BC*

'Though Ovid refers to the young Caesar at Mutina (April 14 and 16), nothing is said about his assumption of imperium on January 7, 43 BC

Not very grave, perhaps.'[1] Three inscriptions datable to the last decade of Augustus' life record the event. The incomplete *Fasti Praenestini* has been reconstructed by Degrassi for 7 January thus: 'Imp. Caesar Augustu[s - - - primum fasces sumpsit] Hirtio et Panso [co(n)sulibus)].' (Imperator Caesar Augustus first assumed the fasces in the consulship of Hirtius and Pansa.) The observer will notice that the appellation 'Augustus' is backdated to 43 BC, and that the calendar makes clear, in naming both consuls, that Caesar's imperium was not conferred upon him as consul. The *Feriale Cumanum* declares: 'VII idus Ianuar(ias) eo die Caesar primum fasces sumpsit. Supplicatio Iovi Sempiterno.'[2] (7 Jan. On this day Caesar first assumed the fasces. Thanksgiving to Eternal Jupiter.) A lengthy inscription from Narbo in Gaul, dated AD 11–13 and celebrating the erection of an altar to the 'numen' of Augustus in thanksgiving for his having reconciled the populace to the decurions, selects certain dates upon which to honour the Princeps. One is his birthday. The other is 7 January, cited as the day upon which he entered upon rule of the world: 'VII quoq(ue) idus Ianuar(ias), qua die primum imperium orbis terrarum auspicatus est . . .'.[3] (Also on 7 January, on which day he first inaugurated his rule of the world.)

The different interpretations of the significance of 7 January are startling. The first two commemorate it as the anniversary of Caesar's first assumption of the fasces (not even as consul after all, but as propraetor to assist the consuls), and simply the first of many *honores* he was to attain in his career. It is given no precedence over his other honours and surely rightly so. On 7 January 43 BC he had not even been saluted as 'imperator' at this point (to occur on 16 April), nor been elected consul (to occur on 19 August). The third—and notably provincial inscription—selects it as the day Augustus began his career as sole ruler. The different perceptions as to the nature of Augustus' rule, even while he was still living, are manifest.

How did Augustus himself perceive the event? Fortunately we have his (public) interpretation on the subject (*RG* i. 2–3):

eo nomine senatus decretis honorificis in ordinem suum me adlegit C. Pansa et A. Hirtio consulibus consularem locum sententiae dicendae tribuens, et imperium mihi dedit. Res publica ne quid detrimenti caperet, me propraetore simul cum consulibus providere iussit.

On that account the Senate, with honorific decrees, enrolled me in its order in the consulship of C. Pansa and A. Hirtius, bestowing on me consular rank in the order of voting, and granted me imperium. It ordered me as propraetor, along with the consuls, to ensure that the Republic should suffer no harm.

---

[1] Syme (1978) 23.
[2] For the quotations from the *Fasti Praenestini* and the *Feriale Cumanum* see Degrassi (1963) 392.   [3] *ILS* 112; Ehrenberg–Jones (1976) 86.

The 7 January 43 BC, had certainly been a red-letter day for Octavian, and obviously still was to the aged Augustus recalling his youth. But not merely because he had had imperium conferred on him for the first time; just as importantly it signified senatorial, and therefore legal, endorsement for his act of having illegally levied troops and made unauthorized use of military force. The 'factio' from which he claims to have saved the state (*RG* I. I) was the legitimate government of the consul, Antonius. If Cicero had not, in the fifth Philippic (I Jan. 43 BC), urged the Senate to enrol Octavian as a senator and ally with *imperium propraetore* against Antony (who had not yet been declared a public enemy), the youthful usurper would have been inviting upon himself the punishment of a brigand.[4]

The *Res Gestae* evinces Augustus' continued preoccupation with the problem of legitimacy which clouded the beginning of his public career. In documenting the circumstances in which he won his first magisterial honours he is saying that his illegal act as a private citizen, his revolutionary beginning, was all for the public good, proven by senatorial recognition. The 7 January was the anniversary of his accession to legal power, authorized by the governing body, and for that reason one of the most important landmarks in his career. But it was by no stretch of the imagination the greatest power or honour he attained. Nor does he say as much.

The *Fasti Praenestini* seems to reflect most accurately the nature of the power Octavian acceded to on that day. The *Feriale Cumanum* is a little less specific but not misleading, as it does record his first consulship on 19 August. So why did the Gallic town of Narbo choose 7 January as the day on which he began his 'imperium orbis terrarum'? His *dies imperii* as it were.

On that day, in 43 BC, Gallia Narbonensis was being governed by M. Aemilius Lepidus, ally of Antony, and now, after the death of Julius, Pontifex Maximus by his ally's contrivance. Antony, after his defeat at the hands of Octavian at Mutina in April of that year, was declared a public enemy and repaired to Gallia Narbonensis where Lepidus joined forces with him. Lepidus' justification for doing so is preserved in a letter he wrote to the Senate on 30 May, explaining how his soldiers refused to war against their fellow citizens and had compelled him to take up the cause of the safety and preservation of so great a number of Roman citizens (Cic. *Fam.* 10. 35. 1).

In his dispatch to the Senate, Lepidus firmly assigned the decision to side with Antony to his troops. This might have been true, as his army of seven legions included some of Caesar's best officers and men, and the enemy they thought they were to confront included the assassin,

---

[4] On the illegality of Cicero's proposal, see Syme (1939) 167–8.

Decimus Brutus. The vicissitudes of politics then brought back both Lepidus and Antony into an *amicitia* with Octavian. When Lepidus' reliability subsequently became suspect and he was removed from his province, Gallia Narbonensis and all of Gaul then passed into Antony's hands. But under Antony, Gaul played an ambivalent role in the Perusine War and its aftermath. Under his legates, P. Ventidias and C. Asinius Pollio, legions from the Gallic provinces marched to the aid of Antony's brother, Lucius, but, lacking direct authorization from Antony himself, failed to engage Octavian's troops in battle. While they awaited instructions, Octavian was able to send his own troops into their Gallic domain, whose depleted garrisons capitulated without resistance. Octavian was eventually able to occupy the whole of Gaul by miraculous good fortune. Calenus, Antony's man holding the fort there, opportunely died, and his son, lacking experience or confidence, was induced to surrender the province and all its legions.[5]

Gallia Narbonensis, having been governed first by Lepidus, then by Antony at a time when they were opposed to Octavian, thus came into the latter's hands under the most inauspicious circumstances. When the passing of time had confirmed the undisputed winner in the contest for power, might there not have been those at Narbo, ex-legionaries perhaps, who were most anxious to compensate for earlier loyalties directed elsewhere? Under such circumstances a desire to eradicate the stigma of a certain embarrassing period in local history would be understandable. Especially now, in AD 11, after Augustus had done the town a favour by sorting out a local dispute. The choice of 7 January 43 BC as Octavian's *dies imperii* was a means of achieving this. It suggests that Narbo, in publicly commemorating, exaggerating, and distorting the nature of the power of Octavian's first magistracy (more possible to do in a province, perhaps), wanted to insist that it really had been loyal to Octavian from the beginning, even while being governed by his opponents.

What is intriguing, however, is that later writers, apparently anxious to find a *dies imperii* for Augustus, also regarded 7 January in such a light. Pliny, for example, refers to this day in connection with Augustus as 'primus potestatis suae dies' (*NH* 11. 190), and 7 January was apparently selected in the third century for the granting of *honesta missio* to the Praetorians and the Equites Singulares.[6] In contrast to this we have Cassius Dio providing various, and inconsistent, dates for the precise beginning of Augustus' sole power, none of which coincides with 7 January 43 BC. At 51. 1. 1. it is said to begin in 31 BC; at 52. 1. 1. the people

---

[5] This is a very bare outline of the most complicated events. For details, see Syme (1939) 165 ff., 173–4, 178 ff, 207 ff. Jones (1970) 25 ff. provides a simplified version.

[6] For sources, see Fink *et al.* (1940) 231.

begin to be ruled by a monarch in 29 BC; at 53. 17. 1 the transfer of power from Senate and people is dated to 27 BC, and the monarchy begins then. The subject clearly posed great difficulties for the early third-century historian.[7]

The conflict is not confined to later sources. In contrast again we have calendars of Augustan/Tiberian dating which preserve 7 January, but neglect to mention Octavian's anniversary at all. First, the *Fasti Maffeiani* (after 8 BC). This calendar marks Augustus' birthday, the day he was made Pontifex Maximus, the day he captured Alexandria, and several anniversaries of Julius Caesar's. But nothing for 7 January. Second, the *Fasti Verulani* (AD 14–37) marks Augustus' marriage to Livia, the dedication of the Ara Pacis and sundry other anniversaries. Again, nothing on 7 January. Third, the *Fasti Aedis Concordiae* (period of the first emperors) preserving only six days but inclusive of 7 January, nothing. Fourth, Ovid's *Fasti*, dedicated to commemorating Augustus' titles of distinction (2. 15–16), makes no mention of his first assumption of the fasces.

It is not possible to account for the omission in the inscriptional calendars mentioned. The provenance of these calendars is not absolutely certain, and the varying interplay between unknowable local factors and central pressures would have undoubtedly played a part in the selection of anniversaries commemorated. But the omission in Ovid, who was writing in Rome with his finger on the pulse of up-to-the-minute calendrical trends, is perhaps explicable.

It is my conjecture that, as Verrius Flaccus recorded the event, and in a manner most similar to that of his patron, Ovid did also—in his first edition prior to exile. But he erased it in the second. The chapter on Germanicus in the present book has demonstrated how the poet completely redesigned an Augustan anniversary for the month of January in order to accommodate his new dedicatee. There is not one anniversary in January, in fact, which lauds Augustus purely in his own right. Ovid clearly struck trouble in incorporating Germanicus, however, when he came to the 30 January, anniversary of the Ara Pacis (1. 709–24). Remarkably the name of Augustus is never mentioned, and his achievement is referred to only obliquely with the mention of Actian laurels. The focus of the passage is more on the services to peace of the 'duces' of the Augustan house (Tiberius and Germanicus), concluded by an exhortation to the reader to pray for the eternal duration of the Augustan dynasty. The passage clearly belongs to the second edition,[8] but Ovid

---

[7] Manuwald (1979) thinks Dio's uncertainty about which date to adopt for the reign's inception, 31, 29, or 27 BC is a result of his use of different sources. See review by Pelling (1983) 221.

[8] See also Fantham (1985) 261, 265 and her discussion of the 'domus Augusta'.

perhaps felt the difficulty of naming his new young dedicatee in a celebration of an altar to peace which had been dedicated as long ago as (by
AD 15) 24 years before.

Ovid could not have excluded the 30 January for the sake of accommodating the person of Germanicus without doing violation to his calendar,
because it was an NP day and a major Augustan festal day. The same did
not apply to 7 January. This day was not a festal day at all, and could be
safely erased without discomfort. As it was too difficult to rework
Octavian's first assumption of the fasces to incorporate Germanicus, this
is what he did. Ovid's omission of 7 January is simply a casualty of
Ovid's rewriting and rededicating of the *Fasti* to Germanicus.

2. Dea Dia

'No sign of Dea Dia, the goddess to whom sacrifice was made by the
Arvales, a confraternity revived by Augustus from ancient desuetude and
intended to convey high prestige. No extant writer knows of Dea Dia,
and she might well baffle the ingenious fancy of Ovid.'[9] The *Acta
Fratrum Arvalium*, inscribed on a series of stone tablets spanning 21 BC
to AD 304, show that the festival of the Dea Dia, extending over three
days, was celebrated annually. The precise dates of those three days,
however, were not made known by the Magister of the brotherhood until
the January of the year in question. This was done by the ceremony of
indictio, usually but not always performed between the nones and ides of
January, usually but not always at the temple of Concord. The names
of members of the brotherhood present at the *indictio* are recorded in the
inscriptions.[10] The dates proclaimed for the festival were usually set for
May. The records show that 17, 19, and 20 May were popular dates, as
were 27, 29, and 30; 25, 27, and 28 were also not uncommon. Yet the first
surviving record of the *indicatio* (20 BC) proclaimed not May but June as
the month of the festival for that year.[11] The fact that the dates were set
and announced annually by the magister assigns the festival of the Dea
Dia to the category of *feriae conceptivae*.

The location of the rites, also proclaimed at the *indictio* varied to a
degree as well. The first day was 'domi, the second 'in luco et domi', the
third 'domi'. The 'domus' was that of the Magister of the Brotherhood,
and as the incumbent of this office changed from year to year, so too did
the location of the 'domus'. The 'lucus' was the Arval Grove, containing

[9] Syme (1978) 23.

[10] The Arval *Acta* are to be found most conveniently in the editions of Henzen
(1874) and Pasoli (1950). For publications of discoveries more recent, see Paladino
(1988) 18.

[11] Paladino (1988) 86 provides a list of variations over the years.

the temple of the goddess, situated approximately seven kilometres west of Rome. The Arval Grove, in which the Acta (with rare exceptions) were discovered, seems to have been the only site predictably associated with the cult. Its central focus, therefore, was outside the city of Rome.

The precise character of the goddess is uncertain, but Varro's discussion of the etymology of the Fratres Arvales ('sacra publica faciunt propterea ut fruges ferant arva', *LL* 5. 85) suggests that the goddess whose worship they conducted was concerned with the safeguard of agricultural production and prosperity.[12] Some of the rites recorded in the Acta reflect an agricultural nature: on day one, for example, corn and bread decked with laurel are consecrated, and on day two wreaths of ears of corn are worn and the corn passed round.[13] The agricultural character of this worship seems to have continued unbroken then, from the Republic to the Principate, notwithstanding that the Arvals also became concerned with rites other than the Dea Dia under the Principate, namely vows and sacrifices performed for the safety of the emperor in the city itself.[14]

The Arval Brothers normally numbered twelve men who served for life. Augustus boasted about being a Frater Arvalis in his enumeration of sacerdotal dignities (*RG* 7. 3). The confraternity was also extremely elitist, the Brothers being drawn from the highest social rank.[15] Others who participated in various ways were cult servants and minor officials. They included four boys from senatorial families with father and mother still alive who assisted at the sacrifices and the communal feasting; kalatores or freedmen of individual priests, publici or public slaves who were attached to the priesthood as a whole, and a notary.[16] The names of the priests who were present at the festival were recorded in the *Acta*. Worship of the Dea Dia seems to have been limited to the brotherhood and a select group of assistants, which would explain how many of the rites could be conducted in as confined a location as the home of the Magister.

Yet on the second day of the festival, held invariably in the Arval Grove, it is mentioned that chariot races were held in the Circus. This aspect is rather intriguing. Despite increased verbosity in the *Acta* as time progressed,[17] details of these chariot races are minimal. We find mention of the presentation of prizes to winners but their names and

[12] Henzen (1876), *Acta* ix: 'Sacra Fratrum Arvalium, ut monstrat nomen eorum Varronisque confirmat testimonium, ad arva potissimum pertinebant et vitam agrestem.'

[13] For details of the rites of each day, see Paladino (1988) 116 ff.

[14] For examples of these rites, see Beard (1985) 117.

[15] Scheid (1975) 106–8 provides the names for the Augustan period.

[16] Beard (1985) 119.   [17] See Beard (1985) esp. 142.

status are not recorded, nor the number of contestants.[18] Presumably, the general public attended the circus games. If so, this seems to have been the only public aspect of the festival of the Dea Dia. We have seen that the first day, the evening of the second, and the third, all took place in the home of the Magister, necessarily restricting proceedings to the Arvals and their attendants. That part of the festival attended by the public therefore occurred only outside the city. But what public? Are we to suppose that the populace of Rome, having taken note of the date from the *indictio* in January, streamed out to the fifth milestone on the Via Campana west of the city to attend these games? Or did the day pass virtually unnoticed in Rome, affecting only those who lived in the neighbourhood in which its rites took place?

There is unfortunately nothing in the evidence to reveal the extent of the importance of the Dea Dia to the general Roman public in relation to the other religious festivals. But if we envisage Augustus and the cream of the Roman nobility trundling out to the Arval Grove every year to preside over circus races, we may be sure that the Dea Dia, whatever her calendrical status, enjoyed a considerable public profile. In view of this it is very doubtful indeed that the goddess baffled the 'ingenious fancy of Ovid', as Syme put it. There must be another reason why he chose to omit the goddess in his calendar. Let us look at the possibilities.

It could be to do with the fact that the festival was *feriae conceptivae*: 'quid a fastis non stata sacra petis?' asks the Muse of Ovid (1. 660), no doubt to explain the poet's reason for not including the moveable festivals of the Compitalia and the Feriae Latinae in the month of January. However, he did include one festival of such a nature, the Feriae Sementivae, under 24 January (1. 657–704). Admittedly this is a special case, as the poet's new circumstances in exile undoubtedly dictated its inclusion. It is reasonably clear that the passage praising Tellus and Ceres as mothers of the corn, offering thanksgiving for the end of war to the Augustan *domus*, and culminating in a celebration of peace, belongs to the second edition dedicated to Germanicus.[19] To a poet hard put to incorporate his new young dedicatee in a calendar in which he did not belong, an extra festival offering added scope for contriving praise must have been a boon. At any rate, his inclusion of the Feriae Sementivae

[18] The circus has not yet been studied by Scheid and Broise (1987), who merely reproduce the plan of A. Pellegrini (1865) on p. 75. John Scheid has informed me in conversation that the area is so built over by modern development that the likelihood of its being excavated in the near future is highly remote.

[19] Ovid apparently included the moveable Feriae Sementivae as a means of praising peace which he reasonably expected after the declaration of a triumph for Germanicus on 1 Jan. AD 15. The passage does not reflect the years AD 6–8, years of war and famine. See also Bömer (1957–8) i. 701, and Fantham (1985) 258–9.

demonstrates that a moveable festival was not an insurmountable obstacle; nevertheless its uniqueness in the poem also demonstrates that it was not Ovid's practice to include such feasts in his first edition.

The fact that the day most central to the festival of Dea Dia was spent outside Rome possibly deterred the poet unwilling or unable to make the effort to witness the event. Yet he did celebrate the extra-urban Robigalia (4. 905 ff.). This was a large-lettered NP festival though, and Ovid could not have done justice to his task had he left out such a major calendrical event. The character of the day of the Dea Dia festival remains unknown to us; if it were not *feriae publicae pro populo* and a holiday for everyone, for example, perhaps the poet felt he could afford to omit it without discomfort.

There is yet another reason which might prove promising. This takes into account the character of the festival of the Dea Dia and the period in which Ovid was writing the *Fasti*. It has already been noted that Dea Dia was more than likely a goddess concerned with the productivity of the earth. Wissowa was convinced that the role of corn in her ritual 'ist leicht verständlich als Dank für die vorjährige und Fürbitte für die diesjährige Ernte'. In conclusion to her study, Paladino found a close connection between the Arvales and the role of 'proprietari di terre coltivabili'.[20]

If Ovid was writing the *Fasti* in the years AD 5–8, is it so surprising that he chose to leave out a festival celebrated by the élite as a guarantee of the gift of grain to the community? The famine of AD 5–6 might have suggested to the public that the Arval brotherhood accorded such prestige by Augustus had not been effective in its task. The fact that Augustus himself was an Arval brother would not have increased public confidence in him as a recipient of divine favour and as guarantor of the grain supply. Dio records that the mass of people suffered grievously from the famine, which generated an atmosphere of crisis. The crisis was exacerbated by a series of natural disasters (fire, flood, earthquake) as well as by additional taxation and conscription as a result of demands of wars in the north, and there was a threat of serious popular unrest (Dio, 55. 26–7; also Pliny *NH* 7. 149). Evidence of Augustus' own concern about the famine comes in the form of his dedication of an altar to Ceres (although he was not a priest of Ceres) and Ops Augusta on the vicus Iugarius on 10 August AD 7, created a new NP day.[21]

Why Ceres and not Dea Dia? Henzen and Warde Fowler thought that the two were identical, that it was only the name Ceres that was wanting

---

[20] Wissowa (1912) 563. Paladino (1988) 265.

[21] See Degrassi (1963) 493 for the calendrical inscriptions. Augustus was not a priest of Ceres. Her priests were 'plebeian aediles Cereris'. See Wissowa (1912) 300; Paladino (1988) 227.

in the Arval ritual, not the *numen* itself. Ceres was simply a different name for, and aspect of, the *numen* whom the Arval brothers called Dea Dia.[22] Wissowa is essentially in agreement, pointing out that Dea Dia is only a 'Beiname einer Gottheit', which he thought originally covered both the closely associated deities Tellus and Ceres.[23]

The theory that the Dea Dia was 'identical' with Ceres, is not wholly convincing, even if the agricultural nature of the two deities are so similar. Especially when a clear difference in the two cults is discernible. That difference seems to lie not so much in the nature of each goddess as in the rank of her worshippers. Ceres was historically associated with the Roman plebs, her temple thought to have been vowed in consequence of a serious famine in 496 BC, and dedicated in 493 BC, the year of the first secession of the plebs and of the establishment of the tribunes and plebeian aediles.[24]

The origins of the cult of Dea Dia on the other hand, are totally obscured to us, but Paladino's study had led her to the plausible hypothesis that the Fratres Arvales under the empire represented a survival of early republican worship by the patriciate or senatorial land-owning nobility, reflected in the élitism of the Augustan membership of the Fratres. Long before the Augustan period, of course, plebeians had access to wealth and power, so that the distinction between the orders as such was by then no longer a criterion. The distinction remained however, in the fact that all the Fratres were senators of the highest rank, which means that socio-political status was still a determining factor in the worship of the goddess of agriculture known as Dea Dia. Ceres continued to be worshipped more by those excluded from land-owning wealth and political power, which naturally meant the majority.[25]

If Dea Dia was associated only with the aristocracy, it makes sense that Augustus dedicated an altar to Ceres, the goddess worshipped by the masses. This act in fact was reminiscent of the circumstances of famine and distress which tradition dictated originally gave rise to the cult of Ceres in Rome. Furthermore, the frequency with which Ovid celebrates Ceres in his half-finished poem certainly attests to her great calendrical importance in the popular consciousness.[26]

The famine of AD 6 was obviously no deterrent to the poet's commem-

---

[22] Warde Fowler (1899) 74.

[23] Wissowa (1912) 195. Other scholars prefer to give her a celestial character: 'Dea Dia est à considérer comme la déesse du ciel lumineux, la déesse du bon murissement' (Schilling (1979) 366–70). See also Scheid (1975) 343–4.

[24] Warde Fowler (1899) 74–5; Wissowa (1912) 300; Nash (1961) 109.

[25] Paladino (1988) 266 ff.

[26] On 24 Jan., 12 and 19 Apr. (1. 657 ff.; 4. 393 ff, 679 ff.). The games of Ceres were celebrated continuously from 12 to 19 Apr. as the inscribed calendars demonstrate.

oration of the 'plebeian' side to her worship. On 12 April there is just the slightest hint that there was a scarcity of grain at the time, attributable to the wars then being waged in the north and their repercussions on the Roman populace. After recounting the history of Ceres' services to mankind, the poet says (4. 405–8):

> aes erat in pretio, Chalybeia massa latebat:
>   eheu, perpetuo debuit illa tegi.
> pace Ceres laeta est; et vos orate, coloni,
>   perpetuam pacem pacificumque ducem.

Bronze was prized. Iron ore was still unknown. Alas, it ought to have remained hidden forever. Ceres delights in peace; And do you, farmers, pray for eternal peace and for a peace-making leader.

and he follows his preface linking agricultural plenty and peace with a long and detailed account of the grief of Ceres (Demeter) at the rape of her daughter Persephone, well known as the event which caused her to withhold from the world her gift of corn (cf. *Met.* 5. 474 ff.). The connection between the preamble and the story itself might well be interpreted as meaning that war caused Ceres almost equal distress, at least enough to induce her to cause a dearth of crops. This interpretation is given support when we see that Ovid carries the theme over into his post-exilic passage for 24 January, where it is clear he thought that Germanicus' coming triumph had signalled the end of warfare. Having harked back to the period of war, when the fields were neglected, he triumphantly concludes (1. 701–4):

> gratia dis domuique tuae: religata catenis
>   iampridem vestro sub pede Bella iacent.
> sub iuga bos veniat, sub terras semen aratas:
>   Pax Cererem nutrit, Pacis alumna Ceres.

Thanks be to the gods and to your house: under your foot wars bound in chains now long lie prostrate. Let the ox come beneath the yoke, and the seed beneath the ploughed earth. Peace nurtures Ceres, and Ceres is the nursling of Peace.

That Ovid did not celebrate Dea Dia could well be a result of the fact that in the years AD 6–8 the goddess tended by the elite brotherhood was not at the time enjoying a great deal of popularity amongst a hungry populace, discontented and openly discussing plans for a revolution (Dio, 55. 27. 1). One wonders how well attended the circus games in the Arval Grove were in the year AD 6. An embarrassingly sparse crowd? With Augustus in his role as Arval brother certain to attend, it would have been an ideal occasion and situation to lodge a protest through non-attendance.

Or were the games cancelled altogether? Cancellation of a festival in time of crisis was not unprecedented. Plutarch (*Fab.* 18. 2) reports that, following the battle of Cannae, a festival and procession for Demeter (Ceres) was omitted lest the magnitude of the disaster should be brought home to the people by the sight of the few persons attending the rites and the gloom on their faces. And Dio reports that, in consequence of the emergency created by the famine, Augustus allowed senators to leave the city and go wherever they chose (55. 26. 1). If any of those senators who did so were Arval brethren, it is surely unlikely that the festival to Dea Dia would have taken place without the full attendance of the confraternity.

To sum up. We have looked at two reasons why Ovid could have chosen to leave out Dea Dia: (a) it was *feriae conceptivae*; (b) it comprised worship by the élite, and, if carried out on behalf not of the people as a whole but on behalf of the land-owning aristocracy, the poet, aware of the contemporary problems encountered by Augustus in dealing with famine and popular discontent with his measures, thought it circumspect to omit it. A celebration of the Arval worship of the Dea Dia may have been too insensitive, given the time of writing.

3. Ludi Saeculares

'More serious, no Ludi Saeculares. This unique festival was celebrated with great pomp, to inaugurate a new age. It began with sacrifices on the first day of June of 17 BC. The college of quindecimviri presided (in their ranks the first men in the state) and the ceremony gave scope for a poet to write about Apollo and the Sibyl. The hymn composed by Q. Horatius Flaccus might not have been forgotten by a fellow bard.'[27] A once-in-a-lifetime event would not be expected to be found in the annual calendar. No record of the Ludi for future remembrance is inscribed in any extant calendar, although economy of space may have dictated the exclusion of the anniversary of a unique festival. But one may well ask why Ovid should include the games.

On the other hand, the memory of the greatest religious festival of Augustus' reign was certainly intended to be preserved. A huge marble inscription survives which records the proceedings as well as details as to the magnitude of the event and the way it was to be remembered in the future.[28] To begin with, the festival, extending over three days and three nights, was intended to be witnessed by as many as possible. A special dispensation was even granted by the Senate to those who were not yet married, to put that intention into practice. Furthermore, the official records of the quindecimviri included a senatorial decree for the erection

[27] Syme (1978) 23 f.

[28] *CIL* vi 32, 323. The text is reproduced in part by Ehrenberg–Jones (1976) nos. 30–2.

on the site of the Games of one marble and one bronze column bearing an inscribed record of the festival 'ad futuram rei memoriam'.[29] Augustus also deemed the event worthy of memorial in the *Res Gestae* (22. 4): 'proconlegio quindecimvirorum magister conlegii collega M. Agrippa ludos saeculares C. Furnio C. Silano cos. feci.'

Against this background, the fact that Ovid did not deem the huge festival worthy of memorial in his poem commemorating religious festivals and dedicated to Augustus is more striking. Though the annual festivals and games of the Roman calendar form the framework of the *Fasti*, the ingenious poet is by no means restricted to them. And economy of space is not his problem. As Syme pointed out, the ceremony did provide great scope for a poet writing on religious themes, as well as the opportunity to remember a fellow bard. Did he then deliberately choose to exclude all recollection of it? Further investigation is required.

The Ludi Saeculares were a spectacular manifestation of Augustus' policy of religious and moral revival, revealed primarily by the text of the *Carmen Saeculare* written by Horace to mark their conclusion and to present their 'ideal image'.[30] The hymn beseeches the gods for the eternal supremacy of the City of Rome (9–12), for the protection of Roman mothers in childbirth (13–16), for the blessing of the 'leges Iuliae' on marriage and childbirth (17–20), for the crowning of Ceres for the bountiful earth (29–32), and for a teachable Roman youth, virtuous in its capacity to emulate the morals of its elders (45: 'di, probos mores docili iuventae'). All these are revealed to be the prayers of the descendant of Anchises and Venus (49–52). Horace then offers a list of Augustus' achievements, invoking them as divinized moral abstractions to propound behaviour desirable to the supernatural powers for the new age (*CS* 57–60):

> iam Fides et Pax et Honos Pudorque
> priscus et neglecta redire Virtus
> audet, apparetque beata pleno
> copia cornu.

Already Faith and Peace and Honour and old-fashioned Chastity and neglected manly Virtue dare to return, and prosperous Plenty with her laden horn is manifest.

The question is, how was this Golden Age faring at the time Ovid was composing the *Fasti*? Nearly a quarter of a century had passed since Horace had celebrated its inauguration in verse. A whole new generation had grown up which had not witnessed the Ludi Saeculares and which had no expectation of ever doing so in the future. How much notice did the youth of the day take of the two columns standing in the Campus Martius, or what efforts were being made by Augustus to instil in the

---

[29] Ehrenberg–Jones (1976) 60 ll. 61, 63.   [30] Fraenkel (1957) 382.

consciousness of the younger generation the notion that they were the products of the Golden Age? Was Horace's heavily moralizing hymn, with its prayer for a virtuous Roman youth, part of the school curriculum, known by heart by every schoolchild? If so, what was the general attitude of the youth towards it?

The most visible representatives of the younger generation in Rome were the younger Julia and Agrippa Postumus. They, with their mother Julia, could not have brought more shame and disgrace to Augustus, nor underlined more heavily his utter failure as pater Familias, or his ineptitude as guardian of future generations. Suetonius claims that Augustus bore the deaths of Gaius and Lucius Caesar far more easily than the misconduct of his family (*Aug.* 65. 2). Agrippa Postumus fell from favour in AD 5, was banished for misconduct in AD 7, and Julia the younger shared the same fate for adultery a year later.[31] Could the youth of the day have read or recited Horace's hymn without suppressing a smirk?

And what of the generation who had witnessed the Ludi? We have seen that the years from AD 5 onwards were among the most critical of the long regime. In addition to the natural disasters and social disorder, there was also intensified discontent with the 'leges Iuliae' of 17 BC.[32] The amendment of AD 9 weakening the *Lex Iulia de Maritandis Ordinibus* had not yet occurred, nor indeed the annihilation of Varus' legions, but it was clear that most of what Horace's hymn had prayed for was in vain, much of what it had given thanks for had disintegrated. That Augustus was acutely aware of this is reflected in the rumour that, even before Varus' disaster, he contemplated suicide (Pliny, *NH* 7. 149):

iuncta deinde tot mala, inopia stipendii, rebellio Illyrici, servitiorum delectus, iuventutis penuria, pestilentia urbis, fames Italiae: destinatio expirandi, et quadridui inedia major pars mortis in corpus recepta; iuxta haec Variana clades et maiestatis eius foeda suggillatio.

then, in addition, such a great number of adversities: lack of funds, the rebellion of Illyria, conscription of slaves, scarcity of young men, pestilence in the city, famine in Italy, a determination to die, and after four-days of starvation he was physically more than half dead; and on top of this the Varian disaster and the foul affront to his authority.

If this rumour was true, Augustus was as good as confessing that the Golden Age had failed to materialize.

Augustus' sensitivity to the failure of the Golden Age is perhaps also reflected in his own record. It is true that he commemorated his celebration of the festival in his *Res Gestae*, but on this E. G. Hardy made a pertinent observation. He noted that, in view of how much the celebration meant to Augustus and what it was intended to promise the Roman

---

[31] Dio, 55. 32. 2; Suet. *Aug.* 65. 4; Tac. *Ann.* 1. 1; Syme (1978) 206 ff.

[32] For references to these events see Wiedemann (1975) 265 ff.

world, 'the brevity and meagreness of his statement are extraordinary'. He wondered at the fact that 'the act symbolic of so much for the present and the future occupies less space in the record of *Res Gestae* than the enumeration of the shows of wild beasts exhibited for the amusement of the Roman rabble'.[33]

Is the 'brevity and meagreness' of Augustus' statement an attempt, while not wishing to obliterate all record of the event, to underplay the great significance it had had at the time it was staged? The Princeps would, in his latter years, be less and less inclined to be reminded of the great hopes of 17 BC. This is suggested by the fact that later writers reflect the brevity and meagreness of his own record of the festival. Suetonius merely mentions it as one of several revivals of obsolete rites (*Aug.* 31. 4). Dio is equally terse: 'and he held the fifth celebration of the Secular Games' (54. 18. 2). The conclusion can be drawn that the true magnitude of the event and the symbolism behind it had been quietly forgotten in the source material left by those taking their lead from an aged and bitterly disillusioned Augustus.

To return to Ovid. It is quite likely that he had attended the three-day spectacle of the Ludi Saeculares in 17 BC. The significance of the occasion would not have been lost on him. Neither would the disenchantment, indeed the embarrassment, of Augustus as the years passed. The *Fasti*, written during these troubled times, reflects a poet anxious to please the dedicatee of his work on Roman festivals. If he had thought that a celebration of the Ludi Saeculares would have been pleasing to Augustus, he would have obliged. Ovid no doubt realized that it would not have been an easy task without reviving memories of the concept behind it, without the faintest echo of the hymn of 'his fellow bard'. Indeed, to celebrate the Secular Games in the *Fasti* would have been a tempting opportunity to highlight and ridicule the spectacular failure of the Pater Patriae in his role as Pater Familias, the most fundamental role of any Roman noble, and to make a burlesque of the whole event. The genre of the poem was admirably suited to such a theme. Ovid somehow managed to resist the temptation. Had Augustus seen the *Fasti*, he would have been vastly relieved.

5. The Adoption of Tiberius, 26 June AD 4

Syme believes that the 'curious phenomenon' of Ovid's omission of the adoption of Tiberius on 26 June AD 4, is an important clue as to the date of the composition of the poem and the reasons for Ovid's renunciation at the end of book 6: he had acquired a distaste for laudations of the dynasty, which must now include the rehabilitated Claudian who had

[33] Hardy (1923) 106.

become Tiberius Caesar. For this reason he not only neglected to mention the event but even decided to abandon his poem altogether.[34]

Syme thus dates the termination of the *Fasti* to AD 4. Ovid on the other hand says it was the fate of exile which interrupted the writing of his poem (*T* 2. 551–1) in AD 8. If the truth of Ovid's claim is accepted (as it has been throughout this work), then his neglect of any mention of Tiberius' adoption needs to be accounted for. If it can, then Ovid's dating for his own poem will earn its deserved credibility. It is for this reason that we proceed.

The earliest extant evidence for the date of Tiberius' adoption comes from the *Fasti Amiternini*, edited and dated AD 20 by Degrassi, which reads thus:

Fer(iae) ex s(enatus) [c(onsulto), q]uod e[o] die (Imp. Caes(ar)] Augus[tus ado]p[tav]it [sibi] filiu[m Ti. Caesarem] Aelio [et Sentio co(n)s(ulibus)].[35]

Holiday by decree of the senate because on that day Imperator Caesar Augustus adopted as his son Tiberius Caesar in the consulship of Aelius and Sentius.

These words cannot be a direct citation of an official decree in AD 4, which must have also included mention of Agrippa Postumus, adopted on the same day (Vell. 2. 104, 112. 7; Suet. *Aug.* 65. 1; *Tib.*, 15. 2). This calendrical entry is therefore unlikely to be a contemporary reflection of the event. It is most unfortunate that, of all the fragments of surviving calendars datable to between AD 4 and 14, not one preserves 26 June. It is thus impossible to know for certain whether the day was made an NP day at the time of the adoption itself, or later in the reign of Tiberius.

Despite such a setback it is possible to conjecture that 26 June was not made an NP day in AD 4, perhaps not before AD 10 or even later. Degrassi, dating the *Fasti Praenestini* to between AD 6 and 9, notes that all references to Tiberius including his earliest anniversaries (such as his assumption of the *toga virilis* on 24 April 27 BC) were added to the inscription at a later date in a different hand. In his transcription of the text Degrassi underlines all references to Tiberius to enhance the difference from that of the original script.[36]

On the evidence of the surviving fragments of the *Fasti Praenestini* we can conclude then that the scholarly Verrius did not incorporate any anniversary of Tiberius' until AD 10 or later, including the adoption in AD 4. Ovid's *Fasti*, in its omission of any mention of Tiberius in the pre-exilic edition, thus has an important factor in common with the calendar of the former live-in tutor to the Princeps' late grandsons, the calendar which, more than any other, we would expect to reflect the wishes of the ruler. If Verrius as definitive authority for the new Julian *feriae* saw no

---

[34] Syme (1978) 34.   [35] Degrassi (1963) 474.
[36] Degrassi (1963) 141–2; 113 ff.

need to celebrate 26 June before AD 10, why should Ovid? His 'negligence' is thus understandable.

If Verrius Flaccus did not incorporate Tiberius' adoption until AD 10 or later, we may be sure that the occasion was not created an NP day in AD 4. No coins celebrated the occasion either. In fact Tiberius received no publicity of any kind on the imperial coinage until AD 10–11.[37] The coincidence of the conspiracy of silence over Tiberius' new name of Caesar and position as Augustus' heir for the years preceding AD 10 in coinage, Verrius' calendrical inscriptions, and Ovid's *Fasti* is striking.[38]

The absence of any official publicity for the adoption of Tiberius excites some curiosity, given that the event was a very public occasion, passed by a bill in the assembly of the *curiae* (Suet. *Aug.* 65. 1). Velleius' record of the extravagant jubilations in the city that day can be taken with a pinch of salt (2. 103. 4). Even so, Suetonius claims that from that time on nothing was left undone which could add to his prestige (*Tib.* 15. 2), and the more sober Tacitus reports that, after the deaths of Gaius and Lucius, Tiberius became the focus of everything. He was taken up as adopted son, colleague in military command, partner in tribunician power, and was paraded throughout the armies (*Ann.* 1. 3).

Any impression of the fuss made of Tiberius on his adoption day comes from authors with the benefit of hindsight, perhaps influenced by the attention they thought should have been lavished on the new Caesar who later became ruler of the world. Cause for doubt in this regard arises when we find no record in the same authors of any attention lavished on the second adoptee, brother of the popular Gaius and Lucius and son of the exiled but still very popular Julia (Suet. *Aug.* 65. 3; Dio, 55. 13. 1), Agrippa Postumus. History had already told posterity that Agrippa was destined for disgrace and extinction. Yet if there were celebrations for Tiberius, one might also expect celebrations for Agrippa from the public who had extravagantly honoured his late brothers and still clamoured for the return of his mother. That no testimony of contemporary sentiment, official or unofficial, exists for either Agrippa Postumus or Tiberius, the latter now restored to public life after ten years of voluntary exile and humiliation at the hands of Gaius[39] is remarkable. Or is it?

Perhaps the circumstances surrounding the adoptions in AD 4 put a damper on any official or unofficial jubilations. Augustus did not hide the fact that, after death had frustrated his hopes for Gaius and Lucius, his stepson was chosen as a last resort (*RG* 14. 1; Suet. *Tib.* 23). To safeguard his dynastic plans he had Tiberius adopt Germanicus to prevent

---

[37] Sutherland (1984) 78 n. 469; cf. 34.

[38] The Athenians, on the other hand, erected a monument celebrating Augustus' new heir as Tiberius Caesar. See *IG* ii (2) 3254.

[39] Details in Syme (1939) 428 ff.

him from transmitting power to those not of his (Augustus') own blood. Even the years following the adoption showed the Princeps to be suspicious and uncertain of his new heir (Dio, 55. 13. 2; 31. 1). Not surprising, perhaps, in view of the last time Tiberius had been given extraordinary powers. Only ten years previously, shortly after having received the *tribunicia potestas* and *imperium maius* which elevated him to near-equality with Augustus himself, Tiberius had withdrawn to private life in Rhodes. The memory of such unpredictable, and what must have been in Augustus' view irresponsible, behaviour, would not have inspired confidence in the future dependability of the man he said he was adopting only in the interests of the state (Vell. 2. 104; Suet. *Tib.* 21).

From Augustus' point of view, 26 June AD 4 was not a happy occasion. It was simply the date upon which he implemented a distasteful but necessary plan to substitute a previous one foiled by 'atrox fortuna'. Where there was no cause for celebration, there was no cause for a new NP day. I suggest therefore that it was not created an NP day. It is also unlikely that there was much in the way of unofficial celebration in the city except perhaps behind closed doors. The recent elevation of Tiberius from a position of discredited *privatus* to that of the second most powerful man in the empire had demonstrated to all observers that nothing was inevitable. A circumspect neutrality would be the wisest course for those without a personal interest at stake in the events of that day. An abstention from a display of approval or disapproval would be most prudent for those with vested interests. The events of AD 8 show that there were those who had refused to accept or believe in the inevitability of the consequences of Tiberius' adoption four years before. It is only in AD 9 in fact, after the elimination of that group that we first hear of a belief in the inevitability of the succession of Tiberus—this from Ovid himself (*T* 2 165, 171 ff.).

The absence of commemoration of Tiberius' adoption may be interpreted as an attempt to curb undue ceremony out of respect for the recently deceased Gaius (only four months previously) and probably reflects the mood of a Princeps unhappy with fate's having forced his hand to a new dynastic scheme. It possibly also reflects the mood of a wary populace, chastened by recent events not to over-indulge in enthusiasm for a current favourite, no matter how certain his prospects seemed. The *Fasti Amiternini* has shown that 26 June became an NP day. This can have occurred only after all opposition had been swept away: perhaps after AD 8, or only after Tiberius' succession. Syme's final omission in Ovid's *Fasti* could be said to reflect the mood before that time, a time of anxiety and uncertainty regarding the succession.

All doubt has not evaporated, however. If Ovid were happily distanced from the vagaries of politics, if he had no vested interest in the events of 26 June AD 4, would it not be possible for him to accord some honour or recognition to the new sons of Augustus in the poem dedicated to him? If he mentioned both Tiberius and Agrippa in accordance with their station, for example (Tiberius being the more senior), could he thereby not claim an unbiased stance and so steer himself a safe course through partisan dynastic squabbles? Then when Agrippa fell while he was still in the process of composition, could he not have excised mention of him and left the remaining honours accorded Tiberius safely embedded in the text?

This possibility is valid only if Ovid were in a position impervious to the vicissitudes of dynastic politics. That Tiberius is never mentioned in his work before AD 9 makes one suspect that he was not. Syme suggests that the adoption of Tiberius caused Ovid to abandon the *Fasti*. I suggest that it was that same event that caused him to begin the work as an attempt to ward off the fate which he knew was surely his after the abrupt change in the political situation in the summer of AD 4.

BIBLIOGRAPHY

Secondary literature on the Augustan Age is vast. The following list is restricted to books referred to in the notes and to books which, although not directly cited, have proved useful in an indirect way for the present study. Articles in Pauly–Wissowa and standard reference works are not included.

ALFÖLDI, A. (1951), 'Der Neue Romulus: Die Geburt der Kaiserlichen Bildsymbolik', *MH* 8, 190.
—— (1954), 'Parens Patriae', *MH* 11, 103.
—— (1975), 'Weinstock, Divus Julius', *Gnomon*, 47, 154.
ALLEN, K. (1922), 'The Fasti of Ovid and the Augustan Propaganda', *AJP* 43, 250.
ALTON, E. H., WORMELL, D. E. W., and COURTNEY, E. (1973), 'Problems in Ovid's Fasti', *CQ* 23, 144.
—— (eds.) (1988), *P. Ovidi Nasonis Fastorum Libri Sex* (Leipzig).
ANDERSON, J. G. C. (1934), 'The Eastern Frontier under Augustus', *Cambridge Ancient History* x. 239.
ANDERSON, W. S. (ed.) (1985), *P. Ovidii Nasonis Metamorphoses* (Leipzig).
BADIAN, E. (1968), 'Sulla's Augurate', *Arethusa*, 1, 26.
BAILEY, C. (1932), *Phases in the Religion of Ancient Rome* (Oxford).
BALSDON, J. P. V. D. (1969), *Life and Leisure in Ancient Rome* (London).
BARNES, T. D. (1972), 'Ultimus Antoninorum', *Historia-Augusta-Colloquium, Bonn 1970* (Bonn).
BARSBY, J. (1978), *Ovid* (Oxford).
BEARD, M. (1985), 'Writing and Ritual: A Study of Diversity and Expansion in the Arval Acta', *PBSR* 53, 114.
—— (1987), 'A Complex of Times: No More Sheep on Romulus' Birthday', *PCPhS* 33, 1.
—— (1990), 'Priesthood in the Roman Republic', in M. Beard and J. North (eds.), *Pagan Priests* (London).
BECKER, P. (1953), 'Ovid und der Prinzipat' (diss. Cologne).
BENNETT, A. W. (1968), 'The Patron and Poetical Inspiration, Propertius 3. 9', *Hermes*, 96, 319.
BICKERMAN, E. J. (1980), *Chronology of the Ancient World*, rev. edn. (London).
BÖMER, F. (1957), 'Interpretationen zu den Fasti des Ovid' *Gymnasium*, 44, 112.

—— (ed.) (1957–8), *P. Ovidius Naso, Die Fasten* (Heidelberg).

—— (1987), 'Wie ist Augustus mit Vesta verwandt?' *Gymnasium*, 94, 525.

BOWERSOCK, G. (1984), 'Augustus and the East: The Problem of the Succession', in F. Millar and E. Segal (eds.), *Caesar Augustus: Seven Aspects* (Oxford).

BRAUN, L. (1981), 'Kompositionskunst in Ovids Fasti', *ANRW* 2. 31. 4, 2344.

BRAUND, D. (1988), 'Ovid as a Source for History', a review of A. V. Podosinov, *Ovid's Works as a Source for the History of Eastern Europe and Transcaucasia* (Moscow), *CR* 102, 28.

BROUGHTON, T. R. S. (1951–2, 1986), *The Magistrates of the Roman Republic* (New York).

BROUWER, H. H. J. (1989), *Bona Dea: The Sources and a Description of the Cult* (Leiden).

BRUNT, P. A. and Moore, J. M. (eds.) (1967), *Res Gestae Divi Augusti* (Oxford).

CARDAUNS, B. (ed.) (1976), *M. Terentius Varro: Antiquitates Rerum Divinarum* (Wiesbaden).

CHAMPEAUX, J. (1982), *Fortuna* (Rome).

CLASSEN, C. J. (1962), 'Romulus in der römischen Republic', *Philologus*, 106, 174.

COARELLI, F. (1974), *Guida Archeologica de Roma* (Verona).

—— (1982), *Lazio* (Rome–Bari).

—— (1985), *Roma*, 3rd edn. (Rome–Bari).

CRAWFORD, M. H. (1974), *Roman Republican Coinage* (Cambridge).

CROON, J. H. (1981), 'Die Ideologie des Marskultes unter dem Prinzipat und ihre Vorgeschichte', *ANRW* 2. 17. 1, 246.

DEGRASSI, A. (1963), *Inscriptiones Italiae*, 13. 2 (Rome).

DUXBURY, L. C. (1988), 'Some Attitudes to Julius Caesar in the Roman Republic', D.Phil. thesis (Oxford).

EHRENBERG, V., and JONES, A. H. M. (eds.) (1976), *Documents Illustrating the Reign of Augustus and Tiberius* 2nd edn. (Oxford).

ENSSLIN, W. (1932), 'Zu den Res Gestae divi Augusti', *RhM* NF 81, 335.

FAIRWEATHER, J. (1987), 'Ovid's Autobiographical Poem, Tristia 4. 10', *CQ* 37, 181.

FANTHAM, R. E. (1985), 'Ovid, Germanicus and the Composition of the Fasti', *PLLS* 5, 243.

FAUTH, W. (1978), 'Römische Religion im Spiegel der Fasti des Ovid', *ANRW* 2. 16. 1, 104.

FEARS, J. R. (1981*a*), 'The Cult of Jupiter and Roman Imperial Ideology', *ANRW* 2. 17. 1, 3.

—— (1981*b*), 'The Cult of Virtues and Roman Imperial Propaganda', *ANRW* 2. 17. 2, 827.

FEDELI, P. (1984), *Propertius* (Stuttgart).

FEENEY, D. C. (1991), *The Gods in Epic* (Oxford).

—— (1992), 'Si licet et fas est: Ovid's Fasti and the Problem of Free Speech under the Principate', in A. Powell (ed.), *Roman Poetry and Propaganda in the Age of Augustus* (Bristol).

FERRARINO, P. (1958), 'Laus Veneris (Fasti 4, 91–114)', in N. I. Herescu (ed.), *Ovidiana, Recherches sur Ovide publiées à l'occasion du bimillenaire de la naissance du poète* (Paris).

FINK, R. O., HOEY, A. S. and SNYDER, W. F. (eds.) (1940), 'The Feriale Duranum', *YCS*. 7.

FISHWICK, D. (1987), *The Imperial Cult in the Latin West: Studies in the Ruler Cult of the Western Provinces of the Roman Empire,* i. 1 (Leiden).

FITTSCHEN, K. (1975–6), 'Zur Panzerstatue in Cherchel', *JDAI* 91, 175.

FLORATOS, CH. (1960), 'Veneralia', *Hermes*, 88, 197.

FLORY, M. B. (1984), 'Sic exempla parantur: Livia's Shrine to Concordia and the Porticus Liviae', *Historia*, 33, 309.

FRAENKEL, E. (1957), *Horace* (Oxford).

FRÄNKEL, H. (1915), *De Simia Rhodio* (Leipzig).

FRÄNKEL, H. (1945), *A Poet between Two Worlds* (Berkeley, Calif., and Los Angeles).

FRASER, P. M. (1972), *Ptolemaic Alexandria,* i (Oxford).

FRAZER, J. G. (ed.) (1929), *The Fasti of Ovid* (London).

GAGÉ, J. (1930), 'Romulus–Augustus', *MEFRA* 47, 138.

—— (1931), 'Les Sacerdoces d'Auguste et ses réformes religieuses', *MEFRA* 48, 75.

—— (ed.) (1977), *Res Gestae Divi Augusti* (Paris).

GAIN, D. B. (1976), *The Aratus Ascribed to Germanicus Caesar* (London).

GALINSKY, G. K. (1975), *Ovid's Metamorphoses* (Oxford).

—— (1990), 'Hercules in the Aeneid', in S. J. Harrison (ed.), *Oxford Readings in Vergil's Aeneid* (Oxford).

GALLOTTA, B. (1987), *Germanico* (Rome).

GANZERT, J., and KOCKEL, V. (1988), *Kaiser Augustus und die verlorene Republik* (Berlin).

GONZÁLEZ, J. (1984), 'Tabula Siarensis, Fortunales Siarenses et Municipia Civium Romanorum', *ZPE* 55, 55.

GORDON, A. E. (1938), *The Cults of Lanuvium* (Berkeley, Calif.).

GORDON, R. (1990), 'From Republic to Principate: Priesthood, Religion and Ideology', in M. Beard and J. North (eds.), *Pagan Priests* (London).

GRANT, M. (1973), *Roman Myths*, 2nd edn. (London).

GREEN, P. (1982), 'Carmen et Error: Prophasis and Aitia in the Matter of Ovid's Exile', *Classical Antiquity*, 1. 2., 210.

GREEN, W. M. (1932), 'Julius Caesar in the Augustan Poets', *CJ* 27, 405.

GRETHER, G. (1946), 'Livia and the Roman Imperial Cult', *AJP* 67, 222.

GRIFFIN, J. (1984), 'Caesar qui cogere posset', in F. Millar and E. Segal (eds.), *Caesar Augustus: Seven Aspects* (Oxford).

—— (1985), *Latin Poets and Roman Life* (London).

GRIFFIN, M. T. (1976), *Seneca: A Philosopher in Politics* (Oxford).

GRUEN, E. S. (1968), *Roman Politics and the Criminal Courts, 149–78 B.C.* (Cambridge, Mass).

GUARDUCCI, M. (1971), 'Enea e Vesta', *Röm Mitt.* 78, 73; repr. in, *Scritti scelti sulla religione greca e romana e sul cristianesimo* (Leiden, 1983).

GUNDOLF, F. (1924), *Caesar: Geschichte seines Ruhms* (Berlin).

HARDY, E. G. (ed.) (1923), *The Monumentum Ancyranum* (Oxford).

HARMON, D. (1978), 'The Public Festivals of Rome', *ANRW* II. 16. 2, 1440.

HARRIES, B. (1989), 'Causation and the Authority of the Poet in Ovid's Fasti', *CQ* 38, 164.

HEINZE, R. (1919), *Ovids elegische Erzählung* (Leipzig).

HELZLE, M. (1989), *Publii Ovidii Nasonis Epistularum ex Ponto liber IV* (Zurich and New York).

HENZEN, W. (ed.) (1874), *Acta Fratrum Arvalium quae supersunt* (Berlin).

HINDS, S. (1992), 'Arma in Ovid's Fasti', *Arethusa*, 25, 81–153.

HOLLIS, A. S. (1973), 'The Ars Amatoria and Remedia Amoris', in J. W. Binns (ed.) *Ovid.*

—— (1982), 'Teuthis and Callimachus, *Aetia* Book I', *CQ* 32, 117–20.

—— (1992), 'Attica and Hellenistic Poetry', *ZPE* 93, 1–15.

HUTCHINSON, G. O. (1988), *Hellenistic Poetry* (Oxford).

JONES, A. H. M. (1970), *Augustus* (London).

JUDGE, E. A. (1974), 'Res Publica Restituta: A Modern Illusion?', in J. A. S. Evans (ed.) *Polis and Imperium: Studies in Honour of E. T. Salmon* (Toronto).

—— (1979), 'Augustus in the Res Gestae', *The Papers of the Macquarie Continuing Education Conference for Ancient History Teachers* (North Ryde, Sydney).

KENNEY, E. J. (ed.) (1961), *P. Ovidi Nasonis, Amores, Ars Amatoria* (Oxford).

—— (1965a), 'The Poetry of Ovid's Exile', *PCPhS* 11, 37.

KERKHECKER, A. (1988), 'Ein Musenanruf am Anfang der Aitia des Kallimachos', *ZPE* 71, 16–24.

LANDI, C., and CASTIGLIONI, L. (eds.) (1950), *P. Ovidii Nasonis Fastorum libri sex*, 2nd edn. (Turin).

LATTE, K. (1960), *Römische Religionsgeschichte* (Munich).

LE BŒUFFLE, A. (ed.) (1975), *Germanicus, Les Phénomènes d'Aratos* (Paris).

LE BONNIEC, H. (ed.) (1965), *Ovide, Fastes lib. 1* (Paris).

—— (ed.) (1969), *Ovide, Fastes, lib. 2* (Paris).

—— (ed.) (1969–70), *Ovide, les Fastes* (Catane and Bologne).

LEFÈVRE, E. (1980), 'Die Schlacht am Cremera in Ovids Fasten 2, 195–242', *Rh.Mus.* 123. 152.

238   BIBLIOGRAPHY

LEFÈVRE, E. (1989), *Das Bild-Programm des Apollo-Tempels auf dem Palatin*, Xenia Heft, 24, (Konstanz).

LEON, E. F. (1951), 'Scribonia and her Daughters', *TAPA* 82, 168.

LEVICK, B. M. (1972), 'Tiberius' Retirement to Rhodes in 6 B.C.', *Latomus*, 31, 779.

——(1975), 'Julians and Claudians', *G&R* 22, 29.

——(1976a), *Tiberius the Politician* (London).

——(1976b), 'The Fall of Julia the Younger', *Latomus*, 35, 301.

——(1978), 'Concordia at Rome', *Scripta Nummaria Romana: Essays presented to Humphrey Sutherland* (London).

LEWIS, M. W. H. (1955), *The Official Priests of Rome under the Julio-Claudians* (Rome).

LIEBESCHUETZ, J. H. W. G. (1979), *Continuity and Change in Roman Religion* (Oxford).

LINDERSKI, J. (1988), 'Julia in Regium', *ZPE* 72, 181.

LITTLEWOOD, R. J. (1980), 'Ovid and the Ides of March' *Studies in Latin Literature and Roman History*, ii (Brussels) 301.

——(1981), 'Poetic Artistry and Dynastic Politics: Ovid at the Ludi Megalenses, Fasti 4. 179–372', *CQ* 31, 381.

LLOYD-JONES, H., and PARSONS, P. (1983), *Supplementum Hellenisticum* (Berlin).

LUCE, T. J. (1965), 'The Dating of Livy's First Decade', *TAPA* 96, 209.

MCKEOWN, J. C. (1984), 'Fabula proposito nulla tegenda meo: Ovid's Fasti and Augustan Politics', in A. J. Woodman and D. West (eds.) *Poetry and Politics in the Age of Augustus* (Cambridge).

MAGUINNESS, W. S. (1932), 'Some Methods of the Latin Panegyrists', *Hermathena*, 47, 42.

MAIR, G. R. (1921), *Callimachus, Lycophron, Aratus*, Loeb Classical Library (Cambridge, Mass.).

MANUWALD, B. (1979), *Cassius Dio und Augustus* (Wiesbaden).

MARSHALL, B. A. (1976), *Crassus, A Political Biography* (Amsterdam).

MEISE, E. (1969), *Untersuchungen zur Geschichte der Julisch-Claudischen Dynastie* (Munich).

MERKEL, R. (ed.) (1841), *P. Ovidii Nasonis Fastorum, libri sex* (Berlin).

MICHELS, A. K. (1967), *The Calendar of the Roman Republic* (Princeton, NJ).

MILLAR, F. (1973), 'Triumvirate and Principate', *JRS* 63, 50.

——(1988), 'Imperial Ideology in the Tabula Siarensis', *Anejos de Archivo Espanol de Arqueologia IX* C.S.I.C. Madrid), 11.

MILLER, J. F. (1982), 'Callimachus and the Augustan Aetiological Elegy', *ANRW* 2. 30. 1, 371.

——(1992), 'The Fasti and Hellenistic Didactic: Ovid's Variant Aetiologies', *Arethusa*, 25, 11–31.

MITCHELL, S. (1976), 'Requisitioned Transport in the Roman Empire: A New Inscription from Pisidia', *JRS* 66, 106.

MYNORS, R. A. B. (ed.) (1969), *P. Vergili Maronis Opera* (Oxford).

NASH, E. (1961), *Pictorial Dictionary of Ancient Rome* (London).

NEWLANDS, C. (1992), 'Ovid's Narrator in the Fasti', *Arethusa*, 25, 33–54.

NEWMAN, J. K. (1967), *The Concept of Vates in Augustan Poetry* (Brussels).

NISBET, R. G. M. (1983), 'Some Problems in Horace Odes 3, 14', *PLLS* iv. 105.

NISBET, R. G. M., and HUBBARD, M. (1978), *A Commentary on Horace: Odes Book II* (Oxford).

NORTH, J. (1986), 'Religion and Politics, from Republic to Principate', *JRS* 76, 251.

OGILVIE, R. M. (1965), *A Commentary on Livy Books 1–5* (Oxford).

—— (1978), *The Library of Lactantius* (Oxford).

OTIS, B. (1938), 'Ovid and the Augustans', *TAPA* 69, 188.

—— (1970), *Ovid as an Epic Poet* (Cambridge).

OWEN, G. S. (ed.) (1915), *P. Ovidi Nasonis Tristium Libri Quinque Ex Ponto* (Oxford).

—— (ed.) (1924), *Ovidii Nasonis Tristium Liber secundus* (Oxford).

PALADINO, I. (1988), *Fratres Arvales: Storia di un collegio sacerdotale romano* (Rome).

PALMER, R. E. A. (1974), *Roman Religion and Roman Empire* (Berkeley, Calif.).

PASOLI, A. (1950), *Acta fratrum Arvalium quae post annum MDCC-CLXXIV reperta sunt* (Bologna).

PEKÁRY, T. (1966–7), 'Tiberius und der Tempel der Concordia in Rom', *Röm. Mitt.* 73–4, 105.

PELLING, C. B. R. (1983), review of Bernd Manuwald: 'Cassius Dio und Augustus', *Gnomon*, 55, 221.

PENSABENE, P. (1979), '"Auguratorium" e Tempio della Magna Mater', *Quaderni del Centro del Studio per l'Archeologia Etrusco-Italica*, 3 (Rome).

—— (1985), 'Area sud occidentale del Palatino', *Lavori e studi di archeologia*, 6, Rome.

—— (1988), 'Scavi Nell'Area del Tempio della Vittoria e del Santuario della Magna Mater sul Palatino' *Quaderni del Centro del Studio per l'Archeologia Etrusco-Italica*, 9, Rome.

PETER, H. (ed.) (1907), *P. Ovidii Nasonis Fastorum libri sex*, 4th ed. (Leipzig).

PFEIFFER, R. (1949–53), *Callimachus* (Oxford).

PHILLIPS, C. R. (1983), 'Rethinking Augustan Poetry', *Latomus*, 62, 780.

PICHON, R. (1917), 'Virgile et César', *REA* 19, 193.

PIGHI, G. B. (ed.) (1973), *P. Ovidii Nasonis Fastorum libri sex* (Turin).

PLATNER, S. B., and ASHBY, T. (1929), *A Topographical Dictionary of Ancient Rome* (Oxford).

PLESSIS, F. (1909), *La Poésie latine* (Paris).

PORTE, D. (1984), 'Un épisode satirique des Fastes et l'exil d'Ovide', *Latomus*, 43, 1, 284.

—— (1985), *L'Étiologie réligieuse dans Les Fastes d'Ovide* (Paris).

POWELL, A. (1983), 'Collectanea Alexandrina', in Lloyd-Jones and Parsons (1983).

PRICE, S. R. F. (1984), *Rituals and Power: The Roman Imperial Cult in Asia Minor* (Cambridge).

PURCELL, N. (1986), 'Livia and the Womanhood of Rome', *PCPhS* NS 32, 77.

QUINN, K. (1982), 'The Poet and His Audience in the Augustan Age', *ANRW* 2. 30. 1, 75.

RAMAGE, E. S. (1985), 'Augustus' Treatment of Julius Caesar', *Historia*, 34, 223.

RAWSON, B. (1986), 'The Roman Family', in B. Rawson (ed.), *The Family in Ancient Rome* (London and Sydney).

RAWSON, E. (1971), 'Prodigy Lists and the Use of the Annales Maximi', *CQ* 21, 158.

—— (1985), *Intellectual Life in the Late Republic* (London).

RICCOBONO, S. (1945), *Acta Divi Augusti* (Rome).

ROGERS, R. S. (1952), 'A Tacitean Pattern in Narrating Treason Trials', *TAPA* 83, 279.

ROMER, F. E. (1978), 'A Numismatic Date for the Departure of C. Caesar?', *TAPA* 108, 187.

RUDD, N. (1976), *Lines of Enquiry* (Cambridge).

RYBERG, I. S. (1955), 'Rites of the State Religion in Roman Art', *MAAR* 22 (Rome).

SABBATUCCI, D. (1988), *La Religione di Roma Antica* (Milan).

SALLER, R. (1980), 'Anecdotes as Historical Evidence for the Principate', *G&R* 2nd ser. 27, 68.

SAMUEL, A. E. (1972), *Greek and Roman Chronology: Calendars and Years in Classical Antiquity* (Munich).

SANTINI, C. (1973–4), 'Toni e strutture nella rappresentazione delle divinità nei Fasti', *G.I.F.* NS 4, 41.

SATTLER, P. (1969), 'Julia und Tiberius: Beitrage zur römischen Innenpolitik zwischen den Jahren 12 v. und 2 n. Chr', *Augustus* (Wege der Forschung, 128), 486.

SCHEID, J. (1975), *Les Frères Arvales: recrutement et origine sociale sous les empéreurs julio-claudiens* (Paris).

—— (1985), *Religion et piété à Rome* (Paris).

—— and BROISE, H. (1987), *Recherches archéologiques à la Magliana: le balneum des Frères Arvales* (Rome).

SCHILLING, R. (1979), 'Dea Dia dans la liturgie des Fréres Arvales', *Hommages M. Renard* 2 Coll. Latomus 102, (Brussels) 1969, 675. Reprinted in R. Schilling, *Rites, cultes et dieux de Rome* (Paris), 366.

—— (1982), *La Religion romaine de Vénus*, 2nd edn., (Paris).

SCOTT, K. (1925), 'The Identification of Augustus with Romulus-Quirinus', *TAPA* 56, 82.

—— (1930), 'Emperor Worship in Ovid', *TAPA* 61, 43.

SCULLARD, H. H. (1981), *The Festivals of the Roman Republic* (London).

SHACKLETON BAILEY, D. R. (ed.) (1985), *Horatius Opera* (Stuttgart).

SIEBLER, M. (1988), *Studien zum Augusteischen Mars Ultor* (Munich).

SIMPSON, C. J. (1977), 'The Date of Dedication of the Temple of Mars Ultor' *JRS* 67, 91.

—— (1991), 'Livia and the Constitution of the Aedes Concordiae. The Evidence of Ovid, *Fasti*, 1. 637 ff.', *Historia*, 40, 449.

SPAETH, J. W. (1933), 'Caesar's Friends and Enemies Among the Poets', *TAPA* 64, 60.

SUMNER, G. V. (1968), 'The Truth about Velleius Paterculus: Prolegomena', *HSCP* 74, 257.

SUTHERLAND, C. H. V. (ed.) (1984), *Roman Imperial Coinage*, i, rev. edn. (London).

—— (1987), *Roman History and Coinage 44 BC–AD 69* (Oxford).

SWEET, F. (1972), 'Propertius and Political Panegyric', *Arethusa*, 5, 169.

SYME, R. (1939), *The Roman Revolution* (Oxford).

—— (1958), *Tacitus* (Oxford).

—— (1974), 'The Crisis of 2 BC', *Bayerische Akademie der Wissenschaften* 7, 3; repr. in *Roman Papers*, iii. 912.

—— (1978), *History in Ovid* (Oxford).

—— (1979), 'Problems about Janus', *AJP* 100, 188; repr. in *Roman Papers*, iii. 1179.

—— (1980a), *Some Arval Brethren* (Oxford).

—— (1980b), 'The Sons of Crassus', *Latomus*, 39, 403; repr. in *Roman Papers*, iii. 1220.

—— (1986), *The Augustan Aristocracy* (Oxford).

TAYLOR, L. R. (1931), *The Divinity of the Roman Emperor* (Middletown, Conn.).

—— (1949), *Party Politics in the Age of Caesar* (Berkeley, Calif., Los Angeles, and London).

THIBAULT, J. C. (1964), *The Mystery of Ovid's Exile* (Berkeley, Calif., and Los Angeles).

TIMPE, D. (1968), *Der Triumph des Germanicus* (Bonn).

TRYPANIS, C. A. (1978), *Callimachus*, Loeb Classical Library (Cambridge, Mass.).

VANGGAARD, J. H. (1988), *The Flamen* (Copenhagen).

VIERNEISEL, K., and ZANKER, P. (1979), *Die Bildnisse des Augustus: Herrscherbild und Politik im kaiserlichen Rom* (Munich).

WAGENVOORT, H. (1966), 'Auguste et Vesta' *Mélanges d'archéologie et d'histoire offerts à J. Carcopino* (Paris); repr. in, *Pietas: Selected Studies in Roman Religion* (Leiden, 1980).

WALLACE-HADRILL, A. (1982), 'The Golden Age and Sin in Augustan Ideology', *Past and Present*, 95, 19.

—— (1983), *Suetonius* (London).

—— (1987), 'Time for Augustus: Ovid, Augustus and the Fasti', in M. Whitby, P. Hardie, and M. Whitby (eds.), *Homo Viator: Classical Essays for John Bramble* (Bristol), 221.

WARDE FOWLER, W. (1899), *The Roman Festivals of the Period of the Republic* (London and New York).

—— (1911), *The Religious Experience of the Roman People* (London).

WEINRIB, E. J. (1967), 'Family Connections of M. Livius Drusus Libo', *HSCP* 72, 247.

WEINSTOCK, S. (1971), *Divus Julius* (Oxford).

WHITE, P. (1988), 'Julius Caesar in Augustan Rome', *Phoenix*, 42, 334.

WIEDEMANN, T. (1975), 'Political Background to Tristia 2', *CQ* 25, 264.

WILHELM, J. (1915), 'Das Römische Sakralwesen unter Augustus als Pontifex Maximus' (Diss. Strassburg).

WILKINSON, L. P. (1955), *Ovid Recalled* (Cambridge).

WILLIAMS, G. W. (1958), 'Some Aspects of Roman Marriage Ceremonies and Ideals', *JRS* 48, 16.

—— (1962), 'Poetry in the Moral Climate of Augustan Rome', *JRS* 52, 28.

—— (1968), *Tradition and Originality in Roman Poetry* (Oxford).

—— (1978), *Change and Decline: Roman Literature in the Early Empire* (Berkeley, Calif., and Los Angeles).

WIMMEL, W. (1960), *Kallimachos in Rom: Die Nachfolge seines apologetischen Dichtens in der Augusteerzeit* (Wiesbaden).

WISEMAN, T. P. (1974*a*), 'Legendary Genealogies in Late-Republican Rome', *G&R* 21, 153; repr. in *Roman Studies* (Liverpool, 1989), 207.

—— (1974*b*), *Cinna the Poet and Other Roman Essays* (Leicester).

—— (1979), *Clio's Cosmetics* (Leicester).

—— (1981), 'The Temple of Victory on the Palatine', *Antiquaries Journal*, 61, 35; repr. in, *Roman Studies* (Liverpool, 1987).

—— (1984), 'Cybele, Virgil and Augustus', in A. J. Woodman and D. West (eds.), *Poetry, Politics and the Age of Augustus* (Cambridge).

WISSOWA, G. (1912), *Religion und Kultus der Römer*, 2nd edn. (Munich).

ZANKER, P. (1968), *Forum Augustum: das Bildprogramm* (Tubingen).

—— (1972), *Forum Romanum*, Monumenta Artis Antiquae, 5 (Tubingen).

—— (1987), *Augustus und die Macht der Bilder* (Munich).

INDEX OF PASSAGES CITED

Figures after the colon denote page numbers

GENERAL INDEX

Acta Fratrum Arvalium 178, 220
Aeneas 53, 54, 61, 62, 66, 67, 71, 72, 83, 89, 90, 94, 114, 162, 195
Agonalia 18, 118
Agrippa 100, 227
Agrippa Postumus 156, 180, 228, 230, 231, 233
Agrippina, granddaughter of Augustus 180, 182, 209, 210
Aitia of Butas 33
  of Callimachus 8, 9, 10, 11, 12, 13, 30, 88, 113, 118
Alexandria, battle of, 47 BC 116–17
Amores 84
Anna Perenna 118
anniversaries, Augustan 32, 107, 219, 220
  Julian 22, 24, 29, 30, 32, 111, 121
Aphrodite 82, 84, 85, 89, 90, 91
Apollo 226
  temple of, 99
Appian 126
April, etymology of 85, 88, 89, 90
Ara Maxima 133, 137
Ara Pacis 61, 219
Ara Pietatis 84
Aratus, *Phaenomena* of 176–7
architecture, influence of on the *Fasti* 28–9
Ars Amatoria 84, 86, 103, 106, 108
Arval Brothers 220–6
Augurate 65
Auguratorium 38, 39, 41
Augustan mythology 52, 61, 62, 72, 81, 108
Augustus
  avenger of Caesar and Crassus 33, 95–108
  and Bona Dea 142–5
  and Ceres 223–4
  as cognatus of Vesta 71–2, 127
  as cognomen 122, 123, 196–203
  contribution to the calendar 25
  and Dea Dia 220
  and deified Julius 124
  as descendant of Venus 81–95

  as Frater Arvalis 221, 223, 224, 225
  and Germanicus 181
  and Golden Age 27, 227–9
  and Janus 187–96
  as Jupiter/Jove 47, 48, 53, 163, 166, 167, 197–204
  a modern concept in calendar 95
  month of 24, 25
  as pater familias 228, 229
  as Pater Patriae 43–8, 52, 54–8, 62–3
  as Pontifex Maximus 27, 28, 33, 63, 66–70, 72–80, 99, 127, 142–3
  as Restorer of Temples 32–6, 42–3
  and Romulus 49, 51–2, 54, 60–2
  will of 169
  see also Octavian
Aventine 136, 137, 140, 141

Basilica Aemilia 29
Bona Dea 131–45
Brutus, Decimus 218
Brutus Ultor 99

Cacus 133, 137, 159
Caecus, Appius Claudius 134, 136
calendar, Roman
  advantage to Ovid 27, 30
  Ceres in 224
  character letters of 17, 19, 22, 23
  and *comitia* 19, 22, 64
  death of Libo in 208
  history and contemporary significance of 15–26
  Julian 17, 19, 20, 21, 22, 23, 42
  Julius Caesar in 111, 127
  Magna Mater in 114
  in poetic tradition 8–14
  Republican 15, 16, 20
  Venus in 85–95
Callimachus, see *Aitia* of
Camillus, M. Furius 56, 164, 166
Campus Martius 222
Carmenta 15, 159–62
Carmentalia 18, 159, 192
Caristia 57